ESPECIALLY FOR

....

FROM

....

DATE

....

DAILY DEVOTIONS FOR MEN

BIBLE ENCOURAGEMENT

FOR EVERY DAY

BARBOUR
PUBLISHING

A list of scripture translations used appears on pages 384.

Cover Design: Greg Jackson, Thinkpen Design

Published by Barbour Publishing, Inc., 1810 Barbour Drive, Uhrichsville, Ohio 44683, www.barbourbooks.com

Our mission is to inspire the world with the life-changing message of the Bible.

Member of the
Evangelical Christian
Publishers Association

Printed in China.

INTRODUCTION

The Bible is filled with thousands of fascinating verses that describe God, people (including ourselves), and the world we live in. Some of them make us confident in our faith, while others puzzle us.

The Old and New Testament scriptures in these pages may be favorite verses you learned as a child or those you've wondered about for a long time. Some you may have never noticed before. Whatever the case, *Bible Encouragement for Every Day: Daily Devotions for Men* is designed to help you appreciate the Word and walk more deeply in it. Here you can daily share the authors' delight in well-known scriptures, come to know some elusive verses better, and feel encouraged to make each one part of your own life.

The Bible is the most wonderful Book on earth. As these verses challenge your faith, encourage your soul, and help you understand more about the God who loves you, His words will touch your heart and soul—and you'll be encouraged to make them an everyday part of your vibrant spiritual life.

THE PUBLISHERS

In the beginning God created the heaven and the earth.
GENESIS 1:1 KJV

Sometimes the simplest things are the most profound.

The Bible begins with a clear, direct statement of where our universe came from: God. What the Bible doesn't try to explain is where God Himself comes from. At the very start, scripture simply assumes His existence.

But read a few pages into the Bible, and you'll find God's explanation of His own being. . .kind of. Though it's tough for the time-bound human mind to understand, God called Himself "I Am" in response to Moses' question, "What is [Your] name?" (Exodus 3:13–14 KJV). Those two little words clearly imply existence, and interestingly, always in the present tense. There was never a time that God wasn't, and there will never be a time when He won't be. God simply *is*.

Scientists and philosophers have debated the origins of the universe and everything in it—including people—for about as long as people have existed in the universe. But the Bible states clearly and simply that everything originated with God.

It takes faith to accept that. But it takes a lot more faith to disbelieve!

Dear God, thank You that You reveal Yourself to me in nature, and thank You that You reveal Yourself to me in Your Word. Amen.

*This is how God showed his love among us: He sent his one
and only Son into the world that we might live through him.*
1 JOHN 4:9 NIV

This short verse packs quite an enormous amount of significance.
God has always been there to guide us, even when we didn't know
He was doing it. He continues to assist us in ways we may never
realize, all because of His love for us. And as we know, He sent
His only Son to this world to offer us salvation.

Many things about God are quite a mystery. We could never
begin to understand the way in which He works and thinks. If
there is anything at all that we can understand for sure, though,
we can know He loves us. For that, we love Him. There is nothing we could ever do to make God stop loving us, because certainly we did nothing to make Him start.

God is concerned about everything we do. He celebrates our
victories and cries with us during our difficult times. As we see in
1 John 4:9, God proved His love for us long before we were ever
born! How could we not love such a God who first loved us so much?

*Lord, You proved Your great love for me before I was born—in fact,
even before the foundation of the earth. Thank You for that.*

Now unto him that is able to do exceeding abundantly above all
that we ask or think, according to the power that worketh in us. . .
EPHESIANS 3:20 KJV

This scripture concludes Paul's prayer for the Ephesian church
for spiritual growth, inner strength, and knowledge of God's love
(verses 14–19). The passage is a doxology giving praise to God and
assurance to every believer of the omnipotence of our loving Lord.

The apostle declares that God is able to do "exceeding abundantly." The Greek word *huperekperissou* is a rare double com-
pound meaning that God is not only able to accomplish all things,
but does so "superabundantly above the greatest abundance"—or
"beyond measure."

"Above all that we ask or think" is just that. Imagine every
good thing that God has promised in His Word—or things you've
only dreamed about. Think of wonderful things that exceed the
limits of human comprehension or description then imagine that
God is able and *willing* to do even more.

The last part of this verse indicates that the Holy Spirit works
within the Christian's life to accomplish the seemingly impossible.
Our highest aspirations are within God's power—but like Paul,
we must pray. When we do, God does far more for us than we
could ever guess.

God, You're far beyond my comprehension. Help me trust that
You're willing and able to do wonderful things in my life. Amen.

Do you not know that you are God's temple
and that God's Spirit dwells in you?
1 CORINTHIANS 3:16 ESV

The Samaritan woman asked Jesus where people ought to worship God—on Mount Gerizim (where a Samaritan temple once stood) or at the Jewish temple in Jerusalem. Jesus surprised her by saying that the time was soon coming when men would not worship God at either spot but "true worshipers will worship the Father in spirit and truth" (John 4:23 ESV). Indeed, as Stephen later said, "the Most High does not dwell in temples made with hands" (Acts 7:48 SKJV).

If God doesn't dwell in temples built by men, where does He dwell? Jesus promised His disciples that although, up to that time, the Holy Spirit dwelled with them, He would soon dwell in them (John 14:17).

Paul stated it clearly when he asked Christians, "Do you not know that you are God's temple and that God's Spirit dwells in you?" (1 Corinthians 3:16 ESV). He further stated, "Your body is a temple of the Holy Spirit within you" (1 Corinthians 6:19 ESV), and emphasized that that was why we ought to live holy lives (2 Corinthians 6:16–17).

What an awesome privilege—to be a temple of the Spirit of God.

God, I praise You for sending Your own wonderful Holy Spirit to
live inside me. Thank You for this unspeakably precious gift.

> *"But they did not listen or pay attention; instead,*
> *they followed the stubborn inclinations of their evil*
> *hearts. They went backward and not forward."*
> JEREMIAH 7:24 NIV

Jews of Jeremiah's time excelled at following the external trappings of the law; as long as they offered the appropriate sacrifices in abundance, they thought they would please God.

In Jeremiah 7:22–23, the Lord told them otherwise. "I did not just give them commands about burnt offerings. . .but. . .this command: . . .Walk in obedience to *all* I command you" (NIV, emphasis added). Instead, they did as they wanted, resulting in a backward religion.

The literal wording of the last sentence reads: "They *were* backward and not forward." They had their religion the wrong way around; they had focused on external actions and not internal obedience.

Earlier, the prophet Isaiah said that the people would fall backward, into captivity, because they had a "little" religion: "The word of the LORD to them will become: Do this, do that, a rule for this, a rule for that; a little here, a little there—so that as they go they will fall backward; they will be injured and snared and captured" (28:13 NIV).

The goal for Christians today remains the same: "This is love for God: to keep his commands" (1 John 5:3 NIV). True devotion will express itself in every area of our lives.

Father, please give me a wholehearted desire to
obey You in all things, great and small. Amen.

*Grace to you and peace from God our Father
and from the Lord Jesus Christ.*
1 Corinthians 1:3 skjv

The Romans had a particular format for beginning a letter. A typical opening line might read: "Hermas, to my dear brother Aristarchus, greetings."

Paul followed this format in his epistles. He began by identifying himself: "Paul," and often as "Paul, an apostle of Jesus Christ." He would then identify the recipient of his letter by saying, "to Timothy" or "to the saints who are in Ephesus."

Instead of simply saying, "greetings," however, Paul invariably invoked blessing upon his readers. "Grace to you and peace from God our Father and the Lord Jesus Christ." The wording is almost identical throughout his epistles. Before anything else, Paul wished believers to have God's grace and peace filling their lives.

In his last letters of Titus and 1 and 2 Timothy—as an aging man looking back over a lifetime of hardships and persecution— Paul added one more blessing. Now he wrote, "Grace, *mercy*, and peace from God our Father and Jesus Christ our Lord" (1 Timothy 1:2 skjv, emphasis added).

God's grace and peace are gifts of His Holy Spirit, helping us make it through difficult times. But sometimes we do fall—and it's good to know God's mercy is there to lift us up.

*God, thank You for Your grace, mercy, and peace—grace that saves
and daily lifts me, peace that fills my heart, and mercy when I stumble.*

In the multitude of my thoughts within me,
Your comforts delight my soul.
PSALM 94:19 SKJV

Do you worry when evil people seem to prosper and when life gets in your way? You are not alone.

We don't know for sure who wrote Psalm 94, but we can be certain that the psalmist was annoyed and anxious when he wrote it. He cries out to God, asking Him to "pay back to the proud what they deserve" (verse 2 NIV). Then, he goes on with a list of accusations about the evil ones. The psalmist's anxiety builds until finally, in verses 8–11, he warns his enemies to shape up and start following God.

Verse 19 is the turning point—the place in the psalm where the writer is at a loss for words. Completely and utterly exasperated, he turns from his rant and starts praising God. "In the multitude of my thoughts within me," he says, "Your comforts delight my soul."

"In the multitude of my thoughts within me." Does that phrase ever describe you? When anxiety overwhelms us, we find relief in the words of Psalm 94:19. When we turn our anxious thoughts over to God, He brings contentment to our souls.

Father, I give all my anxious thoughts to You. I can't bear them any longer. I ask for Your peace. In Jesus' name, I pray.

*They chose Stephen, a man full of faith and of
the Holy Spirit. . .grace and power.*
ACTS 6:5, 8 NIV

From reading Acts 6, one has a suspicion that committees
were the brainchild of the early church. The good news is that
the group described here was assembled to bring help to the
hurting—Greek widows who were not receiving their fair share.
The committee included Stephen, a young man full of faith, grace,
power, and God's Holy Spirit.

What makes this passage so important is its emphasis on
spiritual armor's role in performing good deeds. For Stephen,
that armor included "faith," a conviction that his life was totally
directed by God; "grace," a lifestyle that spoke of Christ, even
when he was silent; and "power," the result of allowing the Holy
Spirit to have His way.

Ultimately, Stephen's uncompromising life so antagonized
his enemies that after a no-holds-barred discourse, he was drag-
ged outside and stoned to death—making him Christianity's
first martyr.

Standing by that day was one Saul, a slayer of Christians.
Undoubtedly, the influence of a young man filled with faith, grace,
and power followed Saul until the day he encountered God on
a road to Damascus. That's when Saul became the apostle Paul.

---

*Lord, please fill me to overflowing with Your Spirit. May Your
grace be upon my life and present in everything I do. Amen.*

"The city and everything in it are to be destroyed as an offering to the LORD."
JOSHUA 6:17 NCV

Fortified with massive walls, Jericho appeared undefeatable. But God miraculously gave the Israelites victory over the city by collapsing that barrier.

In those days, conquering armies would confiscate everything of value from their victims. God, however, instructed Joshua not to take anything from Jericho except articles of gold, silver, bronze, and iron.

The banned spoils included the city's supply of harvested grain, an extremely valuable trading commodity. No doubt some Israelites wondered why God wanted the grain destroyed—especially since their daily manna had ceased only a short time before. Nevertheless, soldiers burned the grain along with everything else in the city.

In recent years, archaeologists have excavated the ancient ruins of Jericho. Their findings match the biblical account right down to clay jars filled with charred grain. Though some consider this battle a myth, the burned jars sit as silent witnesses to the accuracy of the Bible.

Millennia ago, a command to burn grain may have seemed wasteful to some. But God had His purposes. Today, when God assigns us jobs that appear odd or unimportant, believe that He still has His reasons.

God, help me to faithfully obey Your commands—even those I don't fully understand. In Jesus' name. Amen.

But if anyone is deficient in wisdom, he should ask God,
who gives to all generously and without reprimand, and it will
be given to him. But he must ask in faith without doubting,
for the one who doubts is like a wave of the sea, blown
and tossed around by the wind. For that person must not
suppose that he will receive anything from the Lord, since he
is a double-minded individual, unstable in all his ways.
JAMES 1:5-8 NET

James, the half brother of Jesus, was not an early believer. It must have been difficult growing up in a household with perfection personified. But after Jesus' death, burial, and resurrection, James became a strong leader of the church. The book of James reads like a Frequently Asked Questions list for practical Christian living.

At the beginning of this passage, James tells us that if we lack wisdom, we should ask God for it—and He'll grant that request. The three prior verses (James 1:2–4) tell that God gives us wisdom by trials and testing, which produce endurance and finally maturity.

So if you ask, be ready for the storm. When it comes, believe—don't doubt. If we weather that storm, we'll become wise.

Father, I ask You today for wisdom—Your solutions.
Please give me divine insight into the problems that
confront me. I ask this in Jesus' name. Amen.

> *"Study this Book of Instruction continually. Meditate on it day and night so you will be sure to obey everything written in it. Only then will you prosper and succeed in all you do."*
> JOSHUA 1:8 NLT

It is so easy for sin to creep into our lives, particularly in this age of technology in which we live. With a single click of the mouse, we can view anything we wish. We can study any subject and instantly have a library of resources on hand.

Unfortunately, this technology has a dark side as well. A phrase that has been used often throughout the recent years is "garbage in, garbage out." With another click of the mouse, we can allow images and ideas to enter our minds that we know better than to allow.

Joshua 1:8 speaks clearly to the solution to any temptation we may encounter. Just as the Bible is as relevant today as it was when it was written, we can use its instruction to be successful in our Christian walk. When we fill our minds with God's Word, there will be neither room nor desire to fill our minds with the garbage of this world. As Joshua 1:8 points out, only then will we prosper and succeed in everything we do.

Let us thank the Lord for His holy Word.

Dear God, bless me as I fill my heart with Your Word. Guard me and prevent me from being led into temptation. Keep me safe in You, I pray. Amen.

*For God so loved the world, that he gave his only
begotten Son, that whosoever believeth in him
should not perish, but have everlasting life.*
JOHN 3:16 KJV

Every once in a while we find a succinct statement that sums up a series of themes in a neat sentence. No, we're not talking about "Lather, rinse, repeat." John 3:16 is fascinating because in one verse we find the fullness of God's message in a nutshell.

We learn that God so loved. God's love was not a pitying love of pure emotion, but a practical love. God saw our sinfulness, and He loved. He expressed His love by the greatness of the gift of His Son. When sin would drag us down to perish in the awful pit, Christ died and went there as our substitute.

Sin separated us from God. Jesus' resurrection connects us again to a life-giving God, to an eternal life where we know that God is love. By faith we enter into this relationship. In our sin, deserving of death, we could do no good works to dig ourselves out of our hole. By God's grace, He extends salvation as a gift, obtained by believing in His Son. What a message! What a gift!

*Father, I thank You for the wonderful gift You gave
to the world—Your own Son, Jesus. May I be eternally
grateful that He died for my sins. Amen.*

Trust in the LORD with all your heart and lean not on your own understanding; in all your ways submit to him, and he will make your paths straight.
PROVERBS 3:5–6 NIV

Have you ever had to make a decision, but didn't know what to do? As Christians, we have a reliable resource for counsel. When decision-making poses a threat to our serenity and peace, Proverbs 3:5–6 provides sound advice.

First, trust in the Lord. Trusting God is fundamental to our relationship with God. And not just trusting, but doing so with everything within us.

The second bit of advice tells us to avoid the temptation to handle problems or decisions apart from God. Our thoughts and opinions are loaded with misleading personal biases. So King Solomon, author of this proverb, points us to full dependence on the wisdom of God's Word rather than human reasoning. Finally, God provides the solution to decision-making with a promise—namely, if we take all our concerns to God, He will direct our paths.

When we're tempted to act on our own wisdom, the Lord tells us to stop, reflect, and prayerfully consider each matter. He gives us uncomplicated advice for our major and not-so-major decisions. The question is, Will we listen?

Lord, I trust You. I bring my problems to You. Please guide me in my decision-making now, I pray. Amen.

We must pay the most careful attention, therefore,
to what we have heard, so that we do not drift away.
HEBREWS 2:1 NIV

The fishing industry flourished in the Sea of Galilee, since no other freshwater lake existed nearby. This body of water lay nearly 700 feet below the level of the Mediterranean Sea, which was about thirty miles to the west.

The nearby hills reached as high as 1,500 feet. To the east, mountains with peaks of more than 3,300 feet surrounded the sea, whose name means "circle." The geography created a beautiful but dangerous setting, subject to sudden and violent storms.

The fishing boats commonly used held four men, and a boat's typical small size at that time made it quite vulnerable to vicious weather. If fishermen were careless as to what was happening around them—where they were and if the clouds showed signs of changing—they could find themselves in trouble quickly. Their boat would be carried off by the wind and waves.

A similar drifting can easily happen to us as we navigate the sea of life. Keeping an eye open for the early warning signs of danger helps us stay on the course God has given us. We need to pay careful attention to all we learned in order to arrive safely at the end of our journey.

Dear God, I ask You to keep me safe today as I go about
my tasks. Help me to be vigilant. In Jesus' name, I pray.

Then King David went in and sat before the LORD,
and he said: "Who am I, Sovereign LORD, and what
is my family, that you have brought me this far?"
2 SAMUEL 7:18 NIV

It's a very humbling experience when we stop and consider all God has done for us and all He has promised to do.

This is how David felt after Nathan the prophet visited him. Nathan informed David of what God had said concerning him. After reminding David of some of the things He had already brought him out of, God spoke of all that He still intended to do in David's life. God made promises so majestic and full that it must have been overwhelming to this man who had once been a simple shepherd boy.

David wasn't the only one who received promises of God's blessings. Abram (Genesis 15:1–17), Moses (Exodus 3:1–22), and Joshua (Joshua 1:1–9) are just a few of the others who were given promises, promises they were astonished God would offer.

God's willingness to shower His people with such blessings speaks of His wonderful grace, a grace that is generously and daily extended to us. Let us express our appreciation as David did, with a humble attitude and a grateful prayer of praise.

Father, I'm Your small, often wayward child—
unworthy of all the mercies and blessings You have
given me, day after day. Please know that I'm truly grateful.

And this is love: that we walk in obedience to his
commands. As you have heard from the beginning,
his command is that you walk in love.
2 John 6 NIV

"Walk in love." It sounds so easy, so attractive. So why don't more people do it?

Because it goes against our worst instincts. Let's not forget we were rebels from the start. Eve, encouraged by the serpent, feared God was keeping something from her. So she went her own way—and took Adam with her. They ran from God. You might think we would be wiser, but we're all still doing our own thing—and still getting it wrong.

It's human nature to rebel when someone is keeping you down, taking advantage of you, or playing you for a fool. But this is *God* we're talking about, not some con artist, dodgy politician, or tin-pot dictator. He doesn't have anything to prove, and He doesn't have anything to gain. He made everything, so it's already His. To put it bluntly, we can trust Him.

So put aside those fears. If you must rebel, rebel against rebellion. God's "commands" are simply instructions on how to walk beside Him. Stop going your own way and start going His—and you will know what it's like to truly "walk in love."

Lord, help me to walk in obedience to Your commands. Fill my heart
with love for You and for others. In Jesus' name, I ask. Amen.

> *"What is truth?" retorted Pilate. With this he went*
> *out again to the Jews gathered there and said,*
> *"I find no basis for a charge against him."*
> JOHN 18:38 NIV

Most of us are familiar with the trumped-up charges and the kangaroo court that convened to set in motion Jesus' journey to the cross. As Jesus was shuffled from one jurisdiction to another, an interesting conversation begins with Pontius Pilate, the Roman authority figure for the region.

In an attempt to make sense of this latest crisis, which no doubt has interrupted his breakfast, Pilate begins to question Jesus. As Pilate tries to sort out the mayhem the Jewish priests have brought to his door, he finds himself engaging in a philosophical discussion about truth with the prisoner.

Jesus asserts that His purpose is to testify to truth, and for this reason He was born (18:37). The Way, the Truth, and the Life is testifying in a legal proceeding about who He is.

Pilate asks the right question: "What is truth?" He's on the right track, looking for a semblance of justice in the midst of procedural mockery. But he fails in that he doesn't wait for Jesus' answer. Instead, he returns to the bloodthirsty mob who aren't interested in truth—they're only interested in having their position justified.

Jesus approaches all of us with the answer of truth. Will we listen?

Jesus, may I listen to the voice of Your Spirit.
Speak to me from Your Word. Amen.

Hezekiah dammed up the source of the waters of the
Upper Gihon and directed them down to the west side of
the City of David. Hezekiah succeeded in all that he did.
2 CHRONICLES 32:30 NET

Jerusalem sits atop a mountain and has long been a formidable fortress, but it has always had one perennial vulnerability: it must draw its water from the spring of Gihon, which lies outside the walls.

Early in the city's history, a twenty-foot-deep trench was dug and then covered with rock slabs to provide a covered aqueduct draining into the Pool of Siloam, inside the walls. Later it was replaced by the steep Warren's Shaft, which allowed people to get to the spring directly. These weren't very effective, because King David's men first captured the city through one of them.

King Hezekiah solved the problem by covering the exterior access to the Gihon spring entirely and cutting a 533-meter tunnel and aqueduct back to the pool where water could be safely gathered. Jerusalem has been besieged at least twenty-three times, and captured forty-four times, but this solved the water problem.

Tourists in Jerusalem can visit Hezekiah's tunnel today, 2,700 years after it was built!

Father in heaven, give me "knowledge of witty inventions"
(Proverbs 8:12 KJV). Inspire me with solutions
for the problems I face. Amen.

He that dwelleth in the secret place of the most High
shall abide under the shadow of the Almighty.
PSALM 91:1 KJV

What a wonderful promise. God will cover—in a cloud of glory
and protection—anyone who enters into His presence and stays
in continual communion with Him. Under the old covenant, this
applied only to the high priest entering into the Holy of Holies.
But under the new covenant, all Christians can enter into God's
presence through the blood of Jesus Christ.

As we daily abide in the scriptures and come into God's
presence, He assures us safety and security no matter the circumstances. The word *shadow* indicates a shelter, covering, or
protection from the heat and storms of life. Just as a tree's looming
branches shield us from the hot sun, God provides refuge and
protection wherever we are and whatever challenges we encounter.

The names given to God in this verse define the various
aspects of His loving protection and care. "Most High" means that
He is greater than any threat or problem we face, and "Almighty"
emphasizes His power and majesty.

In another verse the psalmist wrote, "God is our refuge and
strength, a very present help in trouble" (Psalm 46:1 KJV). The
Lord is present at all times to help and protect us. He *is* our
dwelling place.

Dear God, grant that I may find perfect peace and rest, abiding
under Your shadow. May I follow You closely today, I pray. Amen.

Let the message about Christ, in all its richness,
fill your lives. Teach and counsel each other with all
the wisdom he gives. Sing psalms and hymns and
spiritual songs to God with thankful hearts.
Colossians 3:16 nlt

As we think about what real wisdom is, we realize that the only wisdom worth having comes from God.

No matter how smart we think we have become, there is nothing compared to God's wisdom. He shares His wisdom with us and instructs us to share it with others.

Colossians 3:16 indicates that we become wise when our lives are filled with God's Word. We need to study and learn and meditate on God's Word. We then will feel moved to sing praises to Him for what He gives us. We need to live the Word of God every day. It will shine through us! The old song says, "They will know we are Christians by our love." This means reflecting the love of God in everything we do.

When we spend time in God's Word, we find peace, wisdom, and contentment that we get from no other place. This is a peace we love to have. This is happiness! Imagine being anything but thankful to God for filling us with His love, peace, and wisdom.

Father, may the simple truth about Your Son, Jesus,
fill my life. May I be truly wise by knowing You through
Him, and may I walk in Your Spirit continually. Amen.

*Jesus reached out his hand and touched the man. "I am willing,"
he said. "Be clean!" And immediately the leprosy left him.*
LUKE 5:13 NIV

This touching verse sums up Jesus' mission. The leper asked for
healing—if Jesus was willing. Of course, Jesus was willing. He
willingly took human form; He willingly suffered ridicule. Willingly
He cured many—and willingly He died.

He didn't have to do any of it, but He did.

In return, God asks the same from us. He can do great works
through us—if we are willing. But that's difficult, isn't it? After
all, who are we? We can't perform miracles. And there lies the
stumbling block—for God to work in the world, we have to get
past thinking of ourselves as His *partners*. The apostles didn't
cure anyone. God used them to perform many cures, but none
of the power came from them. They simply allowed themselves
to be instruments in His hands.

Great things are yet to be done in this world—and we can
be a part of them when we stop worrying about our capabilities
and put more faith in His.

In the quest to be more like Christ, the simplest and most
effective thing we can do is be willing. Then hand that willingness
over to God and see what He does with it.

*Lord, You know my heart. You know I'm willing. And change me in
those areas where I'm not willing. In Jesus' name, I ask. Amen.*

"The Lord bless you and keep you."
NUMBERS 6:24 SKJV

"God bless you." How many times have you said it? How often has it been said to you?

In church you hear this familiar blessing found in Numbers 6:24–26 (SKJV):

> *"The Lord bless you and keep you. The Lord make His face shine on you, and be gracious to you. The Lord lift up His countenance on you, and give you peace."*

God gave the words for this blessing, sometimes called "the priestly blessing," to Moses. It is the oldest blessing in the Bible.

What does it mean for the Lord to bless you? Webster's defines the word *bless* as "to hallow or consecrate by religious rite or word." To be blessed by God is to be granted His favor and protection. In Matthew 5, Jesus offers illustrations of those who are blessed. He tells the blessed ones, "Rejoice and be exceedingly glad" (verse 12 SKJV). The result of God's blessing is happiness. We find joy knowing that God loves and protects us.

Paul says in Ephesians 1:3 that we should react to God's blessings with praise: "Praise be to the God and Father of our Lord Jesus Christ, who has blessed us in the heavenly realms with every spiritual blessing in Christ" (NIV).

How has the Lord blessed you today? Praise Him for it.

God, I praise You for the many ways You've blessed me. Thank You for supplying all my needs.

When he had received the drink, Jesus said, "It is finished."
With that, he bowed his head and gave up his spirit.
JOHN 19:30 NIV

"It is finished"—Jesus' words on the cross have inspired music and thrilled the hearts of Christians ever since His death.

John wrote his Gospel in Greek, a language rich with possibilities. The original word translated "It is finished" is *tetelestai*. This verb in the perfect tense implies an action completed in the past with continuing results in the present. When Jesus died, God's plan for our salvation had come to fruition—and we are still saved today by that one-time sacrifice.

More meaning comes through when we consider the actual Hebrew words Jesus spoke on the cross. "*Tam ve'nishlam*" is taken from the prayer offered at the conclusion of a book of the Torah: "*Tam ve'nishlam Shevach La'el Boreh Olam.*" Translated into English, it means "It is completed and fulfilled, blessed be God, the Creator of the world." The high priest spoke the "*Tam ve'nishlam*" at the end of Passover.

In saying "it is finished," Jesus not only said He had completed the work of our salvation, He also said His death fulfilled the law and identified Himself with the Passover lamb. Once again, He staked His claim as the Jewish Messiah.

Let us give thanks for Jesus, our Passover Lamb.

Jesus, thank You for dying as the Passover Lamb. Thank You that my sins are forgiven, once and for all, by Your sacrifice.

DAY 24

One night the Lord spoke to Paul in a vision: "Do not be afraid; keep on speaking, do not be silent. For I am with you, and no one is going to attack and harm you, because I have many people in this city."
ACTS 18:9–10 NIV

Ever feel like you're surrounded by troubled, troublesome people? In less charitable moments, you might say "lunatics."

Well, you are—that's the nature of our fallen world. But never think you're totally alone. Of course, Jesus promised, "Surely I am with you always, to the very end of the age" (Matthew 28:20 NIV). But He has also placed flesh-and-blood fellow believers in strategic places to help you on your way to heaven.

Remember Elijah? After defeating Baal's prophets at Mount Carmel, his life was threatened by the evil Jezebel. Suddenly terrified, he complained that he was the last remaining God worshipper. But the Lord told Elijah, "I reserve seven thousand in Israel—all whose knees have not bowed down to Baal" (1 Kings 19:18 NIV).

The apostle Paul referenced that story in his letter to the Romans (11:1–5). And Paul received a similar encouragement from God while facing harassment in Corinth: "I am with you, and no one is going to attack and harm you, because I have many people in this city."

God has many people, everywhere, available to encourage you. Keep an eye out—you're surrounded!

Lord, please send a fellow believer my way today—or vice versa.

> *"But God raised him from the dead, freeing him from*
> *the agony of death, because it was impossible*
> *for death to keep its hold on him."*
> ACTS 2:24 NIV

According to science and the natural order, which statement is true?

- It is impossible for the dead to return to life.
- It is impossible for the dead to stay dead.

Even movies like *The Night of the Living Dead* play on our rock-solid assumption that dead people are meant to remain in the graves.

In his sermon on the day of Pentecost, Peter told his audience that Jesus of Nazareth had indeed died, put to death at their hands only weeks before. For the members of that audience, that should have been the end. If even the great King David's body lay entombed in Jerusalem, how much more this troublesome prophet from Galilee (Acts 2:29)?

But in Jesus, God turned the normal course of nature on its head. He reversed the poles; He turned the impossibility of coming back to life to the impossibility of staying dead. He raised Jesus to life and exalted Him to His right hand (Acts 2:32–33).

May we bow in worship to the one who turned His funeral upside down and opened a new world of (im)possibilities.

> *Jesus, I praise You for rising from the dead and*
> *conquering death. Thank You that death's power*
> *is shattered! May Your kingdom come on earth.*

But when Peter came to Antioch, I had to oppose him
to his face, for what he did was very wrong.
GALATIANS 2:11 NLT

When Peter first arrived in Antioch, Jewish and Gentile believers fellowshipped together during mealtime. Although the food preparation didn't follow Jewish dietary laws and Jewish law considered Gentiles unclean, Peter didn't hesitate to participate in these meals. After all, God had declared Gentiles and all food to be clean in Peter's vision at Joppa.

However, when James and other Jewish Christian leaders came to Antioch, Peter stopped eating and fellowshipping with the Gentile believers. Then the other Jewish Christians followed Peter's hypocrisy, and even Barnabas was influenced to join them in their hypocrisy (Galatians 2:13).

Alarmed by Peter's behavior and its influence on others, Paul confronted him face-to-face. If left unchecked, Peter's actions could have resulted in a heretical teaching that claimed there were two bodies of Christ, one for Jews and the other for Gentiles.

Out of fear of what others would think, Peter, a pillar of the early church, shrank back from doing the right thing.

We all want to fit in. However, compromising God-given convictions isn't the answer. To combat compromise, pray for guidance, memorize appropriate scripture, and stand firm. Anything less is hypocrisy.

Father in heaven, guide me in the stands I take.
May I be motivated by Your truth. Amen.

Uzziel son of Harhaiah, one of the goldsmiths, repaired the next section; and Hananiah, one of the perfume-makers, made repairs next to that. They restored Jerusalem as far as the Broad Wall.
NEHEMIAH 3:8 NIV

When Nehemiah started rebuilding the walls of Jerusalem, he used all sorts of people. The perfume makers and goldsmiths may have supplied the means, or they may actually have put stone upon stone. Beside these artisans were merchants and rulers of districts. Men of different tribes worked side by side. Some repaired areas they had a personal interest in. Shallum repaired a section, "with the help of his daughters" (verse 12 NIV). Priests and temple servants labored. Some were less than diligent; others were zealous.

Nehemiah called all believers to do the Lord's work. And, working together, they rebuilt the city walls in an amazing fifty-two days! The fact that they were surrounded on all sides by enemies may have been a further incentive.

Faith is in a similar position today. We only have one enemy, but we make him stronger when we treat our brothers and sisters as Satan's reinforcements. By allowing politics and interpretations to divide church from church we only weaken the city of God.

Make the common denominator belief in Him and we will build a wall with all His people on the inside and only Satan left on the outside.

Lord, change any bad attitudes in my heart toward fellow Christians. I ask You to bless them. Amen.

But Mary treasured up all these things
and pondered them in her heart.
LUKE 2:19 NIV

The Bible records two different accounts of Mary pondering events surrounding her son Jesus. The first was at the Savior's birth—following the angels' appearance to the shepherds—when she carefully weighed every circumstance she'd experienced and seen.

The second time was when the twelve-year-old Jesus separated from His parents to sit at the feet of teachers in the temple. When Jesus' anxious parents found Him in Jerusalem, they scolded their son. His response? "Why were you searching for me? . . . Didn't you know I had to be in my Father's house?" (Luke 2:49 NIV). Then He obeyed and went with them.

The Bible portrays Jesus' mother as a tender, loving, patient, and humble woman. Yet she was still very human. On one hand, she knew Jesus was the Messiah; on the other, Jesus was her son—the boy she nurtured, taught, and cared for. So Mary stored in her memory the things that had already taken place, to try to understand the divine nature and mission of her beloved son.

We have no record of Mary verbalizing questions, thoughts, and perhaps—at times—concerns. But we know she pondered (and undoubtedly prayed) as all good Christian parents do.

Dear God, I have questions that I've been pondering in my heart for many years. Shed light on them and give me answers, I pray.

And the LORD said unto him, What is that in thine hand?
EXODUS 4:2 KJV

God astonished Moses by miraculously appearing as a flame in a desert bush. He told Moses that He was sending him to Egypt to liberate the Israelites and lead them to the promised land. When Moses objected that he was nobody, God assured him, "Certainly I will be with you." Again Moses protested: "But, behold, they will not believe me" (Exodus 3:12; 4:1 SKJV).

God did not need to "suppose" any such thing. He had just said, "*Certainly* I will be with you." Nevertheless, God was willing to throw in an extra sign to strengthen Moses' faith and asked, "What is that in your hand?" (Exodus 4:2 SKJV).

Well, what *was* it? It was a shepherd's staff, a rod made of an almond sapling. God told Moses to cast it down, and when he did, it transformed into a serpent. When Moses seized its tail, it morphed back into a wooden rod.

This verse is often used to teach: "Help yourself with what you have on hand," but that's missing the point. The real point is that even after we have a show-stopping "burning bush" encounter with God, even after God assures us He's with us to help us—we *still* doubt. And God often then does another miracle to reassure us.

Lord, forgive me for the times You've shown me what to do and I still doubted. Help me have the faith to obey You. Amen.

In your hearts revere Christ as Lord. Always be prepared to give an answer to everyone who asks you to give the reason for the hope that you have. But do this with gentleness and respect.
1 PETER 3:15 NIV

Isn't the relevance of God's Word amazing? This verse is part of a letter, written by the apostle Peter, for Christians living in a non-Christian society. His letter is filled with encouragement and advice. Peter gives three parts of advice with several key words.

First, Peter advises, set God apart from everything else in your heart; in other words, "sanctify," or recognize God's holiness, and treat Him with deserved awe.

Second, be prepared to explain your hope in Christ and eternal life, having a full grasp of what and in whom you believe.

Finally, remember *how* you say something is equally important as *what* you say. Peter instructs believers to explain Christ with "gentleness and respect."

In other words, we must walk the walk before we can reveal the hope we have in Jesus Christ. And when God's ready for us to speak on His behalf, we will know whom we represent, and we will do so with utmost respect and gentleness.

Father, help me know what I believe. And help me present the truth to others gently and respectfully. In Jesus' name, I ask. Amen.

For God so loved the world, that he gave his only begotten Son, that whosoever believeth in him should not perish, but have everlasting life.
JOHN 3:16 KJV

In the Chestnut Grove Cemetery in Ashtabula, Ohio, a small grave marker carries an interesting inscription:

SPENCER E. PIERCE
1922–∞

We can hope that infinity symbol represents Christian faith on Mr. Pierce's behalf. As believers, we have staked our eternal hope on Jesus' famous words to Nicodemus, captured in John's Gospel and reproduced above. By believing in the Lord's teaching, death, resurrection, and ascension, we gain a life that never ends, a place in God's presence where we'll enjoy "pleasures for evermore" (Psalm 16:11 KJV).

This reality should strengthen us for life on this earth, where the pleasures are not lasting—where we may, in fact, face some extremely difficult and disappointing things. Our human existence, as we currently know it, is not infinite, and we can actually be grateful for that. Who would want to live forever in a broken, sinful world that grows darker by the day?

But a day is coming when Jesus, the spiritual light of this world (John 8:12), will be the "light"—in every sense of the term—of a renewed, sinless world (Revelation 21:22–23). That day will be perfect, and it will be infinite. And as a believer in Jesus, you will be a part of it.

Lord Jesus, come quickly.

*Jesus answered them, "You are deceived, because you
don't know the scriptures or the power of God."*
MATTHEW 22:29 NET

The Sadducees were trying to trap Jesus.

They asked Him question after question to try and make
Him contradict Himself. They wanted to show the crowd the
importance of their religious ways and their superiority over
Jesus. It irritated them that Jesus drew a big crowd everywhere
He went with His teaching. They wanted to be the authority, but
instead it seemed that the crowds preferred to listen to every
word that came from Jesus. Imagine being alive during the time
Jesus was teaching and being able to hear the voice of the Son
of God as He spoke!

On this occasion, as recorded in Matthew 22, Jesus again could
see the motivation behind the Sadducees' questions. His answer
to them amazes us even today. These self-righteous Sadducees
must have thought very highly of themselves to try to trip up
Jesus the way they did. What better answer could there be for
such a person than to be told, "You are deceived, because you
don't know the scriptures or the power of God"?

The scriptural illiteracy these men displayed was certainly not
impressive to Jesus. This is just another illustration of why we
make the written Word of God our standard for living.

---

*Savior, help me to soak in Your Word so that my life is full of
Your truth. Drench me in Your Holy Spirit today, I pray. Amen.*

Now the Israelites were in distress that day, because Saul had bound the people under an oath, saying, "Cursed be anyone who eats food before evening comes, before I have avenged myself on my enemies!" So none of the troops tasted food.
1 SAMUEL 14:24 NIV

Just imagine the trouble we'd avoid if we all stopped shooting off our mouths. Individually, culturally, worldwide—how helpful to recognize the truth of Proverbs 13:3 (NIV): "Those who guard their lips preserve their lives, but those who speak rashly will come to ruin."

King Saul spoke rashly when he pronounced a curse on any soldier who ate before nightfall. Israel's troops could have enjoyed the refreshment of plentiful honey they found in the woods, "yet no one put his hand to his mouth, because they feared the oath" (1 Samuel 14:26 NIV). Jonathan, the king's son who'd been out successfully fighting Philistines when Saul issued his foolish order, *did* eat some honey, and his "eyes brightened" (verse 29 NIV). He recognized that the soldiers would have been more effective with food in their stomachs.

Saul's order resulted in a death penalty on Jonathan, and the mass disobedience of the rest of the army to save the young man's life. How unnecessary it all was.

Today, let's commit ourselves to James's wisdom: "Everyone should be quick to listen, slow to speak and slow to become angry" (1:19 NIV).

Lord, may my thoughts be many and my words few.

I say to myself, "The LORD is my portion;
therefore I will wait for him."
LAMENTATIONS 3:24 NIV

For the Israelites, the word *portion* held multiple meanings. It could refer to a piece of land or an inheritance. Portions could also imply the necessities of life like daily food, water, and clothing. Old Testament writings often designate the kind of life one was born into and the family one was raised in as our portion in life.

In today's scripture, the writer declares that the Lord is his portion. He states clearly that he inherited the right to worship God, and that God provides the essentials to support his life. He is also welcomed to be a part of the family of God.

The Lord is our portion too. But when will we fully receive this inheritance and celebrate with Him? We know it is coming, but it's difficult to wait.

Hope gives us strength as we anticipate our return to God. We belong to God and know someday we will worship Him face-to-face. Knowing God will keep His promise, we can say with confidence, "The LORD is my portion; therefore I will wait."

Lord, because of what Jesus has done, You are my portion also.
Thank You that You have chosen me to share in Your great riches.

Let the morning bring me word of your
unfailing love, for I have put my trust in you.
PSALM 143:8 NIV

How did your day begin today? Did you arise early and enjoy the peaceful quiet of the morning after a good night's sleep? Or maybe you spent a sleepless night tending to the needs of a sick family member, and you faced the day running on empty.

We don't know if David was a morning person or a night owl, but he chose to start his day looking for visible reminders of God's unfailing love. It might have been easy to remember God's love for him if he had witnessed a glorious morning sunrise, but if the night had been stormy and he was dealing with spooked sheep in the midst of a downpour, God's unfailing love may have felt a little distant.

Regardless of the circumstances, David decided to trust in God first thing in the morning. Whether or not conditions were favorable for faith, David believed in God's unfailing love—even if he couldn't see it in the world around him.

Dear God, all night You kept me in Your care. And this day I entrust
my soul to Your keeping as well. Guard me with Your unfailing
love. Give me wisdom to deal with today's problems. Amen.

"The one who is victorious I will make a pillar in the temple of my God. Never again will they leave it. I will write on them the name of my God and the name of the city of my God, the new Jerusalem, which is coming down out of heaven from my God; and I will also write on them my new name."
REVELATION 3:12 NIV

An old hymn by C. Austin Miles states, "There's a new name written down in glory, and it's mine." In Revelation 2:17 (NIV), Jesus promised to give the one who overcomes "a white stone with a new name written on it, known only to the one who receives it." In the Old Testament, God promised a new name to Zion when "the nations will see your vindication" (Isaiah 62:2 NIV).

But God's people weren't the only ones to receive a new name. In the message to the church at Philadelphia, the one "who is holy and true, who holds the key of David" (Revelation 3:7 NIV) spoke of *His* new name (verse 12). Both God the Father and God the Son will mark their own with their names: their names will be inscribed on the 144,000 (Revelation 14:1) and those who are allowed into the New Jerusalem (Revelation 22:4).

Our Savior has adopted us (Ephesians 1:5) and bestowed His name on us. What an amazing blessing it is to share in God's great name.

Jesus, I thank You that You'll write Your name on me. I thank You that You'll do this to show the world that I'm Yours.

> *"But will God really live on earth? Why, even the highest heavens cannot contain you. How much less this Temple I have built!"*
> 1 KINGS 8:27 NLT

A masterpiece of quarried stone, wood paneling, and carvings with gold overlay, Solomon's temple required over thirty thousand men, working seven years, to complete.

During the temple's dedication service, the priests carried the ark of the covenant into the Most Holy Place, and "the glorious presence of the LORD filled the Temple" (1 Kings 8:11 NLT).

Offering a prayer of dedication, Solomon recognized that God isn't confined to one place. Perhaps he had memorized his father's words, written years before, "I can never get away from your presence! If I go up to heaven, you are there. . . . If I dwell by the farthest oceans, even there your hand will guide me, and your strength will support me" (Psalm 139:7–10 NLT).

God himself says, "Am I not everywhere in all the heavens and earth?" (Jeremiah 23:24 NLT).

Out of love for the Israelites, God displayed His presence in their temple through a brilliant cloud.

Our God is not some impersonal force that considers us mere specks of humanity existing on the earth. He sees and cares for us as individuals. And more comforting, He knows our whereabouts at all times and is at hand to guide us through good and bad times.

Lord, You are the eternal God—abiding forever, filling up all eternity. Holy God, reveal Yourself to me, I pray.

"For my yoke is easy and my burden is light."
MATTHEW 11:30 NIV

Ever felt like a beast of burden? With all the pressures and expectations of this life, it would be hard not to sometimes. If you had to be such a creature, what kind of master would you choose?

Horses and oxen still plow fields all around the world. They wear yokes across their shoulders, and their burdens are not light. We who feel wearied by the world might sympathize with them as they drag plows through hard, stony ground. They don't get to choose their masters. They can only walk where the reins or the whip make them go. And when their working life is over. . .

So, why would anyone chose to wear a yoke?

Because the one Christ offers really is light. So light in fact that He actually carries our burdens! There is no harness; there is no whip. We get to choose our Master.

All He asks for a lifetime of companionship followed by an eternity of bliss is that we wear the "yoke" of the love of God. With Jesus guiding our steps, plowing a straight furrow will be our pleasure. And when our working life is over, we'll find the furrow led all the way to heaven.

Master, I choose to be yoked to do Your work. Help me, I pray, to please You in all things. Keep my eyes focused on the great reward You'll give me at the end of life's journey. Amen.

"He performs wonders that cannot be fathomed,
miracles that cannot be counted."
JOB 5:9 NIV

In Job 5, Job's friend Eliphaz tries to put in plain words the reason for Job's suffering. In his opinion, Job must have done something sinful to be in such a dreadful state. Eliphaz tells Job what he would do if he were suffering because of his sins. He would appeal to God. He would confess his sins and hope for God's mercy. After all, God "performs wonders that cannot be fathomed, miracles that cannot be counted."

In other words, Eliphaz says Job should seek God's justice, because God is greater than anyone can imagine. He alone is the one who forgives our sinfulness and heals our suffering.

Job's afflictions were not due to anything that he had done. Eliphaz's instructions would have been good, if Job *had* sinned. We see them again in 1 John 1:9 (NIV): "If we confess our sins, he is faithful and just and will forgive us our sins and purify us from all unrighteousness."

Are you feeling guilty about some sin in your life? Remember the greatness of God. Romans 10:13 (NIV) says: "Everyone who calls on the name of the Lord will be saved."

Lord, You perform such amazing wonders they can't be
fathomed, so many miracles that they can't be counted.
Work in my life now. Forgive my sins, I ask You. Restore
Your favor and blessings to me. In Jesus' name. Amen.

*For our conversation is in heaven; from whence also
we look for the Saviour, the Lord Jesus Christ.*
PHILIPPIANS 3:20 KJV

In this passage, the Greek word translated "conversation" is *politeum*, meaning "citizenship." The word is broad in its translation, indicating our citizenship, thoughts, and affections are already in heaven.

For every Christian, heaven is home. From the moment we accept Christ, we are adopted into God's family with the promise of spending eternity with Him and all the saints who have gone before us. We are no longer citizens of this earth; we are born from above, and our names are written in God's celestial register.

Because our citizenship is in heaven, so are our hopes, thoughts, and affections. We are *in* the world, but not *of* it any longer. In the letter to the Hebrews, we read about Abraham and his descendants "looking forward to the city with foundations, whose architect and builder is God" (Hebrews 11:10 NIV). They considered themselves strangers on this earth because "they were longing for a better country—a heavenly one" (Hebrews 11:16 NIV).

As heaven's citizens, we will enjoy all the rights and privileges of our heavenly Father. Meanwhile, we look to Jesus and stay steadfast to His Word until He ushers us home.

*Dear Lord, I thank You that I'm already a citizen of
Your eternal kingdom. And I thank You that I shall
rule and reign with You forever. Amen.*

"For the eyes of the LORD range throughout the earth to strengthen those whose hearts are fully committed to him."
2 CHRONICLES 16:9 NIV

God is on a quest. He explores throughout the world and searches in every corner. He is relentless in His pursuit for something.

What is the object of His exploration? He wants people with a particular type of heart condition—hearts fully devoted to Him. God seeks a relationship with those who have open and receiving hearts. He is not looking to condemn or judge, but to find hearts committed to knowing Him and learning His way. He desires people who want to talk and listen to Him and who have a deep thirst to serve and please Him.

God gives loyal hearts a gift—His strength. He eagerly pours His spirit into these open hearts in order to draw closer and build an intimate relationship with them.

God looks for us, and the only requirement is for each of us to have a fully devoted heart. We open our hearts and hands to receive Him, and He will find us.

Lord, help me to be yielded to Your Holy Spirit, open and attentive to Your slightest bidding. Soften my stubborn heart, I pray. In Jesus' name, I ask. Amen.

When Jesus heard what had happened, he withdrew
by boat privately to a solitary place. Hearing of this,
the crowds followed him on foot from the towns.
MATTHEW 14:13 NIV

Jesus went out onto the sea in search of peace in which to mourn John the Baptist. He must have been distraught. But might He also have spared a thought for Himself? After all, both He and John had been gifts from God and heralded by angels. They were both part of the same plan.

John had prepared the way—and now he was gone. Jesus must have felt alone in a way He never had before. Perhaps there was a sense of "Now it's My turn." The prospect of the long walk to the cross must have seemed, somehow, more real at that moment.

Did He gather His strength on that boat?

Then He came back to the shore. The crowd swept away any possibility of self-pity. Seeing them and their needs, "He had compassion on them" (Matthew 14:14 NIV). Then, in one of His best-remembered miracles, He went on to feed five thousand of them.

When He stepped onto the shore, Jesus encapsulated one of the most important tenets of Christianity: it isn't about you; it's about the wonderful things you can achieve for God when you put your own fears behind you and have compassion on others.

Jesus, You desired to get away and rest but put others'
needs first. Help me learn from Your example. Amen.

*Jesus Christ our Lord, who was. . .declared to be the
Son of God with power, according to the Spirit of
holiness, by the resurrection from the dead.*
ROMANS 1:3–4 SKJV

When Jesus was baptized and the Holy Spirit descended upon Him, God the Father declared out loud, "This is My beloved Son, in whom I am well pleased" (Matthew 3:17 SKJV).

Jesus also declared to the Jewish people, "I am the Son of God," and said that if they didn't believe it when He *said* so, to at least believe because of the miracles (John 10:36–38 SKJV). Jesus' miracles also declared that He was the Son of God.

But when the Holy Spirit of God raised Jesus back to life after He had lain dead in the grave for three days, this was the final and greatest proof that Jesus was the long-awaited Messiah, the Son of God. Jesus Christ was "declared to be the Son of God *with power*" (Romans 1:4 SKJV, italics added).

This final declaration has great personal relevance to us who believe on Jesus, for if the Spirit of God had the power to raise Jesus from the dead, and that same Spirit dwells in our hearts, He will raise us to endless life as well (Romans 8:11).

*God, I praise You for raising Jesus from the dead. And I thank
You that You will one day raise me to new life also. Thank
You that I have that wonderful future to look forward to.*

 DAY 44

If you fulfill the royal law as expressed in this scripture,
"You shall love your neighbor as yourself," you are doing well.
JAMES 2:8 NET

Sometimes we wonder if we are doing enough for God. We think about the commandments and the teachings of Jesus and wonder if we are living "Christlike" lives.

A rich, young ruler came to Jesus one time and asked Him what he must do to be saved. But the answer Jesus gave reflected the idea that He always taught: there is nothing we can do to earn our way into heaven. It is not a matter of earning our salvation, and certainly God is not impressed by our work. Our walk with Jesus is about a real relationship. It is about loving Him and loving others as ourselves. Isn't it wonderful that we have a God of love?

As we see in James 2:8, we are living as we should if we obey God's law to love one another. We know that this is not always easy to do. It seems that the way we love the person we like the least is how we love God the most. Sometimes it is quite challenging to look upon others as Jesus does. If we see people through the eyes of Jesus, though, in His words we are "doing well."

Father, may I love others as I love myself—and think
of their needs and feelings as much as I think of
my own. In Jesus' name, I ask. Amen.

And the LORD God planted a garden eastward in Eden;
and there he put the man whom he had formed.
GENESIS 2:8 KJV

Adam wasn't created in the garden of Eden. He was formed from the dust somewhere to the west of the garden. The first thing God did, after giving him life, was to lead the father of mankind to paradise.

Then Adam and Eve blew it and were thrown out. God could have let it go and left mankind scrabbling in the dust, but He didn't. He sacrificed His Son to give us another way to paradise. That's how much He wants us there. . .because that's where we were meant to be.

But mankind has been fallible from the start, and as a result, we often don't think we deserve that kind of love. The dust of this world is all many ever aspire to. Heaven is for better folk, special folk, saints perhaps, not weak, inconsistent, scared people like us. And when we think like that, we break God's heart. He's not waiting for us to prove ourselves worthy. He made the invitation and it's still valid. We just have to accept.

The garden was planted for *you* to walk in. Not some "better" person. You have another chance. Take it. Head eastward or upward. God wants you to come home.

Lord, I thank You that You created paradise for
sinners just like me. Thank You for making a
way there—through Your Son, Jesus.

Blessed is the man whom You choose and cause to approach
You, that he may dwell in Your courts. We shall be satisfied
with the goodness of Your house, even of Your holy temple.
PSALM 65:4 SKJV

Many people struggle with the idea of God choosing His own, yet the idea appears throughout scripture. Certainly God chose David, the author of today's scripture, for relationship and blessing in a very powerful way.

The Bible also teaches human responsibility for sin. It goes to our very conception (Psalm 51:5), affects everyone (Romans 3:23), and puts us all under a sentence of death (Romans 6:23). Apart from God's intervention, we are doomed.

Exactly how and why some people are saved is known only to God—and His grasp of such mysteries is a huge distinguishing factor between Him and us. If we could understand everything about God, He wouldn't be God. . .we would. Clearly, that's not the case.

So, trusting as Abraham did that "the Judge of all the earth" will do right (Genesis 18:25 SKJV), let's be grateful that God looked with kindness on each of us who follow Jesus. We as Christians enjoy God's greatest mercies—which we should be eager to pass along to others.

Heavenly Father, thank You for choosing me and causing me to
approach You. May I always appreciate Your gift of salvation.
Please empower me to share this good news with others.

> *"Should you then seek great things for yourself? Do not seek them. For I will bring disaster on all people, declares the LORD, but wherever you go I will let you escape with your life."*
> JEREMIAH 45:5 NIV

Sometimes life doesn't go as we expected. Whether we'd set goals and made plans to achieve them, or just had a feeling that we'd own, do, or be something by a certain age, we find ourselves disappointed.

It's not a new problem. Some twenty-six hundred years ago, Jeremiah's scribe wrestled with similar frustrations. Baruch wrote down the messages God gave to Jeremiah, and occasionally even spoke for the prophet. Apparently, Baruch had personal expectations that weren't playing out. In a very short chapter of a very long book, God had a specific message for him, the words of today's scripture.

God also said, "I will overthrow what I have built and uproot what I have planted, throughout the earth" (Jeremiah 45:4 NIV). That ominous promise was fulfilled in spades when Babylon invaded Judah and overran Jerusalem.

But there was good news, of a sort. Jeremiah 45:5 ends with the promise, "I will let you escape with your life" (NIV). No matter how bad things got, God still had His eye and His hand on Baruch. That's also true for you today.

Lord God, You never promised ease and pleasure in this life. That comes in eternity! Please keep me faithful until the day You make everything right.

*"Neither," he replied, "but as commander of the army of
the Lord I have now come." Then Joshua fell facedown
to the ground in reverence, and asked him, "What
message does my Lord have for his servant?"*
JOSHUA 5:14 NIV

Oh, Joshua really did the right thing here! He'd wanted to know
if this strange man with the drawn sword was on his side or the
enemy's side. But the "man" was above and beyond such concepts.

Even though the Israelites were God's chosen people, He
wasn't on their side. Their enemies were being destroyed—and
the man with the sword would tell Joshua how to do that—
because they worshipped false gods. It was up to the Israelites
to be on God's side.

We sometimes fool ourselves into thinking that because God
loves us He must hate our enemies. Armies have often marched
to war under the same mistaken premise. But if we neglect our
duties to the Lord and our enemies are diligent in theirs, then
we become the enemy, no matter how much He has blessed us
in the past.

There *are* two sides we should be interested in, but they aren't
ours and our enemy's—they are God's and His enemy's. Joshua
wasn't so proud as to think it was all about him and his victories.
Neither should we be.

---

*God, convict my heart anytime I'm not on Your side—whether that
happens to be the side of love, forgiveness, justice, or mercy.*

And He said, "Come." And when Peter came down out of
the ship, he walked on the water to go to Jesus.
MATTHEW 14:29 SKJV

Maybe you've seen the bumper sticker: IF YOU THINK YOU'RE SO
PERFECT, TRY WALKING ON WATER. It refers to that time in the
Bible when Jesus, the perfect Son of God, broke the rules of physics
by hiking over the waves. But there was someone far from perfect
who also walked on water.

Earlier, Jesus had told His disciples to get into a boat and go
on without Him to the other side of the lake. He stayed behind
to send the crowds away—and then to pray. Later that evening,
the disciples, wrestling their boat against a contrary wind, saw
a ghostly figure approaching. Jesus assured them it was He, and
Peter asked the Lord to command him to come. Jesus did—and
Peter, briefly, walked on water.

What does it take for an ordinary person to walk on water?
A command of God. By the power of God, ordinary men and
women, responding to God's call, have successfully accomplished
difficult, even impossible, tasks.

Don't give up when things seem worst. That's the time to find
the strength of God.

Jesus, if and when You call me to do some difficult task, grant
me the faith to obey, knowing that You will empower me. Amen.

*But just as he who called you is holy, so be holy in all
you do; for it is written: "Be holy, because I am holy."*
1 PETER 1:15-16 NIV

Peter reiterates one of God's seemingly impossible commands in
his epistle: be holy.

God had first given the command to the nation of Israel. He
emphasized it by repeating "be holy" three times in the book of
Leviticus alone (11:44; 19:2; 20:7).

The word *be* can also be translated "become." We are in the
process of becoming holy. "Perfecting" holiness involves purifying
ourselves from contaminants of body and spirit (2 Corinthians
7:11)—empowered by the refining fire of the Holy Spirit. When
Christ returns, we will be like Him. That hope encourages us to
purify ourselves in the here and now (1 John 3:3).

Perhaps the meaning of the word *holy* becomes clearer when
we examine the companion command to "consecrate yourselves" (Leviticus 11:44 NIV). We dedicate ourselves to God—100
percent pure. No impurities (1 Thessalonians 4:7). No distractions.
Just 100 percent commitment to God.

One hundred percent? We're not there yet. But we will be.
"For he chose us in him before the creation of the world to be
holy and blameless in his sight" (Ephesians 1:4 NIV).

*Lord, help me take steps—starting today—to get rid of sins or habits
that are preventing me from partaking of Your holiness. Amen.*

*Peter said, "I don't have any silver or gold for you.
But I'll give you what I have. In the name of Jesus
Christ the Nazarene, get up and walk!"*
ACTS 3:6 NLT

Financially, Peter and John might have felt right at home in a slumping economy. But unlike many in our world, they had other wealth to spend—the riches found in Jesus Christ.

Setting: The temple gate. Beneficiary of the disciples' generosity: A crippled beggar. Results: A lame man healed, the opportunity to share Jesus with the crowd that gathered—and a jail sentence.

It's Peter's confidence that fascinates most readers. Temple leaders demand that Peter keep quiet about Jesus, but the disciple had experienced too much with Jesus to keep quiet. When the leaders tried to minimize the miracle, Peter pointed out irrefutable evidence—the man was walking! Finally, Peter was asked his secret, which enabled the disciple to speak of the inexhaustible power found in Jesus Christ (Acts 4:7–12).

What a contrast: a circle of sophisticated temple leaders attempting to silence two country fishermen who could not help speaking about what they had seen and heard (Acts 4:20).

Christian friend, don't let a checkbook dictate your generosity; share what you have with the spiritually crippled and those who hunger and thirst after righteousness.

You can do it through the power of Jesus Christ.

*Father, I often feel I have little to give. Show me
the riches that I can share with needy souls. Amen.*

Deborah, a prophet, the wife of Lappidoth,
was leading Israel at that time.
JUDGES 4:4 NIV

How did a woman end up ruling Israel, a culture steeped in patri-
archy? Who is this prophet, Deborah?

A leader of Israel around 1200 BC, Deborah is described as a
prophet, a judge, and a military leader who delivered God's word
to Barak and inspired him to follow God. She must have been a
remarkable woman, to be accepted by men and given power at a
time in history when women were rarely seen in leadership roles.

A prophet is one called by God to speak on His behalf. Deborah
inspired people to turn their hearts toward God. She joins only
a few other biblical women described as prophets—Miriam,
Huldah, the wife of Isaiah, and Anna.

Deborah serves as a role model for men and women today in
our witness for God. Our simple daily acts of kind service inspire
others. We can speak God's Word, sharing hope and encouragement with others in letters, texts, and even simple conversations
in the grocery line. Simply being present with a grieving friend
often shows Christ to others when words seem inadequate.

We may not see ourselves as prophets or leaders, but we can
all draw others closer to God through our prayers and service.

God, help me share an inspiring thought with some
discouraged person—however trivial it may seem to me.

*This gospel of the kingdom shall be preached in all the world
for a witness unto all nations; and then shall the end come.*
MATTHEW 24:14 KJV

If you ask many people if we're already living in the end times,
they'll answer, "Yes, we are, and Jesus can come any day now."
However, Jesus tells us that the gospel must first "be preached in
all the world for a witness unto all nations"—and only then the
end will come.

We tend to think that in this modern era the gospel has surely
already been preached in all nations—thanks to radios, television,
and the internet—even in nations closed to the message of salvation. But the Greek word translated as "nations" is *ethnos* and
literally means "ethnic groups" or "people groups." Many closed
nations are made up of dozens of people groups and tribes in
remote mountain valleys and hinterlands who don't have access
to modern media—yet they, too, need to hear the gospel.

We desire Jesus to return, and when He declares, "Surely
I come quickly," we pray, "Amen. Even so, come, Lord Jesus"
(Revelation 22:20 KJV). But we must do our part to hasten that
day: we must help see to it that the gospel goes to the ends of
the earth (Acts 1:8).

*Jesus, help me to do my part in preaching the gospel—by speaking
it, writing it, or giving financial support to those who do. Amen.*

One man was there who had been an invalid for thirty-eight years. When Jesus saw him lying there and knew that he had already been there a long time, he said to him, "Do you want to be healed?" The sick man answered him, "Sir, I have no one to put me into the pool when the water is stirred up."
JOHN 5:5–7 ESV

At the Pool of Bethesda in Jerusalem, blind, lame, and paralyzed people waited. Occasionally, the waters would stir. Word on the street was that an angel was causing the movement, and the first person into the pool would be healed.

Jesus, in Jerusalem for "one of the Jewish festivals" (John 5:1 NIV), saw a particular man who had been disabled nearly four decades. The Lord asked a simple question: "Do you want to be healed?" Notice the man's answer: not an immediate "Yes!" but a roundabout "Sir, I have no one to put me into the pool when the water is stirred up."

Compare this man's reply with a blind man Jesus met in Jericho. The Lord asked the begging Bartimaeus, "What do you want me to do for you?" His answer was as specific as Jesus' query: "Rabbi, I want to see" (Mark 10:51 NIV).

Both men received a miraculous healing. But how much better is Bartimaeus's example? Be specific in your prayers, then thank God for His specific answers.

Father, help me to pray clearly and with a heart of expectancy for Your particular answers.

Whoever claims to love God yet hates a brother or sister is a liar. For whoever does not love their brother and sister, whom they have seen, cannot love God, whom they have not seen.
1 JOHN 4:20 NIV

This is the verse that risks making hypocrites of us all. Who among us does not know someone we'd cross the road to avoid? That person might be obnoxious, a liar, might have caused all sorts of grief—but is still beloved by God, and He wants that soul brought home.

What about the guys begging on the street? There are so many these days, and lots of them are con artists, so we preserve our dignity by walking on by. Well, some of them are in real need, and God values the saving of even a con artist above your dignity. Don't put yourself in danger, but engage with these wayward children of the Lord.

Then there are the ones who hurt us, people we trusted once and can never forgive for their betrayal. They weren't born cruel and callous. They were hurt, so they inflict hurt. God wants *you* to break that chain, to replace hurt with love.

It's a big task and one we might never be able to live up to, but we will be nearer to God for having tried.

God, help me, when appropriate and wise, to reach out and help those I'd rather avoid. May I show Your love to everyone, I pray.

If your enemy is hungry, give him food to eat; if he is thirsty,
give him water to drink. In doing this, you will heap burning
coals on his head, and the LORD will reward you.
PROVERBS 25:21–22 NIV

This verse defies human nature. The world's way is to bless one's friends and curse one's enemies. Forgiveness and mercy are foreign concepts. However, God's thoughts and ways are higher than man's (Isaiah 55:8), and this passage directs Christians to provide their enemies with subsistence and care.

God desires that believers resist carnal thinking and embrace the message of the cross. Namely, "Love your enemies. . .and pray for them which despitefully use you, and persecute you" (Matthew 5:44 KJV).

The end result of our humanitarianism is that we will heap burning coals on our enemy's head. This isn't backhanded benevolence intended to impose affliction on our enemies; it's a metaphor.

In Bible times, burning coals were placed below and heaped above metals placed in a furnace. In doing so, the metal was liquefied and the dross fell to the bottom. In the same manner, loving our enemies will either melt them into repentance and lead them to God or aggravate their condemnation, making their malice even more inexcusable.

Today's scripture presents an interesting paradox: those that revenge are the *conquered*, and those that forgive are *conquerors*.

Father, help me to love my enemies and do good to
them, even as You extend kindness to them. Amen.

*Walk with the wise and become wise, for a
companion of fools suffers harm.*
PROVERBS 13:20 NIV

Some biblical principles are easier to live by than others. Today's scripture is one of them.

While God will always provide the strength we need to do what He says, certain duties require a lot of faith. Shadrach, Meshach, and Abednego couldn't have stood tall in that crowd of prostrate Babylonians without some serious commitment to their Lord.

But walking with the wise? That's easy.

If you want to be wise, just make sure you're hanging out with the right crowd. Look for other Christian guys who have a clear passion for the Lord and His Word. In this world, they'll be pretty obvious. . .and because they are wise, they'll be happy to include you in their lives. True Christianity is never an exclusive club.

As you walk with the wise, the proverbs say you'll become wise. Then you can pass your wisdom along to other Christian guys, who will in turn do that for others. On and on the cycle goes until Jesus returns.

Really, it's a pretty ingenious system. But wouldn't you expect that from our all-wise God?

---

*Heavenly Father, I want to be wise. Please lead me
to wise men with whom I can walk. . .then help me
to pass along the wisdom I gain to others.*

Jesus looked at them and said, "With man this is
impossible, but with God all things are possible."
MATTHEW 19:26 NIV

The rich young ruler's conversation with Jesus had not gone as expected. Instead of learning that he had fulfilled all the requirements of the law—which he thought would admit him to heaven—the young man was told to sell his possessions and give to the poor. Dejected, he gave up and went home.

This turn of events prompted much discussion between Jesus and His disciples, centering on the difficulties of being admitted to heaven. Frustrated with the impossible scenario Jesus was painting, complete with camels going through the eye of a needle, the disciples finally asked: "Who then can be saved?" (Matthew 19:25 NIV).

With the question finally asked, Jesus zeroed in on the heart of the matter: no one can be saved by their own efforts! The rich young ruler had tried everything humanly possible, and still he came up short. Man's greatest efforts pale in comparison to the requirements of a holy God.

But grace, freely offered by God and accepted by individuals, will admit us to heaven. With God, all things *are* possible—especially enabling forgiven sinners to live eternally. Realizing we can do nothing is the key to gaining everything.

God, I still don't understand how You can save sinners like
me, but I'm very glad that You do. I praise You for it.

Go to the ant, you lazy one, observe its ways and be wise.
PROVERBS 6:6 NASB

Each species of ants—over ten thousand—includes one or more queens, a few males, and numerous female worker ants.

The queen ants do not lead or rule. They simply spend life laying eggs to populate the colony. The workers perform the bulk of the labor necessary for the colony to survive and diligently carry out their tasks without any leadership.

In some species, worker ants keep aphids the way people keep cows. The ants care for the aphids over winter and in spring place them outside on plants. When rubbed, these aphids secrete a sweet liquid used as a beverage by the ant colony.

In leaf-cutting species, worker ants cut leaves to grow fungus underground while other workers tend these subterranean gardens. Larger workers patrol the colony, keeping a sharp lookout for enemy insects.

Proverbs contrasts the hardworking ant with a sluggard.

The term *sluggard*, as used in this verse, implies irresponsibility and the lack of ambition to be successful, while the ant's ability to accomplish a task without oversight is applauded.

Do you procrastinate or feel overwhelmed by certain tasks? Break the chore into smaller segments and celebrate each completed part. Become wise by anticipating future needs and planning for them. Study the ant and learn from her.

Lord, ants are truly marvelous creatures. How they live and farm and work shows that an intelligent Being created them.

Jesus did many other things as well. If every one of them were written down, I suppose that even the whole world would not have room for the books that would be written.
JOHN 21:25 NIV

The Bible contains four Gospels, but it doesn't have a single biography of Jesus.

Aren't the Gospels biographies?

Not exactly. Two of the Gospels ignore Jesus' birth completely, and only Luke makes any mention of His childhood years.

Carl Sandberg needed six volumes to write a biography of Abraham Lincoln. The apostle John said that to write a definitive biography of Jesus would require more room than is available in the whole world. So he chose which details of Jesus' life to include—and with great care.

All of the Gospel writers did. They each had a particular purpose in writing their accounts of Jesus' life. John spells his out clearly: "That you may believe that Jesus is the Messiah, the Son of God, and that by believing you may have life in his name" (20:31 NIV).

Jesus' story continues to be written—in us. May our lives lead others to faith in Him.

Jesus, thank You for the four Gospels and the varied accounts they give of Your life. I look forward to learning more about You in heaven.

Never stop praying.
1 THESSALONIANS 5:17 NLT

Several passages of the Bible tell us clearly that God listens to us when we pray. He hears every word and is compassionate.

Sometimes the answer to our request is "not yet." Sometimes the answers are even a flat "no." But when we come before the Lord and lay what is in our hearts at His feet, He always finds a way to bless us and make everything work out for the best. He does this even when we don't get exactly what we want.

God is so much smarter than we could ever hope to be. He knows what is best for us and provides it each time. All we have to do is share our concerns with Him and wait faithfully for what He will provide.

God wants to be involved in our daily routines. He wants to hear from us and waits for us. God never promised an easy life to Christians. If we will allow Him, though, God will be there with us every step of the way. All we need to do is to come to Him in prayer. With these three simple words from 1 Thessalonians 5:17, our lives can be fulfilling as we live to communicate with our Lord.

*Father in heaven, help me to constantly follow
the advice in this verse, to seek Your face and
to draw close to You. In Jesus' name. Amen.*

*Fix these words of mine in your hearts and minds; tie them
as symbols on your hands and bind them on your foreheads.*
DEUTERONOMY 11:18 NIV

Have you ever seen a person of the Jewish faith wearing a small
box attached to his forehead? Phylacteries or frontlets are tiny
leather boxes worn by Orthodox Jews, tied to the forehead and
left arm and worn at prayer times.

Each box holds scrolls of parchment containing key Old
Testament verses. The frontlets provide a method of carrying
God's Word with them all the time. When they cross their arms,
they draw the scriptures closer to their hearts. They believe this
practice helps them fulfill the commandment in Deuteronomy.

How can we as Christians carry God's Word with us all the
time? This verse provides the answer: fix them in our hearts
and minds.

Maybe memorizing Bible verses isn't a fashionable thing in
today's world, but learning key verses plants the Word of God
deeply in our hearts.

We draw strength and nourishment in dark times from
remembering what God told us in the Bible. In times of crisis
we recall God's promises of hope and comfort. In our everyday
moments, repeating well-known verses reminds us that God is
always with us—whether we feel like it or not.

*Dear God, help me to hide Your Word in my heart so that it can
comfort and strengthen me during times of testing. Amen.*

*"Where is your faith?" he asked his disciples. In fear and
amazement they asked one another, "Who is this? He commands
even the winds and the water, and they obey him."*
LUKE 8:25 NIV

It was calm on the lake that day when the disciples and Jesus
set out in their boat to sail across to the other side. It was such a
leisurely boat ride that Jesus fell asleep as they went along. Then it
happened.

Calmness was replaced by a squall. The boat began taking
on so much water that it was going under. The disciples woke
Jesus up and pleaded with Him to do something because they
were going to drown.

Jesus got up and spoke to the wind and the powerful water.
The storm ceased and calmness was restored. After Jesus stilled
the storm, He questioned His followers about where their faith
was. Stunned at this new aspect of Christ they had seen, they
could only marvel at His ability to control nature.

Jesus used the terrifying boat ride that day not only to display
His power over all creation but to provide an opportunity for the
disciples to look at the depth of their faith.

We would be wise to do likewise, for the question "Where is
your faith?" is one Jesus still asks today.

*Jesus, I don't know how I would have reacted during
that storm. I probably would have been afraid.
So please strengthen my faith, I pray.*

Do not answer a fool according to his foolishness,
lest you also be like him. Answer a fool according
to his foolishness, lest he be wise in his own eyes.
PROVERBS 26:4–5 SKJV

Skeptics love to point out what they believe are contradictions in the Bible. Well, here's one if ever there was one. The only problem is, of course, that this is no contradiction. Solomon gave these two contrasting pieces of advice, deliberately stating one right after the other, to make it clear that we are to respond differently in different circumstances. Solomon later pointed out, "There is a time for everything," and "the wise heart will know the proper time and procedure" (Ecclesiastes 3:1; 8:5 NIV).

The kind of answer you give a fool (the word here means a "self-confident person") depends on how caught up in his self-confident opinions he is, what the circumstances are, and who's standing around listening. God may lead you to give him a serious answer (in contrast to his proud chatter) or a humorous, foolish answer (to show him how foolishly he's talking).

With a full-blown fool, it's best to bite your tongue and refrain from saying anything at all (Proverbs 23:9). No matter what you say, it won't persuade him.

Lord, give me the wisdom to know how to answer each person.
Please inspire me with the right words by Your Spirit, I pray. Amen.

Jesus wept.
JOHN 11:35 KJV

If you've attended church for any amount of time, you probably recognize John 11:35 as "the shortest verse in the Bible."

For accuracy's sake, we should actually say John 11:35 is the shortest verse in many English translations of the Bible, including the venerable King James Version. But some modern translations, such as the New International Version, have an even shorter verse, Job 3:2: "He said."

Wherever it stands statistically, John 11:35 is a memorable and powerful verse. Jesus, the Son of God, Creator of the universe (John 1:1–3), actually cried when He saw the pain caused by the death of His friend Lazarus.

John 11 goes on to say that Jesus raised Lazarus back from the dead, restoring him to his grieving sisters, Mary and Martha. That showed Jesus' power as God—but before that, in a moment of pure humanity, He wept over the loss of a friend.

These days, those of us who obey Jesus' commands are His friends (John 15:14), and He still feels our pain, sorrow, and temptations (Hebrews 4:15). This is no cold, aloof, angry God that we serve!

Jesus, I'm moved by Your love for Lazarus and his sisters. This shows that You know and care for people individually—including me.

"Then you will know which way to go, since you have never been this way before. But keep a distance of about two thousand cubits between you and the ark; do not go near it."
JOSHUA 3:4 NIV

We have numerous tools these days to help us navigate through places we're unfamiliar with. Maps, GPS systems, and cell phones give us confidence that we won't get lost. The Israelites didn't have such tools; instead they had something better for guidance—the ark of the covenant.

The time had come for Joshua to lead the Israelites across the Jordan River into a new land. The people hadn't journeyed in this direction, so the plan was for them to follow the ark, which the priests would be carrying. When they saw the direction the ark was going they would know which way to go.

The Israelites could only safely travel into the unknown by believing in what was known: that God was leading them. Earlier in scripture it was their ancestor Abraham who had taken a walk of faith into unknown territory under God's guidance (Genesis 12).

Many times in our lives we're going to find ourselves heading in a direction we're not familiar with. When God's the one who has brought us to that unknown territory, we can be sure He'll guide us through it.

Lord, You promised to send Your angel before me and said You Yourself would be with me and never forsake me. Thank You for that.

"But I tell you, do not resist an evil person. If anyone slaps you on the right cheek, turn to them the other cheek also."
MATTHEW 5:39 NIV

There was one four-letter word Jesus hoped would forever be on the tips of our tongues: *love*.

The Lord had more to say about love than almost any other topic. His advice was straightforward: Jesus said we should love God (Matthew 22:36–37), love our neighbors (Matthew 22:39), and love our enemies (Matthew 5:44).

Our enemies? Now that's called "pushing the envelope."

In theory, it sounds wonderful. But in reality, it can feel impossible. Take the disciple Peter, for example. For years, he had heard Jesus' teachings on love, but when the high priests came to arrest Jesus (John 18:10), Peter resisted love and defensively cut off the enemy's ear. Jesus corrected him saying, "Put your sword away" (verse 11). Then He healed the man.

God knows we live in a world where walking away is often judged spineless. That's why He sent Jesus to really "push the envelope" and become the definition of love.

Because God extended us His grace, we, too, can courageously accept the enemy's strike and "turn the other cheek."

Father, help me to be motivated by love, not pride, in all my interactions. Help me to love even my enemies. In Jesus' name, I pray.

Do everything without grumbling or arguing.
PHILIPPIANS 2:14 NIV

Pollyanna is a classic children's story about a young orphan whose sunny outlook on life fueled an unstoppable optimism. Regardless of the challenges she encountered, Pollyanna met each circumstance with a commitment to look for the best. Her "Glad Game" reached out to others and encouraged her community.

The apostle Paul knew of hardship and challenges long before the character Pollyanna appeared in a novel. Having endured shipwrecks and imprisonment, Paul's life circumstances were far from a carefree existence. Surely there were moments when he wanted to argue and complain at the harsh circumstances he was experiencing. And yet, after asking the difficult questions, his response was to hold to his faith in the God who knew him by name and who had called him to take the gospel to the Gentiles.

Try this experiment today: Every time you notice you are complaining or arguing, switch your watch (or a bracelet, or a rubber band) from one wrist to the other. When the day is over, reflect on how many times you made the change. How often did you catch yourself in a negative pattern?

Paul's instructions to do everything without complaining or arguing are a central component in Pollyanna's Glad Game. Perhaps we would all do well to play it daily.

God, please be with me today. Keep my mind focused on happy, positive thoughts. Help me even to encourage and cheer others. Amen.

*While Paul was waiting for them in Athens, he was deeply
troubled by all the idols he saw everywhere in the city.*
ACTS 17:16 NLT

While exploring Athens, Paul discovered the appalling truth
of a common Roman saying, "It's easier to find a god at Athens
than a man."

Burdened for the Athenians, Paul began proclaiming Christ in
the Jewish synagogue and every day in the agora (marketplace). As
a result, Epicurean and Stoic philosophers met Paul and brought
him to Mars Hill to hear his teachings.

Previously, Paul had noticed an Athenian altar to *agnostos
theos*, "the unknown god." In his address on Mars Hill, Paul used
this unknown god as a bridge from the Athenian idols to God and
His Son, Jesus. Paul also quoted Epimenides and Aratus, poets
familiar to the Athenians.

Rather than condemning the people and spouting dire warnings, Paul looked for common ground and built his case for Christ
from there. As a result, several men and women believed his
message.

Are you around people whose beliefs differ greatly from yours?
Do you sometimes feel lost as to how to turn a conversation to
Christ? Copy Paul's approach. Look for a shared viewpoint or
familiar truth and slowly build from there.

*Dear Lord, inspire me with ways to build cross-cultural
bridges. Show me common ground with those of
different mind-sets and beliefs. Amen.*

Turn my eyes from worthless things,
and give me life through your word.
PSALM 119:37 NLT

How's your spiritual eyesight? Are things in focus, or is your life a little blurry? Are worthless things impeding your vision?

The psalmist recognized that many things in life vie for our attention. Some have little value and take us farther away from God's transformational power—hence the "worthless" designation. Myopic distractions may foster a selfish, nearsighted focus. A farsighted focus can keep us so busily distracted with others that we have no time to reflect and grow in our own lives. Astigmatism reflects the struggle for balance between the two extremes.

But some things bring us closer to God and preserve our life—life that comes through God's Word. To turn away from worthless things, let's focus our eyes on Jesus, "the pioneer and perfecter of faith" (Hebrews 12:2 NIV). Let's allow our lives to be changed by the power of His Word as we encounter Him each day.

Please, God, search my thoughts. Reveal areas where
I have an imbalance, and show me how to bring them
into proper focus. In Jesus' name, I ask. Amen.

Do not get drunk on wine. . . . Instead, be filled with the Spirit.
EPHESIANS 5:18 NIV

On the day of Pentecost, when those gathered together saw and felt the presence of God's Holy Spirit, they became hilarious. There was a nonalcoholic response to the exciting Third Person of the Trinity. The only hangover experienced was lingering joy.

There was a day when Spirit-filled believers gave expression to their joy in Christ. It was impossible to be blasé about God's transforming work. He is still making "all things new." Nothing is different today: when one has a brand-new start in life, well, that's to be celebrated!

While the doctrine of the Holy Spirit varies slightly from denomination to denomination, all Christians understand the great influence He has in the life of God's children. In New Testament Greek He is described as the Paraclete, the one who is beside us. Celebrate that.

When Jesus returned to the Father, God gave the Holy Spirit to the world (Acts 2), with responsibility for comfort, guidance, direction, and the empowerment of believers. Celebrate that. You can sing,

> *The Comforter has come! The Comforter has come!*
> *The Holy Ghost from Heav'n, the Father's promise giv'n!*
> *O spread the tidings 'round, wherever man is found;*
> *The Comforter has come!*

FRANK BOTTOME

*Father, fill me with Your Holy Spirit. Pour Your
joy into me, and help me to obey You. Amen.*

"For by your words you will be acquitted,
and by your words you will be condemned."
MATTHEW 12:37 NIV

Remember when you realized that a certain childhood expression—"Sticks and stones may break my bones, but words will never hurt me"—was a lie?

Words can act as a gentle spring rain or a thunderous storm. Words can stir things up or settle things down. Our words are so important that James spent most of a chapter in his book detailing the nature of the tongue and its power. The book of Proverbs warns us repeatedly to give careful thought to the way we speak.

Before telling a crowd that their words would prove their guilt or innocence, Jesus said that people would someday give account of all the careless words they'd ever spoken (Matthew 12:36).

According to Jesus, our words are a reflection of what we've stored up in our hearts. Good brings out good, evil brings out evil. Other people, who can't see into our hearts, clearly learn what's there by the way we speak.

What is your heart saying today?

Almighty God, help me to guard what comes out of
my mouth. Keep me from uttering foolish things.
Prevent me from speaking hastily, I pray.

Now may the Lord of peace himself give
you peace at all times and in every way.
2 THESSALONIANS 3:16 NIV

Had the apostle Paul lived in modern America, Second
Thessalonians might have been Second Chicagoans, Second
Angelenos, or Second New Yorkers. As it is, his first-century
letter still speaks powerfully to Christians everywhere.

The Macedonian believers who originally received Paul's
message were suffering from persecution and trials (1:4), false
teaching (2:2), and the misbehavior of fellow Christians (3:6).
Some in the congregation had become lazy and disruptive, to the
point of mooching food off of others. "Such people we command
and urge in the Lord Jesus Christ," Paul wrote, "to settle down
and earn the food they eat" (3:12 NIV).

All of these things contributed to the Thessalonians' suffering
for God's sake. If we're committed to living godly lives in our
culture, we'll suffer too.

But Paul offered hope in the form of God's peace. Notice how
extensive it is: this peace comes from God Himself, "the Lord of
peace," and it's available "at all times and in every way." Whatever
frustrates and troubles us is more than offset by the peace of
God—which, Paul said elsewhere, "transcends all understanding
[and] will guard your hearts and your minds in Christ Jesus"
(Philippians 4:7 NIV). All you have to do is ask.

Heavenly Father, there are more than enough troubling things
in life. Please control my reactions and give me peace.

*Paul looked straight at the Sanhedrin and said, "My brothers,
I have fulfilled my duty to God in all good conscience to this day."*
ACTS 23:1 NIV

After his arrest, Paul, a Jew and Roman citizen, stood before
the Sanhedrin and chief priests to plead his case. The apostle
declared—with a clear and good conscience—his commitment
to God, his fervent determination to serve and please Him, and
his faultless life even before his conversion to Christ.

Before Christ, Paul lived according to the Jewish law and
ordinances and remained true to those teachings. He was void
of hypocrisy or dishonesty and acted from his conscience. After
Paul's conversion, he was a warrior of faith resolute to serve the
Lord with all holiness and zeal, ever mindful of his call to God
and service to others.

The translation of the Latin word rendered "conscience" is
"what one knows with oneself." The conscience is the inner faculty
that decides the moral quality of our thoughts, words, and actions.
Our consciences are seared with remorse when we do wrong and
endowed with peace and satisfaction when we choose right. All
of us must live with our own consciences, whether good or bad.

In another passage Paul said, "So I strive always to keep my
conscience clear before God and man" (Acts 24:16 NIV). May
we all do likewise.

---

*Lord, You promised that You would wash my
conscience clean (Hebrews 10:22). Forgive my sins,
O God, and give me peace within. Amen.*

There is a way that appears to be right,
but in the end it leads to death.
PROVERBS 14:12 NIV

Why do we love a glorious last stand? General Custer's final defeat is a revered part of American history. The poet Tennyson glorified the Light Brigade for charging into rows of Russian cannons. Butch Cassidy and the Sundance Kid will forever be remembered in freeze-frame just before the Bolivian soldiers shoot them down.

Each time you watch the film, don't you wish Butch and Sundance could find another way out? Don't you still hold your breath to see if Steve McQueen will make it over the barbed wire to freedom in *The Great Escape*? And if only those reinforcements had reached Little Bighorn in time!

Why does the last stand appeal to us so much? Because we know our stubbornness could easily put us in the same position. Our insistence on going the "way that seems right to a man" might satisfy our rebel souls, but we weren't made to be rebels.

Despite our insistence on going our own way, we still long for a last-minute rescue. No matter how far into the Valley of Death we ride, there is a God we can count on to save us. Jesus pulls off more rescues than the US Cavalry ever has, and His way leads to life.

Jesus, You've rescued me time after time. I thank You for that—
but please help me simply to obey You, the first time, every time.

*Consider it pure joy, my brothers and sisters, whenever
you face trials of many kinds, because you know that
the testing of your faith produces perseverance.*
JAMES 1:2–3 NIV

This verse comes from a letter written by James, most likely the brother closest in age to Jesus. If you remember, James did not always believe Jesus was the Messiah (John 7:5). Perhaps he was speaking from experience when writing these words.

God spoke through James, to encourage Jewish Christians who were worn out from persecution for their faith. Likewise through these same words, God encourages us when we're tired and beaten down with life's challenges.

Initially, the suggestion that we consider trials as "pure joy" doesn't feel encouraging. Enduring difficulties in order to achieve a stronger faith seems futile. But the apostle Peter says, "Trials. . .have come so that the proven genuineness of your faith—of greater worth than gold, which perishes even though refined by fire—may result in praise, glory and honor when Jesus Christ is revealed" (1 Peter 1:6–7 NIV).

God promised that He will never leave or forsake us (Hebrews 13:5). So when we feel the heat, may we call on God's power to help us persevere. And may we consider it pure blessing to have faith that's refined, genuine, and honorable to Jesus Christ our Lord.

*Father, please give me joy when I'm going through severe tests.
Remind me that You're with me and refining me. In Jesus' name. Amen.*

> *Return unto me, and I will return unto you,*
> *saith the LORD of hosts.*
> MALACHI 3:7 KJV

After God spoke through His prophet Malachi, the Lord went silent for about four centuries. Then John the Baptist appeared, preparing the way for the ultimate expression of God's truth—His Son, Jesus Christ.

So what was the Lord's final Old Testament spokesman saying? What message did "My messenger" (the meaning of Malachi's name) have for God's people?

As with all of the prophets, Malachi warned the people of Israel about their sin. But he also reminded the chosen ones of the love of their heavenly Father. They had wandered far from God, been punished by Assyrian and Babylonian invaders, and been restored to their homeland. Sadly, their hearts still strayed from true worship.

So Malachi appeared with God's final word before the "Word" finally appeared. "Return unto me, and I will return unto you," the Lord said.

It was a promise to the people of ancient Israel but also a glimpse into the heart of a loving heavenly Father. It's a promise we can still count on today.

Lord, thank You for this beautiful promise. Help me to wholeheartedly return to You so that I may see Your work in my life.

So then, just as you received Christ Jesus as Lord, continue to live your lives in him, rooted and built up in him, strengthened in the faith as you were taught, and overflowing with thankfulness.
COLOSSIANS 2:6–7 NIV

How do we live as disciples of Christ? This verse gives us four simple guidelines to follow.

First, we reach out to Jesus in daily prayer, as He is now living within our hearts. Living with someone means spending time together so we can learn His ways.

Second, we nourish our roots to grow deeper for a strong foundation. Mighty trees have deep roots to support them in turbulent winds and terrible storms. Our roots are nourished with the waters of prayer and the food from studying the Bible. This stabilizes us to face the storms in life.

Next, we draw strength by remembering what we have learned in the past and what we have been taught by others. Their words or the example of how they lived fortifies our faith.

Finally, we give thanks in all circumstances. Gratitude flows easily during good times. But even in difficult circumstances, expressing appreciation renews our spirits.

How do we live for God? He guides our lives through prayer and study, the fellowship of others, and practicing daily gratitude.

Jesus, help me to live my entire life in You. Help my faith roots to go deep down in Your love and Your Word. Amen.

Oh, the joys of those who do not follow the advice
of the wicked, or stand around with sinners,
or join in with mockers.

PSALM 1:1 NLT

There are few joys greater than that of having done the right thing, even if those around you have not.

God knows what is in our hearts and minds. He loves us and cares about us so much that He takes an intimate interest in everything we do. May He never see us making bad decisions or following those who are obviously making bad choices.

Unfortunately, this is exactly what He sees at times. Christianity is for intelligent people. It is available to everyone. It is a party to which everyone is invited. But not everyone chooses to make smart decisions. Sometimes it is so much easier to simply go along with the crowd.

This seems to take pressure off us and makes us feel better in the moment. Later, though, we realize what we have done and how we have pushed ourselves away from God.

The next time we are tempted to follow the crowd, it would be wise to remember the very first verse of Psalms. What a joy it is to do the right thing.

God, please surround me with those who will give me
good, honest advice. Help me not to be swept along
by peer pressure, I ask. In Jesus' name. Amen.

Jesus turned and said to Peter, "Get behind me, Satan!
You are a stumbling block to me; you do not have in mind
the concerns of God, but merely human concerns."
MATTHEW 16:23 NIV

That was a bit harsh, wasn't it? Poor old Peter meant well.

But, of course, Jesus was right. He knew death was waiting for Him. He also knew it was an important part of His Father's plan.

Peter was acting out of love, but it was human love with a fair portion of self-interest. He didn't want to lose his friend.

We forget sometimes how far above us God really is. Our version of love is nothing compared to His, and while we see the death of someone close to us as a tragedy, to God it's surely a glorious homecoming by one of His own.

This is a beautiful world and we, understandably, hate the thought of losing some of the people in it. Satan relies on that. He takes our attachments and weaknesses and uses them as stumbling blocks between us and heaven.

But, wonderfully, Jesus turns stumbling blocks into stepping stones. When, thanks to Him, we arrive up above, hopefully we will find, like Peter, that we didn't really lose anyone after all.

Lord, I often see circumstances through a narrow,
skewed perspective. Give me faith to take the
long view. Show me Your viewpoint. Amen.

And the LORD said unto Satan, Behold, all that he hath is in thy power; only upon himself put not forth thine hand. So Satan went forth from the presence of the LORD.
JOB 1:12 KJV

Many people picture God and Satan as opposing forces locked in eternal combat. When the good times roll, then God must be having the upper hand. When things go south, Satan is winning.

Today's scripture opens a window to the inner workings of God's day-to-day administration. In Job 1, Satan first gave an account to God of his travels through the earth. Then God informed Satan of Job's uprightness. Satan replied that Job was on God's side because the Lord had blessed him so much: "Just take away his goods and watch what happens then." At that point, God allowed Satan to test Job, but issued a strict charge not to touch his person.

Clearly, Satan is under God's complete authority. The devil can't work without God's permission. No matter how bad things may get, they are never out of control. And a day is coming when God will rid the universe of Satan, casting him into eternal fire.

One final thought: Job was blessed more at the end of his life than the beginning (Job 42:12).

Dear God, I'm so grateful that You're in control, that the devil isn't free to harm Your children. Protect me from his attacks, I pray.

Who is he who condemns? It is Christ who died, yes, rather, who was raised again, who is even at the right hand of God, who also makes intercession for us.
ROMANS 8:34 SKJV

When Jesus Christ died on the cross, He paid the price for our sins, and when He rose from the dead, He broke the power of death in our lives. If that wasn't enough, now that He's in heaven, sitting at the right hand of God, He constantly intercedes to God for us.

So who is he who condemns us? The devil does, of course. He's called "the accuser of our brethren," and day and night he accuses Christians before God. But we can overcome him with the blood of Jesus Christ—the same blood that paid the price for our sin (Revelation 12:10–11).

People sometimes condemn us, but Paul said that we shouldn't pay attention to them (1 Corinthians 4:3). And we in turn are commanded not to judge others (Matthew 7:1).

We often condemn ourselves, but even "if our heart condemns us, God is greater than our heart and knows all things" (1 John 3:20 SKJV).

How can *anyone* really condemn us when Christ Himself took away our sin and never ceases to intervene to God His Father on our behalf?

Thank You, Jesus, for constantly interceding with the Father on my behalf. Thank You that no one— not even myself—has any grounds to condemn me.

*"If anyone asks you, 'Why are you doing this?' say,
'The Lord needs it and will send it back here shortly.'"*
MARK 11:3 NIV

The Lord Jesus knew the triumphal entry awaited Him when He borrowed a donkey.

David worshipped this same Jesus, God the Son in the flesh, saying, "The heavens are yours, and yours also the earth" (Psalm 89:11 NIV). As God said to Job, "Everything under heaven belongs to me" (Job 41:11 NIV). Yet the God who owned the world told His disciples to borrow a colt and to tell the owner, when asked, "The Lord *needs* it" (italics added).

The Greek word *chreia*, translated elsewhere as "business," appears forty-nine times in the New Testament. Its primary use refers to things humans need: the sick need a physician (Matthew 9:12). John needed to be baptized by Jesus (Matthew 3:14). God supplies all our needs (Philippians 4:19). Twice, John uses the word to describe Jesus' omniscience (John 2:25; 16:30).

Only in this passages about the triumphal entry do we read that Jesus needed something from us: something as simple as a ride into town, on loan, to be returned shortly.

Everything belongs to God by right. But He grants us the privilege of sharing out of our poverty to join Him in conducting His business.

*Jesus, may I give my all for Your service! Help me to do whatever
You desire, whenever You ask me. Help me to give cheerfully.*

There happened to be a Jewish man in Susa the citadel whose name was Mordecai. He was the son of Jair, the son of Shimei, the son of Kish, a Benjaminite, who had been taken into exile from Jerusalem with the captives who had been carried into exile with Jeconiah king of Judah, whom Nebuchadnezzar king of Babylon had taken into exile.
ESTHER 2:5-6 NET

We should never forget that the Bible tells the story of real people, set in real history.

The book of Esther takes place in 460 BC, against the backdrop of Persian military aggression against Greece. Ancient tablets found by archaeologists confirm that Mordecai was a scribe or minister at the royal court of King Xerxes in Susa, where Nehemiah also served and Daniel had prophesied. Over and over again, the Bible is shown to be true and trustworthy.

"Now there happened to be. . ." Isn't it amazing how God's providence works, even in secular places where He isn't welcomed by name? The book of Esther never once mentions God directly, yet His hand is clearly at work throughout the story.

In the same way, we should be a light in our world, even where we can't discuss God openly.

Lord, may I always "happen to be" in the right place at the right time, that You may freely use me. In Jesus' name. Amen.

*And he said: "Truly I tell you, unless you change
and become like little children, you will never
enter the kingdom of heaven."*
MATTHEW 18:3 NIV

On the road to Capernaum, Christ's disciples were arguing among themselves about which of them was the greatest. When Jesus asked what they had been arguing about, they kept quiet (Mark 9:33–34). Maybe they were embarrassed to say.

Matthew 18 provides more insight into this story. It says that the disciples asked Jesus, "Who is the greatest in the kingdom of heaven?" (Matthew 18:1 KJV). In other words, "What do we have to do to attain greatness when we get there?"

In Matthew 18:3, Jesus answers their question by using little children as examples. He tells His disciples that they need to change their attitudes and think with the righteous heart of a child.

Very young children approach the world with innocence. They are free from selfish ambition, are humble and dependent on their parents. This simple, meek spirit is what God requires of us. Instead of worrying about being great here on earth or when we get to heaven, Matthew 18:3 indicates we should be concerned about whether we will enter His kingdom at all.

*Father, please give me the humble, trusting, innocent attitude of a
small child so that I'll refrain from seeking my own glory. Amen.*

When they had crossed, Elijah said to Elisha, "Tell me, what can I do for you before I am taken from you?" "Let me inherit a double portion of your spirit," Elisha replied.
2 KINGS 2:9 NIV

What a bold request.

Elijah offered a blessing to Elisha. Elisha responded, "Let me inherit a double portion of your spirit."

Elijah filled the role of leader, prophet, and miracle worker. Why would Elisha want the heavy responsibilities and difficulties involved in this type of work?

Elisha could have asked for wealth, unlimited power, or a life with no problems. Even the ability to live each day in peace was within his reach.

Yet Elisha asked for Elijah's spirit. He did not ask to have a larger ministry than Elijah—he was only asking to inherit what Elijah was leaving and to be able to carry it on.

What might God give us if we asked boldly for the impossible? God deeply desires to bless us. If our hearts line up with His will and we stay open to His call, He will surprise us. God takes the ordinary and through His power transforms our prayers into the extraordinary—even double-portion requests.

God, increase my faith so that I can boldly ask You for great things. May You use me mightily for Your purposes, I pray. Amen.

Don't be ashamed of me.
2 TIMOTHY 1:8 NLT

Who could be ashamed of the apostle Paul—especially his almost-son Timothy?

Speculation about the younger man's background includes a sickly childhood, a doting Jewish mother and grandmother, and an absentee Greek father. Perhaps, as the only child in a wealthy family, he was shielded from many of life's vicissitudes; he was timid and undisciplined. Yet Paul saw in Timothy the potential for servanthood.

In this "farewell letter," the apostle is introspective, remembering the boy Timothy used to be. He reminds Timothy that "the Spirit God gave us does not make us timid, but gives us power, love and self-discipline" (2 Timothy 1:7 NIV). *Don't let my present condition deter you from proclaiming Jesus.* Implied: Do not be ashamed of our Lord.

Older people can be a great influence on the younger generation, but as the apostle Paul illustrates, it remains the child's task to "fan into flame" the sparks lit by others (1:6 NIV).

Let's all live up to our spiritual responsibilities—whether we're fanning the flame ourselves or igniting the spark in others.

Lord, anoint me to send sparks of inspiration into people's lives, and fan the flames of the fires they already have burning. In Jesus' name. Amen.

He has made everything beautiful in its time. He has
also set eternity in the human heart; yet no one can
fathom what God has done from beginning to end.
ECCLESIASTES 3:11 NIV

Our souls know there is a God. The souls of unbelievers know it
too. By setting "eternity in the human heart" God gave us a longing
for Him. That deep desire is fulfilled in those who accept Jesus,
but those who deny Him have to find something else to scratch
the itch. That unfulfilled longing is the best explanation for abuses
of alcohol, drugs, sex, and power.

Of course, earthly desires are traps, but sometimes they are
even used by believers to bolster faith weakened by a lack of
understanding.

Our human nature needs to understand. It's a problem that
holds many a believer and unbeliever back. No one can completely
"fathom what God has done." That's what makes Him God. And
yet, still we try.

Thankfully, our hearts don't need to understand; neither do
they need earthly "fixes." They just need to be set free, to find God
and revel in the beauty of His never-ending creation. Believer,
stop letting unanswerable questions prevent you from loving
God more completely. And if you're an unbeliever, ask yourself:
If you had every material thing you could want, wouldn't your
heart still be reaching out for eternity?

Lord, help me to seek those treasures and rewards that are above,
with Christ. Help me to always have my eyes on heaven and eternity.

He existed before anything else,
and he holds all creation together.
COLOSSIANS 1:17 NLT

Jesus holds our world together in both the spiritual and the physical realm. It's not that He wraps His arms around our universe to keep it from falling apart. Rather, Jesus fine-tuned our planet for life and continually preserves those conditions.

Earth's precise distance from the sun is essential to life. If it were 5 percent closer, rivers and oceans would evaporate from a strong greenhouse effect. Move 5 percent farther away, and both water and carbon dioxide would freeze. Too cold or too hot means no life.

Even our sterile moon makes life possible by stabilizing the tilt of Earth's axis. Without the moon's steady pull, the earth's tilt could randomly swing over a wide range, resulting in erratic seasons, with temperatures too hot and too cold for life.

Astronomers are also discovering how other planets in our solar system actually help the earth. For example, the huge planet Jupiter deflects many comets from entering the inner section of the solar system, where they could easily hit our planet with devastating results.

Through science we discover the physical laws Jesus designed for our universe. Through Bible study we unearth the spiritual laws Jesus designed for us. Look to Jesus to hold your life together.

Jesus, I praise You for how You set up the universe
and keep it running smoothly day by day.

"When they were discouraged, I smiled at them.
My look of approval was precious to them."
JOB 29:24 NLT

This verse prompts a question: If, without the luxury of words, we communicated solely through our actions or mere presence, what message would our lives convey?

It is said that a smile is the light of one's countenance. Job was a righteous, well-respected man of God. His friends and countrymen lauded him for his wisdom, and all men listened to him, heeding his instruction. Prior to Job's afflictions, the people sought his favor. Consequently, his smile was enough to encourage and lighten their loads (verses 21–24).

Our preoccupation with words often obscures a simple truth: *what we say is not as important as who we are.* Job's smile made a difference because of the life he led.

Our most authentic forms of communication occur without a word. Rather, they flow from an understanding smile, a compassionate touch, a loving gesture, a gentle presence, or an unspoken prayer.

God used Job, an ordinary man with an extraordinary amount of love and wisdom—a man whose only adornment was righteous living and a warm smile. And He wants to use us too. So keep smiling. Someone may just need it.

Lord, overshadow me with Your presence, so when people consider my life, they see someone full of Your Spirit, gentleness, and love. Amen.

"My sheep listen to my voice;
I know them, and they follow me."
JOHN 10:27 NIV

Sheep graze in large flocks. They often spread out finding the best
spot for some tasty grass or cool water to drink. They wander down
gullies and ruts, oblivious to dangers such as pits or wild animals.

Sheep are not very smart animals. They need someone to
watch over them and lead them to the best places.

But sheep do know one thing quite well: the sound of the
shepherd's voice. They hear him call, even from great distances.
His voice directs them back to safety. They know to bleat for his
help when they get into trouble.

We humans aren't always smart, either. We get lost as we seek
the glittering attractions of the world. We wander off our spiritual
path, distracted by our own desires and ignoring the dangers.

We also have a good Shepherd to watch over us and gently
call us to safety. If we listen, we can hear His voice even when
we drift away.

Jesus wants us to hear Him and to follow His path. What will
we choose to listen to? The noisy sounds of the world or His soft
whisper to join Him?

Jesus, You are the good Shepherd. Help me always to hear Your
voice calling me back to You. And help me to obey it. Amen.

"But LORD!" Moses objected. "My own people won't listen to me anymore. How can I expect Pharaoh to listen?"
EXODUS 6:12 NLT

The story of the Exodus is familiar to many of us. Called out of the wilderness, Moses was dispatched by God to rescue the Israelites from the oppressive Egyptians. Returning to the country he had fled as a fugitive, Moses no doubt presumed that he would go in, do what God said, and get out as quickly as possible.

Instead, Moses faced down Pharaoh on multiple occasions, with the Israelites' oppressive workload doubling as a result of the negotiations. Instead of smooth sailing, Moses saw circumstances deteriorate—even as he followed God's instructions verbatim. The dark hour in Israel's history. . .became even darker!

Moses' discouragement is evident. He was sent to deliver Israel, and they weren't listening to him. Pharaoh wasn't listening. Conditions were worsening instead of improving. It would have been easy for him to say, "Obviously this isn't working, God. Find someone else who can succeed with this."

Stuck in the middle, Moses didn't give up. Instead, he kept the lines of communication open between himself and God. Moses chose to persevere through the hardships of dealing with difficult people.

Who are the difficult people in your life? What impossible situation is God calling you to persevere through?

God, give me the patience to put up with difficult people. And help me to persevere when circumstances become trying, I ask. Amen.

I do not want you to be ignorant, brothers, concerning those
who are asleep, lest you sorrow as others who have no hope.
For if we believe that Jesus died and rose again, even so
God will bring with Him those who sleep in Jesus.
1 THESSALONIANS 4:13-14 SKJV

Of all great promises in scripture, here is one of the greatest.

We Christians know that this world is not everything. Death is not the end. Life, now such a strange mixture of joy and sorrow, will one day be completely good. Our Christian family and friends who have died on earth are fully alive in heaven, awaiting the day they return with Jesus, when He comes back to make everything right.

All of these things are based on the reality of Jesus' resurrection. We believe that He died a real death on a real cross in a real time and place. And we believe that He really came back to life to demonstrate His infinite power. Death and Satan have no hold on Jesus, and He promises the same protection and victory to those of us who trust in Him.

We do not "sorrow as others who have no hope." The Christian's sorrow points toward an ultimate joy. So the apostle Paul says, "Comfort one another with these words" (1 Thessalonians 4:18 SKJV).

Lord Jesus, You showed the way by Your death and resurrection.
Thank You for promising me life after death—with You, forever!

Jesus replied, "But even more blessed are all who hear the word of God and put it into practice."
LUKE 11:28 NLT

Money, it is said, makes the world go 'round. But a good argument can also be made for connections.

Successful people make sure their relatives are well provided for. Kings hand down the throne to their own offspring. Business leaders make sure their families have jobs (or simply cash). Influential people engineer opportunities for their spouses, siblings, and kids. If you're "in," life is good.

It's nice to know that Jesus takes an entirely different approach.

One time when He was teaching, a woman in the crowd interrupted Jesus by shouting, "Blessed is the mother who gave you birth and nursed you" (Luke 11:27–28 NIV).

What the woman said was true. Mary herself, after learning she would give birth to the Messiah, praised God by saying, "From now on all generations will call me blessed" (Luke 1:48 NLT).

But Jesus' response to that enthusiastic follower—the words of today's scripture—broadened the opportunity for blessing. You don't have to be Jesus' flesh-and-blood kin to enjoy God's favor. Just listen for His voice and apply His Word to your life. No special connections are needed. *Anyone* can be blessed.

Lord Jesus, it's so nice to know that You welcome everyone. I don't have to be "anyone special" to be blessed. I just need to follow You.

> *No one who is born of God will continue to sin,*
> *because God's seed remains in them; they cannot*
> *go on sinning, because they have been born of God.*
> 1 JOHN 3:9 NIV

The Greek word translated "seed" in this verse is none other than *sperma*. One born of God has His "seed" in him, a spiritual DNA that marks us as belonging to Him. One of these DNA markers changes our awareness of sin. John repeats his assertion that God's child will not continue sinning twice more in this epistle (3:6 and 5:18).

Paul talked about the constant tension between knowing what is right yet doing what is wrong (Romans 7:7–25). Only as we live by the Spirit can we put our sinful natures to death (Romans 8). John also acknowledged this tension—and ultimate victory—when he stated that "everyone [who is] born of God overcomes the world" (1 John 5:4 NIV).

People have always been tempted to claim to know God while doing evil. Back in Jeremiah's day, people called the Lord Father and friend. Jeremiah said, "This is how you talk, but you do all the evil you can" (Jeremiah 3:5 NIV).

In Christ and by the Spirit, we have overcome the world. May our lives reflect this truth in increasing measure.

Jesus, You said that You have overcome the world—
and Your Spirit lives in me. May I be yielded to You
and become an overcomer also. Amen.

I often think of the heavens your hands have made,
and of the moon and stars you put in place.
PSALM 8:3 CEV

Almost three thousand years ago, the psalmist David looked with awe at the clear night sky. He gazed at the moon and the twinkling stars and marveled at the greatness of God. How could someone so immensely creative care about us lowly humans?

In the summer of 1969, another man wondered the same thing. American astronaut Edwin "Buzz" Aldrin saw the night sky with a new perspective—from the surface of the moon. Aldrin and Neil Armstrong were the first humans to walk on the moon. One can only imagine the thoughts that filled their minds.

For Aldrin, it was a deeply religious experience. As he stood on the moon's surface and gazed up at the sky, he remembered the words of the psalmist David as written in the King James Version of the Bible. He quoted those words in a television interview from space. Aldrin said, "When I consider thy heavens, the work of thy fingers, the moon and the stars, which thou hast ordained; what is man, that thou art mindful of him? and the son of man, that thou visitest him?" (Psalm 8:3–4 KJV).

Three thousand years apart, two different men looked up at the sky—and they saw the same God.

Heavenly Father, I'm thrilled when I view the stars, planets, and other
mysterious objects of the universe You have created. I praise You!

A fool spurns a parent's discipline, but whoever heeds correction shows prudence.
PROVERBS 15:5 NIV

Maybe *heed* isn't the most common of words. Meaning "to give consideration or attention to," its synonyms include *regard*, *note*, and *listen to*. However we say it, though, guys should take the idea to heart.

Proverbs 15:5 says men who heed correction show prudence— other Bible versions say they're "sensible" (HCSB) or "wise" (NLT). Today's verse declares that it's folly to ignore or turn aside "instruction and correction" (AMPC), and scripture overall comes down hard on fools. Resentment kills them (Job 5:2); their mouths invite ruin (Proverbs 10:14); honor does not befit them (Proverbs 26:1); they will be servants to the wise (Proverbs 11:29).

We might be tempted to think Proverbs 15:5 is only for teenagers, young bucks who live at home and play tug-of-war over Dad's rules. But many of us older men have a "father in the faith," as Timothy did with the apostle Paul (1 Timothy 1:2). And even if we're old as Methuselah, we still have a Father in heaven. When any of these parent figures speak, it behooves us to listen. . .to heed what they say.

Never let pride prevent you from hearing the loving discipline of someone who cares deeply for you. Heeding their words today can save you a ton of grief tomorrow.

Father in heaven, may I always heed Your correction—and the discipline of those parent figures You've put in my life.

Be merciful to those who doubt.
JUDE 22 NIV

Jude wanted to discuss the joys of salvation, but first he had to warn his readers of the dangers posed by those who follow a more worldly path.

He cautioned the faithful to be cautious—but didn't say, "Stay away from those heathens!" Instead he recommended building ourselves up in "holy faith" because there is work to be done. God doesn't want to lose anyone—and with His help, we might be "snatching them from the fire" (verse 23 NIV).

Not all of those faithless folk are intentionally evil or wicked. Many have been fooled into thinking God is for others. Some have doubts and questions and might come to faith if only they could see how it applied to a life like theirs. The world certainly isn't going to show them that—and if we just walk on by, they might never know.

Like Jude, we might want to celebrate our salvation. But, just as he found, there is something more important to be concentrating on. Rubbing shoulders with some worldly people might be a risk worth taking if, in the process, a few doubters can be saved.

After all, if Christianity consisted only of those who never doubted, there would be very few going to heaven—and a lot more feeling the heat.

Lord, let the joy, the peace, and sense of purpose I have in You be contagious. Let me shine brightly for You. Amen.

"You shall love your neighbor as yourself."
LEVITICUS 19:18 SKJV

Most Christians have never actually read the book of Leviticus. As far as they can see from skimming its pages, it contains endless lists of laws and regulations, tedious, outdated instructions on how to sacrifice animals and stay ritually pure. The book of Deuteronomy, they feel, is almost as irrelevant to life in the modern world.

Yet the two greatest commandments in the Old Testament are found in Leviticus and Deuteronomy.

When a Pharisee asked Jesus, "Which is the great commandment in the law?" Jesus didn't quote any of the well-known Ten Commandments that most of us would have repeated. Instead, He quoted Deuteronomy 6:5: "You shall love the Lord your God with all your heart" (Matthew 22:37 SKJV). Jesus then stated emphatically, "This is the first and great commandment. And the second is like it: 'You shall love your neighbor as yourself'" (Matthew 22:38–39 SKJV, quoting Leviticus 19:18).

If the two most important commands in the Law are found in these "dull, dry" books, what else might be found there that can inspire and guide us? Stray off the beaten path of your scripture reading and explore the remote corners of your Bible. There are wonderful gems hidden there.

God, open my spiritual eyes. Guide me so that I discover wondrous truths in Your Word. May I search for Your truth like hidden treasures. In Jesus' name, I pray. Amen.

Herein is love, not that we loved God, but that he loved us,
and sent his Son to be the propitiation for our sins.
1 JOHN 4:10 KJV

My Utmost for His Highest points out that we have the wrong
theology when we say that God forgives us based on His love.
Put it this way: Suppose in court the man on the stand exclaims,
"I confess! I killed him!" Then the judge rises up and says, "I love
you, sir, so I will pardon your crime. Go free!" Well, where would
be the justice in that?

God does not forgive based on His love, for then His justice
would be unfair. So God sent Jesus to die for our sins. Now
God forgives on the basis of the cross. Our sins were punished
when Jesus was crucified. Now when God forgives, justice is
still satisfied.

Perhaps we are judging God's love based on how much He
has blessed us in this life. We forget that we come before Him
as sinners in need of a Savior. God, in love, has provided that
Savior—at a great cost to Him. Let's treat sin with the loathing it
deserves and God with the love due Him.

Thank You, Jesus, for allowing Yourself to be so savagely
beaten, then dying an agonizing death on the cross to
pay the price for my sins against Your Father.

> *"For as the heavens are higher than the earth, so are my ways higher than your ways and my thoughts than your thoughts."*
> ISAIAH 55:9 ESV

God tells us, "My thoughts are not your thoughts, neither are your ways my ways" (verse 8 ESV). Then He goes on to describe the vast difference between the way He thinks and the way we mortals think, between the way He operates and the way people try to work things out. God reasons and works on such a higher level that He compares it to the heavens, which are immeasurably higher than the earth.

God has given us intelligence and common sense, and He intends us to use our brains to think through everyday problems and come up with solutions. We are not infinitely smart, however, and sometimes the solution to our problems may be different from anything our minds can envision. A good example is Jesus' command to love our enemies (Matthew 5:44). It runs contrary to normal human logic.

God, of course, knows best—and though we may feel certain that His way won't work or even seems downright foolish, we do well to remember that "the foolishness of God is wiser than men" and that compared to God, "the thoughts of the wise. . .are futile" (1 Corinthians 1:25; 3:20 ESV).

Lord, I thank You that I can understand many of Your thoughts and ways. So I trust You for those that are beyond my comprehension.

Let us, therefore, make every effort to enter that rest.
HEBREWS 4:11 NIV

How often have you heard it said, "If it seems too good to be true, it probably is"? That's a great perspective when you're shopping for used cars or considering a "can't miss" investment opportunity. But don't allow that generally accurate statement to color your understanding of the Christian life. Salvation is totally free, a generous gift from a merciful God, an offer of everlasting life that requires nothing but your acceptance.

Why, then, does Hebrews urge us to "make every effort" to enter God's rest?

We must recognize that our salvation is not *by* works but *to* works. We are saved by God's grace, which empowers us to do good things. Sometimes those good things will require "every effort." Growth in grace, the process called *sanctification*, is actually hard work.

According to Hebrews, the work is now, in this life. We must keep our hearts soft before God (Hebrews 4:7). We must allow God's Word to fill and change us (4:12). We must "hold firmly to the faith we profess" (4:14 NIV). We must regularly, confidently, approach God in prayer (4:16).

Having done these things (and many others as taught in scripture), we can be assured of "a Sabbath-rest for the people of God" (Hebrews 4:9 NIV). The rest is coming. Now is the work.

Father in heaven, empower me for the good work You call me to do.

> *"We saw the Nephilim there (the descendants of Anak
> come from the Nephilim). We seemed like grasshoppers
> in our own eyes, and we looked the same to them."*
> NUMBERS 13:33 NIV

Moses sent spies to explore the land of Canaan. Returning, the men said, "We went into the land to which you sent us, and it does flow with milk and honey! . . . But the people who live there are powerful, and the cities are fortified and very large" (verses 27–28 NIV).

Compared to Canaan's current inhabitants—especially the Anakims, who were known for their tall and robust stature—the Israelites were grasshoppers. And that shook their faith to its core. But amid the clamor, Caleb silenced the crowd saying, "We should go up and take possession of the land, for we can certainly do it" (verse 30 NIV). And Joshua agreed.

The ten spies believed only in what they saw, while Joshua and Caleb believed God. They dared to oppose the majority with a firm commitment to God and an unwavering confidence in God's promises to them.

Are your trials and problems too overwhelming to face? Like the ten spies, do you feel as if there is no way to conquer them? Stand on God's Word, and He will bring you to the promised land. In the process, your faith will transform you from a grasshopper into a spiritual giant.

*God, please strengthen me and assure me that You're with me,
even though I face huge foes and obstacles. Help me trust You. Amen.*

"When you pass through the waters, I will be with you;
and when you pass through the rivers, they will not
sweep over you. When you walk through the fire, you will
not be burned; the flames will not set you ablaze."
ISAIAH 43:2 NIV

This is one of the most comforting verses in the Bible. It is God's promise that when we face trials in our lives, He will not abandon us.

The Bible offers literal examples of this. When Moses and the Israelites approached the Red Sea, with the Egyptian army in hot pursuit, God literally parted the water and allowed the Israelites to escape from their enemies (Exodus 14:10–31). When Shadrach, Meshach, and Abednego were cast into a fiery furnace for refusing to bow down to a golden idol, God brought them out of the fire unscathed. He was literally there in the fire with the three young men, seen as a fourth person (Daniel 3).

Isaiah 43:2 doesn't say *"If* you pass through the waters." It says "when." When we face trouble in our lives, God is with us. Jesus repeats this promise in John 16:33 (NIV), "In this world you will have trouble. But take heart! I have overcome the world."

Lord, thank You for always being with me. I praise You for
how You've repeatedly delivered me in times past. And I
praise You because You will yet deliver me in the future.

*He was despised and rejected by mankind, a man of suffering,
and familiar with pain. Like one from whom people hide their
faces he was despised, and we held him in low esteem.*
ISAIAH 53:3 NIV

Eight hundred years before Christ, the prophet Isaiah was predicting that He would take on the sins of the world for our salvation.

Isaiah's description of a man we would rather not look at, a man bent under the burden of sin, might apply to lots of people in the world today. We probably all know someone we would rather not talk to: nasty people, evil people, or just plain unpleasant people. But they weren't meant to be like that! Sins, theirs and others', have twisted their lives.

They didn't take that burden on board for us, and they certainly didn't do it for our salvation. But that doesn't mean we should look away or walk around. We tend to do so because they are dangerous. If we reach out to them, they might well bring us down. People certainly felt the same about Jesus.

But knowing there is a soul God loves in there, knowing that in the least of these the Lord is to be found, our reaching out to them in His name might just be the saving of us—whether they take us down or not.

*Lord, give me love and courage to reach out, even to nasty or evil
people. And give me wisdom to know when I should refrain.*

*"Isn't this the carpenter's son? Isn't his mother named Mary?
And aren't his brothers James, Joseph, Simon, and Judas?
And aren't all his sisters here with us? So where did he get all this?"*
MATTHEW 13:55–56 NET

Can you imagine growing up in the same household with Perfection? Your mother only thinks you're perfect. . .Mary *knew* her eldest son was. But His brothers and sisters were not. The sibling rivalry must have been intense.

Mark 3:20–21 (NET) says, "Now Jesus went home, and a crowd gathered so that they were not able to eat. When his family heard this they went out to restrain him, for they said, 'He is out of his mind.' " Jesus' own family rejected Him. James didn't even come to the crucifixion; Jesus asked His best friend, John, to look after Mary.

It was only after the resurrection that they believed. Jesus appeared to James (1 Corinthians 15:7). We don't know anything about the meeting, but James quickly became a leader in the early church. Jesus' other brothers apparently also served in the church (1 Corinthians 9:5).

Many of us have been praying for our relatives' salvation. Jesus knows what that's like and cares just as much as we do.

---

*Jesus, You know what it's like to pray for unsaved loved ones.
Help me not to give up. Work in their lives, I pray, and open their
hearts to hearing about You. Reveal Yourself to them. Amen.*

I waited patiently for the LORD; and he inclined
unto me, and heard my cry. He brought
me up also out of an horrible pit.
PSALM 40:1–2 KJV

Bible heroes often went through times of great testing. You'd tend
to think that because they were close to God that they would have
been spared most of life's adversities. They weren't. Or you might
assume that because they had great faith they would have been
speedily delivered from whatever pitfalls they fell into. Not so.

David found himself trapped in a "horrible pit" with no appar-
ent way out, and he cried loudly to the Lord to rescue him. Then
he waited. It took time for God to answer. David undoubtedly
learned more patience in the process and probably had to endure
doubts, wondering if God cared about the dilemma he was in.

Nor did Jeremiah always get immediate answers to prayer.
One time he and some Jewish refugees were in a dire situation
and were desperate to know what to do. Yet after Jeremiah prayed,
the Lord took ten days to answer (Jeremiah 42:7). But the answer
did come. . .in time.

We today sometimes find ourselves in a "horrible pit" as well
and pray desperately for God to bring us up out of it. He will. We
often just need to be patient.

God, I'm in dire circumstances. I'm sinking in a horrible
pit. Rescue me! Don't delay, God, or I won't make it.

For the word of God is alive and powerful.
HEBREWS 4:12 NLT

The Bible is many things. May we never overlook the fact that of all the things that can be said about it, God's Word is an incredible work of art.

The measure of a good work of art is whether it is fresh and relevant each time it is experienced. Is the work powerful and moving? Certainly the Bible is. Each time we read it, we can discover new things relevant to our current position in life. It is new and different each time we read it. It is *alive*.

How many books can boast such a property? God does not change, but everything else does. People change, technology changes, schools of thought change. . .but the Word of the Lord does not change. It will be as relevant two thousand years from now as it was two thousand years ago.

The Word of God says several things about itself. As we are reminded in Hebrews 4:12 that God's Word is alive and powerful, we can meditate on just how relevant it continues to be. Even now, we can still communicate with our Lord through prayer and by reading and filling our minds with His words. Let us remember to praise God for this opportunity He has provided us to hear from Him.

---

*Father, I thank You that Your Word never ages or becomes
irrelevant. I thank You that it still gives spiritual life to
those who read it. Bless my reading of it today, I pray.*

"Rather, let the greatest among you become as the youngest, and the leader as one who serves."
LUKE 22:26 ESV

Sometimes when we're wrong, we're *really* wrong. We look at the map and turn right, thinking we are headed west. After driving for miles, we find we're going in the opposite direction. It is the same thing when it comes to being great. We think being great involves commanding hundreds of people, of being in a place of authority.

Surprise! If we wish to be great in the kingdom of God, we may have to do a U-turn. Greatness is found in being a servant. The leader is not one who tells others what to do; the leader leads and teaches by example. He doesn't point the way to go; he simply does what must be done.

Jesus did not simply tell His disciples how to live. He humbled Himself to serve, and He never rose above that station. Because He left us an example of humble service, shall we exalt ourselves? We have the promise that as Christ served even to death, and God therefore highly exalted Him, we who serve Him faithfully shall reign with Him.

Dear Lord, help me understand with my heart the importance of serving others. Teach me to set an example of how Your sons should live. Amen.

"If anyone forces you to go one mile, go with them two miles."
MATTHEW 5:41 NIV

Going the extra mile. The Romans adopted the ancient Persian custom of forcing someone to carry their baggage for them while they traveled. Against their will, people were compelled to lug these conquerors' belongings the length of a mile or one thousand paces.

In the book of Matthew, Jesus said in the Sermon on the Mount to surprise your enemies. Don't just go the minimum distance—be willing to double the effort and walk two miles.

God's love exceeds our wildest imagination. He pours out His blessings, forgiveness, and strength upon us even in our toughest circumstances. He goes the extra mile.

God calls us to do likewise and live to a higher standard. We choose not to retaliate when we have been wronged. We volunteer for two shifts when others leave early and don't complete their assignments. We help someone without any thought of what we may get in return. We pray for people others ignore. We strive to love the unlovable.

God expects us to go beyond all expectations and to go the extra mile.

Father, help me to go the extra mile, to do more than my share if I'm able to. Help me to walk in Your footsteps.

> *"If anyone comes to Me and does not hate his own father, mother, wife, children, brothers, sisters, yes, and even his own life, he cannot be My disciple."*
> LUKE 14:26 NASB

Jesus must have seriously wanted to discourage people from following Him. He told the crowds following Him, "If you don't hate your family, you can't be My disciple."

Ouch.

But Jesus was using hyperbole to make a point: love Me so deeply that your love for your family will seem like hatred by comparison. When He gave the twelve disciples instructions before sending them out, He repeated the point in less strident terms: "Anyone who loves their father or mother more than me is not worthy of me; anyone who loves their son or daughter more than me is not worthy of me" (Matthew 10:37 NIV).

Jesus applied the same hyperbole to the consequences of loving Him. He told the crowds, *Unless you do this, you will not be My disciples.* He told the twelve, *You are My disciples; now act in a way worthy of your calling.*

Love for Christ and love for others flows in a circle. The more we love Christ, the more we love others. . .and the more we love others, the more we show our love for Christ.

Dear Jesus, help my love for You to grow day by day. May I love You more than anyone I know on earth. Be close to me, I pray. Amen.

*"The LORD your God is with you, the Mighty Warrior who saves.
He will take great delight in you; in his love he will no longer
rebuke you, but will rejoice over you with singing."*
ZEPHANIAH 3:17 NIV

God's passion for His people shows itself in many ways.

His mighty power saves us. He delights in us. His love brings
peace and quietness to our hearts. And His pleasure is revealed
as He rejoices over us with singing.

Angels sang the night Jesus was born (Luke 2:13–14). The
psalms are full of lyrics people have used to praise God over the
centuries. And Revelation 5:11–12 paints a glorious picture of
heaven, complete with continual songs of praise.

But there is a song that's been written just for you. It has your
name as its title. And the composer, God Himself, sings your song
over you as you go about life here on earth.

Close your eyes. Listen carefully. Do you hear God's voice?
He's singing your song. Raise your voice and join Him in the
heavenly music.

*Lord God, help me daily to remind myself that You take great
delight in me—so much so that You rejoice over me with
singing. Reveal to me what this means, I pray. Amen.*

Jesus replied, "You do not realize now what I
am doing, but later you will understand."
JOHN 13:7 NIV

It was an emotional time for the disciples as Jesus was frequently speaking of His upcoming death. How hard it must have been for these men to believe Jesus would soon be killed, when people had just recently greeted Him with shouts of "Hosanna."

And now another jolt. During dinner, Jesus got up from the table, wrapped a towel around His waist, and began washing the disciples' feet. Peter responded not with humbleness or praise, but with questioning, and then refusal. Peter had a vision for himself, and it didn't include Jesus washing his feet.

Jesus told Peter that he wouldn't understand until later what He was doing. This is a response Jesus could easily give to each of us when we're facing hard or unpleasant events in our lives or seeing them in the lives of others. For which one of us hasn't at least once lifted our eyes to heaven and asked, "Why, God?"

Peter did get his feet washed and eventually came to understand why Jesus did what He did. Until that time of understanding came, Peter had to choose to trust and obey.

Will we make that same choice?

Father, there are so many things You do that I can't understand.
Enable me to trust You and obey until the day I do understand.

*But Moses told the people, "Don't be afraid. Just stand
still and watch the LORD rescue you today. The Egyptians
you see today will never be seen again."*
EXODUS 14:13 NLT

On the night of the tenth plague, God brought the Israelites out of
Egypt. Under Moses' leadership, God took them across the Sinai
Peninsula to the edge of the wilderness. From there they marched
toward Pi-hahiroth to camp along the sea.

Meanwhile, back at the palace, Pharaoh regretted freeing the
Israelites and ordered his entire army after them. The warriors
reached the Israelites as they approached the Red Sea.

According to the historian Josephus, the Egyptian army
trapped the Israelites between the Red Sea and a ridge of impass-
able mountains.

The people panicked, but not Moses. God had promised to
deliver the Israelites from the Egyptians, and he believed Him.

God instructed Moses to hold his staff over the water.

In an awesome display of power, God divided the sea. The
Israelites walked to the other shore on dry land. When Pharaoh's
warriors followed, the walls of water collapsed, drowning the
entire army.

Moses acted courageously because he believed God. We, too,
can be fearless when holding on to His promises.

---

*At times I feel overwhelmed by my foes. Please, God, stop them
from carrying out their evil schemes. In Jesus' name, I pray.*

*Now I want you to know, brothers and sisters,
that what has happened to me has actually
served to advance the gospel.*
PHILIPPIANS 1:12 NIV

Early Christians were mistreated, even tortured and killed, because of their faith in Jesus Christ. The apostle Paul, author of the book of Philippians, was no exception. He was stoned, imprisoned, and shipwrecked during his missionary journeys. But all his sufferings had a purpose—to advance the gospel he preached.

Paul could have escaped his suffering by turning away from his faith, but he did not. He endured persecution, boldly shared the gospel, and grew even stronger in his Christian convictions. More than preserving his own life, Paul desired to lead others to salvation through Jesus Christ (Romans 1:16).

After Jesus rose from the dead, He said to His disciples, "Go ye into all the world, and preach the gospel to every creature" (Mark 16:15 KJV). It is our duty as followers of Christ to share the gospel proudly and without reservation.

Who can you approach with the gospel today?

*Lord, give me opportunities to share the gospel today. And anoint
me with the courage to speak out boldly for You. Amen.*

Even fools are thought wise when they keep silent;
with their mouths shut, they seem intelligent.
PROVERBS 17:28 NLT

Here's a little grammar lesson: the word *even*, which begins today's scripture, is an adverb. Merriam-Webster's dictionary says it is "used as an intensive to stress an extreme or highly unlikely condition or instance."

The highly unlikely instance here is that a fool is considered wise. A buffoon comes across as intelligent. What causes that unexpected circumstance? Silence. When the fool stops talking, his perceived IQ skyrockets.

Hopefully, you're no fool. But if "even" a fool is considered wise in his silence, how much wiser would a good man seem by simply talking less? Think how often Peter and some of Jesus' other disciples embarrassed themselves by blurting out foolish, impetuous words. Or think about those times *you've* said things you wish you could take back. The wisdom of Proverbs 17:28 becomes crystal clear.

The good news is that this advice can be followed by any man at any time. Silence takes no special knowledge or skill, just an intentional commitment to slow down, listen more, and talk less.

Just think: If others view you as wiser and more intelligent, they may even ask what makes you different. Then you can speak up to tell them about "wisdom itself," Jesus Christ (1 Corinthians 1:30 NLT). What could be smarter than that?

God of wisdom, may I use my words sparingly—
but when I do speak, talk of You.

Immediately he spoke to them and said, "Take courage! It is I. Don't be afraid." Then he climbed into the boat with them, and the wind died down. They were completely amazed.
MARK 6:50–51 NIV

Imagine being on a big lake during a storm. The waves and the wind seem to be having a contest to see which can overturn the boat first. The fishermen in the boat hold on as tightly as they can. Just as they are sure it will be their final fishing trip, the very Son of God appears outside the boat, walking on the water! He identifies Himself and reassures the men. At this, He climbs into the boat, and everything becomes calm. The storm is no more, and the danger is gone. Imagine how those fishermen must have felt.

This is what actually happened as described in Mark 6, but Jesus continues to work this same way in us. We occasionally have so much trouble, and we see no way out of it. Jesus walks directly across our personal storm and reminds us that He is still there. Then, just as He climbs aboard "the boat," He fills us with His presence and shows us that there is nothing to fear if only we will trust Him. Just as we read in Mark 6:50–51, we have no choice but to be completely amazed.

Lord, come to me, I pray, across the stormy waters. My life is in upheaval. Bring peace and trust where there is none now. In Jesus' name, I pray. Amen.

*And the manna ceased on the next day after they had eaten of the
old wheat of the land. The children of Israel no longer had manna.*
JOSHUA 5:12 SKJV

For forty years, while the children of Israel wandered in the deserts of Sinai, God miraculously provided manna—"bread from
heaven"—for them to eat (Exodus 16:1–16). This wonder bread
continued to appear all around them while they marched south
around Edom and through the deserts east of Moab. The manna
even continued to cover the ground when they camped in the
fertile land near Jericho.

For forty years, or some 14,600 days, day after day, the manna
had continued to appear (Deuteronomy 8:2–3). But the day after
the Israelites ate the Passover meal in the promised land, this
continuous forty-year miracle ceased. Before the manna stopped
appearing, God had already begun to provide food that grew by
natural means.

This same thing happened in the life of Elijah: when the
water in the Cherith Brook dried up, God told him it was time
to move to Zarephath, where a widow would now provide for
him (1 Kings 17:5–9).

This principle often applies to us today. God provides for us in
different ways at different stages in our life, and when one means
of supply dries up, He has another means ready.

*Father, I thank You for supplying all my needs. And I know
You won't fail me in the future. May I always trust You. Amen.*

*"Blessed are those who mourn,
for they will be comforted."*
MATTHEW 5:4 NIV

Jesus began His Sermon on the Mount with nine blessings, or "Beatitudes." The Amplified Version suggests that *blessed* means "enviably happy [with happiness produced by the experience of God's favor and especially conditioned by the revelation of His matchless grace]" (Matthew 5:4 AMPC).

Apparently Jesus' interpretation of happiness doesn't match ours: Happy are the poor? The hungry and thirsty? The persecuted? Happy are those who *mourn*?

Yes, for they will be comforted.

Jesus would "comfort all who mourn. . .to bestow on them. . .the oil of joy instead of mourning" (Isaiah 61:2–3 NIV).

The psalmist frequently praised God as the source of comfort (23:4; 71:21; 86:17). Isaiah commanded the mountains to burst into song because of the Lord's comfort (49:13). Even Jeremiah, the weeping prophet, called God "my Comforter in sorrow" (8:18 NIV). In Jesus, Christians receive comfort "in all our troubles" (2 Corinthians 1:4 NIV).

The earth will experience the final fulfillment of that promise in heaven, when "God will wipe away every tear from their eyes" (Revelation 7:17 NIV).

In this life, tears will come—but so will God's comfort.

*Lord, You are my Comforter. You're with me in my trouble,
feel my pain, and console me with Your love. Thank You.*

*"Are not five sparrows sold for two pennies? Yet not
one of them is forgotten by God. Indeed, the very
hairs of your head are all numbered. Don't be afraid;
you are worth more than many sparrows."*
LUKE 12:6–7 NIV

In the late 1970s, rocker Bob Seger's "Feel Like a Number" lamented the depersonalization of human beings. "I got the idea for the song after watching a show about computer banks and how many names were in them," he said. "It's about identity and trying to survive."

And that was years before the internet, before your every web search was tracked by a multidigit IP address, before every purchase identified by your fifteen- or sixteen-digit credit card number. We simply can't avoid being a number.

Unless. . .we're part of God's family through faith in Jesus Christ. Sure, God is numbering our hairs—a relatively easy job with many of us. But the awesome Creator who "brings out the starry host one by one and calls forth each of them by name" (Isaiah 40:26 NIV) also knows exactly who His children are. Jesus, having described Himself as the good shepherd, said He "calls his own sheep by name" (John 10:3 NIV). And someday, He'll even give each of us a new name, "known only to the one who receives it" (Revelation 2:17 NIV).

You're not just a number. You're a completely known, much-loved son of God.

Lord, thank You for paying such deep, personal attention to me.

Christ was sacrificed once to take away the sins of many;
and he will appear a second time, not to bear sin, but to
bring salvation to those who are waiting for him.
HEBREWS 9:28 NIV

This world will never encourage you to "wait for Jesus." To pursue money and possessions? Yep. To drink and party and chase after sex? For sure. To lose yourself in every imaginable form of entertainment? Uh-huh. But to wait for Jesus? Not a chance.

This idea of waiting and watching for Jesus' return, however, appears throughout the New Testament. Besides today's passage, you'll find variations on the theme in Matthew, Mark, Luke, Romans, 1 Corinthians, 1 Thessalonians, Titus, and Jude. Some have said that anything God says is important, but if He repeats Himself, you should really pay attention. Jesus is coming back! And, as Christians, we are instructed to keep that promise front of mind.

So how exactly do we "wait" for Jesus? Well, how would you wait for any loved one returning from a long absence? You'd eagerly anticipate that person's return. You'd prepare yourself, your family, and your home for the big reunion. You'd avoid any distractions that would interfere with the joyful moment you were together again. It's not rocket science—though you will want to keep your eyes on the skies: "Look, he is coming with the clouds" (Revelation 1:7 NIV).

Lord Jesus, keep me focused and true as I wait for Your return.

"Be still and know that I am God."
PSALM 46:10 SKJV

David experienced a great deal of trouble, and the only way he survived was by trusting in the Lord. He had to believe that God was indeed God, the Creator of the heavens and the earth, powerful enough to help him out of his difficulty. To gain such confidence, David had to turn away from his problems, stop fretting, quiet his heart, and focus on God. Only when he was perfectly still and trusting could he know in a very real way that God was God.

David also wrote, "Speak with your own heart on your bed and be still" (Psalm 4:4 SKJV). Many of us have lost the ability to meditate on God. We either tell ourselves that meditation is something Eastern religions do, or else we cry out frantic prayers while distracted by the careening roller coaster of life. When we lie down in bed at night, instead of meditating calmly and trusting in God, we fret and toss and turn.

When we learn to trust that God can protect us and work out our problems, then we can lie down peacefully and sleep (Psalm 4:8). That same trust gives us the strength to face our days with confidence.

God, help me to meditate on You, to think deeply about who You are and Your attributes. May I truly come to know You in a profound way, I ask in Jesus' name. Amen.

"I will give them an undivided heart and put a new spirit in them; I will remove from them their heart of stone and give them a heart of flesh."

EZEKIEL 11:19 NIV

When a person has a heart attack, a portion of the heart muscle dies—making the organ less efficient in pumping life-giving blood throughout the body.

A heart of stone—cold, hard, and immovable—cannot pump life and love within us, either. We are born needing a heart transplant. Our naturally divided hearts chase after the glittering desires of the world, jealous of the success of others, harboring deep resentments, bitterness, and anger in their dark chambers. We think the world will satisfy the emptiness we feel inside.

God is willing to give us an undivided heart—a heart that is open and ready to see, hear, and love God. This heart has a single focus: loving God and others with a tenderness that we know comes from Someone beyond us.

The good news is we have already had successful surgery, and our donor heart is within us. We received our heart transplant when Jesus died for us, creating new spirits within us.

God's heart changes everything and creates us as new people with living hearts.

Thank You for giving me a new heart and a new spirit, Lord. Help me to worship You with all my heart and soul, I pray.

*And it shall come to pass, that all they that look upon thee
shall flee from thee, and say, Nineveh is laid waste: who will
bemoan her? whence shall I seek comforters for thee?*
NAHUM 3:7 KJV

If the Old Testament's prophetic books were movies, Nahum would
be the sequel to Jonah.

You remember *Jonah*, the action/adventure movie with the
anticlimactic ending? The star of the film reluctantly challenges
Nineveh, the world's center of evil, with a message from God:
"Turn from sin, or you're history." Amazingly, the capital of the
brutal Assyrian empire repents and God relents. As the movie
ends, Jonah watches in disappointment as Nineveh lives to
see another day.

Actually, it'll live another century or so. But in *Jonah II*, Nahum
warns Nineveh that it's on God's wrath list again for, among other
things, its bloody victimization of other nations. Though this
movie doesn't show the actual destruction, history records that
the Babylonians flattened Nineveh in 612 BC.

Nahum's "it shall come to pass" does. . .and God's justice is
fulfilled, as it always will be in His good time.

The End.

*Lord, I'm troubled that evil men do so much wrong in this
world. Help me trust that You'll judge them in due time.
In the meantime, help me to stand up for justice. Amen.*

> *"Therefore I tell you, do not worry about your life,*
> *what you will eat or drink; or about your body,*
> *what you will wear. Is not life more than food,*
> *and the body more than clothes?"*
> MATTHEW 6:25 NIV

This verse is part of Jesus' Sermon on the Mount, which addresses the moral expectations He has for His followers. Jesus' speech consisted of five great dissertations that—if followed—would ultimately give us inner peace.

Picture those gathered on the mountainside, adorned in robes and sandals, nodding their heads as they identified with Jesus' words over two thousand years ago. What's fascinating is the relevance of this verse to our "red carpet" obsessed society. What if we removed our hunger for possessions and our desire to look a certain way and focused on God instead? What would we be left with?

Jesus said we would be left with a treasure, one that never goes out of style. A treasure that moths and rust can't destroy and thieves don't break in and steal (Matthew 6:20). And the best part is—it's free.

Jesus, the Sermon on the Mount is so beautiful but so difficult to put in practice. May Your Spirit help me to live it. Amen.

The LORD is close to the brokenhearted and
saves those who are crushed in spirit.
PSALM 34:18 NIV

Some versions of the Bible provide a clue about when this psalm was written. They begin with an introduction: "A Psalm of David, when he pretended to be insane before Abimelech, who drove him away, and he departed" (NASB). You can read more about this time in David's life in 1 Samuel 21.

Psalm 34 is an acrostic poem. When written in Hebrew, the verses begin with the successive letters of the Hebrew alphabet. It is David's song of praise and thanksgiving for God's redemption. In some ways, it is like the book of Proverbs, because it teaches the reader about the character of God.

"The LORD is close to the brokenhearted and saves those who are crushed in spirit." This reassuring verse guarantees that God is close to us when we are sad. It promises to save us from despair.

Jesus restated these words in His Sermon on the Mount: "Blessed are the poor in spirit: for theirs is the kingdom of heaven. Blessed are they that mourn: for they shall be comforted" (Matthew 5:3–4 KJV).

Are you brokenhearted? Is your spirit weighed down with despair? Then meditate on Psalm 34:18. Ask God for help. He cares about you (1 Peter 5:7).

God, this is me—my spirit is weighed down with despair. I desperately
need hope. Help me to trust that You're with me. Amen.

*I have no greater joy than to hear that
my children are walking in the truth.*
3 JOHN 4 NIV

People speak of what they see others doing and hear them saying.
John had received reports that his friend Gaius was living out his
faith. So pleased was John over this that he wrote Gaius a letter
in order to praise him.

First, John was pleased that Gaius was not only walking in
the truth but that he was faithful to the truth. Second, John was
delighted that Gaius was showing hospitality to those who were
doing the work of the church. John encouraged Gaius to continue
living in such a manner.

John wasn't encouraged, however, about something else he had
been hearing. A man named Diotrephes was hurting the church
with his bad behavior. He was engaged in gossiping and wasn't
welcoming people. John condemned Diotrephes for his actions
and wrote that he would hold him accountable.

While John took a few lines of his correspondence to address
Diotrephes' situation, this letter really focuses on Gaius and the
encouragement others were receiving because of his faithfulness.

Are we living out our faith in such a manner that others are
uplifted and encouraged? Do our choices bring God joy? These
are questions worth considering.

*Father, help everything I do and say to be an encouragement and
an example to fellow believers. Help me to walk in truth. Amen.*

"Take my yoke upon you and learn from me."
MATTHEW 11:29 NIV

The setting is Galilee, where Jesus meets John the Baptist's disciples. Their leader, in Herod's prison, wants verification that Jesus is the Christ of whom he has preached. Besides John's followers, there are many who come out of curiosity as well as need.

Standing with the gathered crowd, Jesus is moved by their burdened spirits. "For my yoke is easy, and my burden is light," He adds, after calling them to yoke up with Him (verse 30 NIV). One imaginative writer described a hanging shopkeeper's sign that swung in the breeze, reminding Jesus of the sign outside Joseph's carpentry shop that read MY YOKES ARE EASY.

A yoke is not worn by one animal—it unites two, to perform a task. For thousands of years the yoke was a symbol of labor and hardship; Jesus turns the familiar implement into a metaphor for uniting oneself with His heavenly Father. Such a union is a light burden.

In verse 28 Jesus tells the crowd that such linkage is available by coming to Him and accepting His way. In a team relationship with Jesus, one discovers His gentleness, humility, and rest.

Jesus, help me to take Your yoke upon me, to be united with You in everything I do. Help me not to burn out. Amen.

Wanting to satisfy the crowd, Pilate released Barabbas to them.
He had Jesus flogged, and handed him over to be crucified.
MARK 15:15 NIV

Pilate didn't want anything to do with this Jesus fellow. Even his wife had warned him not to get involved. So he stalled. Then he released a murderer and killed an innocent man.

Why? Because Pilate was a bad man? Partly. But largely to please a crowd.

The people in the crowd, whipped into a self-serving frenzy, chose what they knew—a sinner like them—instead of reaching for something better. That's what crowds do. With few exceptions, most mobs appeal to the lowest in us.

We deal with crowds like that all the time, even though they might not be howling in the street. The "crowd" might be school friends who want to ostracize someone, the party crowd who want you to get as drunk as them, even fellow church members who focus on earthly traditions above heavenly love.

As sociable beings, we often enjoy being in groups. Usually they're fun and harmless, and because of that, it's often tempting just to go with the flow. But when the crowd laughingly suggests something that makes your soul hesitate, ask yourself: Are you choosing Barabbas or Jesus?

God, help me to obey You and not the crowds. Give me the
moral strength to buck the mob and do what is right. Amen.

And around the throne, on each side of the throne,
are four living creatures, full of eyes in front and behind.
REVELATION 4:6 ESV

When John visited heaven, he saw four amazing "living creatures" surrounding the throne of God, almost like the majestic lions some kings used to keep chained near their thrones—only these bizarre beasts were unchained and far more majestic! One creature was like a lion, another like an ox, another like a man, and another like an eagle. Each beast had six wings and was covered with eyes all over its body—even under its wings.

These creatures are also described in the book of Ezekiel where they are called *cherubim* and described as having human bodies (Ezekiel 1:5; 10:1). Here, too, they are covered with eyes, even on their hands, wings, and backs. In Ezekiel's visions instead of having six wings they have four wings, and *each* creature had all four faces: the face of a man, an eagle, an ox, and a lion (Ezekiel 1:5–10; 10:8–14).

Despite the striking similarities, there are differences. Either this is because the descriptions are symbolic (quite likely), or the living creatures, like other angelic beings, are capable of morphing (quite likely).

These incredible heavenly beings are a testament to the unparalleled imagination and creativity of our God.

God, I marvel at Your creativity. You have created many
awesome and unique creatures. You alone are God!

*Remember those earlier days after you had received the
light, when you endured in a great conflict full of suffering.
Sometimes you were publicly exposed to insult and persecution;
at other times you stood side by side with those who were so
treated. You suffered along with those in prison and joyfully
accepted the confiscation of your property, because you knew
that you yourselves had better and lasting possessions. So do
not throw away your confidence; it will be richly rewarded.*
HEBREWS 10:32–35 NIV

American Christians have generally been spared the persecution
believers in other times and nations have suffered. But those days
of ease may be passing. Now, in what some call a "post-Christian
culture," committed Jesus followers may soon find themselves like
their New Testament forebears. The big question is whether we'll
respond with joy and hope.

Nobody wants to be insulted. Or to end up in prison. Or to
have his home or livelihood stolen away by haters of Jesus. But
the early Christians accepted these things "joyfully."

That's only possible by taking the long view of life. If this world
is everything, persecution is a tragedy to be avoided. But if we
have "better and lasting possessions" in a world to come (and we
do), our losses on earth are so minor as to be almost invisible.
Pray with the apostle Paul:

*I consider my present sufferings not worth comparing
with the glory that will be revealed in me (Romans 8:18).*

*"But the Advocate, the Holy Spirit, whom the Father
will send in my name, will teach you all things and
will remind you of everything I have said to you."*
JOHN 14:26 NIV

Jesus' earthly missionary journey was about to end and—in this
passage—the Master prepared His disciples for His departure.

The disciples were confused and frightened, so Jesus comforted
them with words of assurance, comfort, and hope: "Do not let
your hearts be troubled and do not be afraid" (14:27 NIV).

At first, Jesus' followers thought they would be left alone.
But Jesus assured them He would send the Father's Ambassador
to teach, direct, guide, and remind them of every word He had
told them.

Jesus called the Holy Spirit "the Advocate," a translation of
the Greek word *parakletos*: "one called alongside to help." It can
also indicate strengthener, comforter, helper, adviser, counselor,
intercessor, ally, and friend.

The Holy Spirit walks with us to help, instruct, comfort, and
accomplish God's work on earth. Through His presence inside
us, we know the Father. In our deepest time of need, He is there.
He comforts and reveals to us the truth of God's Word.

Jesus is always with us because His Spirit lives in our hearts.
No Christian *ever* walks alone.

---

*Lord, I praise and thank You for sending the Holy Spirit, the Spirit
of Christ, into my life. Thank You for not leaving me alone.*

Even though I walk through the darkest valley,
I will fear no evil, for you are with me; your
rod and your staff, they comfort me.
PSALM 23:4 NIV

Do a rod and a staff sound comforting to you? These well-known Bible verses bring hope to many people, yet little is mentioned about the shepherd's tools—the rod and staff.

Sheep traveled into valleys for food and water, but the valley also contained danger. The high ridges created perfect places for lions and coyotes to wait to snatch an innocent lamb.

Anticipating new grass, sheep often wandered away where they slipped into swamps or fell down steep cliffs. Tiny flies bit their ears.

But the shepherd was prepared. He constantly watched over his flock for any signs of danger. With his tall staff with crooked end, he could snare a sheep from a swamp or guide him in fast-moving waters. His rod, a short stick with leather strips on the end, kept the flies and mosquitoes away—and could be used in cleaning and grooming.

As stubborn, somewhat dumb creatures, we (like sheep) get into dangerous situations in the valleys of life. But the Lord stays with us, protecting us from the nuisances, cleaning us of our sins, and redeeming us when we fall.

Lord, even though I walk through dark valleys
or stray into dangerous terrain, You are always
ready to rescue me. I thank You for that.

*"The blind receive sight, the lame walk, those who have
leprosy are cleansed, the deaf hear, the dead are raised,
and the good news is proclaimed to the poor."*
MATTHEW 11:5 NIV

What did Jesus say when the Pharisees and Pilate asked Him if
He was the Son of God? Well, let's just say He didn't give them
any answers they understood. Those powerful questioners were
left deeply frustrated.

But when John the Baptist sent messengers to ask, "Are you
the one who was to come?" Jesus specifically tells them about the
work He is doing. Why the difference?

Well, the Pharisees and Pilate were asking for reasons of
earthly power. They didn't really want to know the Lord, while
John, helplessly chained in a cell, wanted nothing more. Within
days of death and with doubts gnawing at his soul, John asked
for words of comfort. Jesus' reply must have made the Baptist's
beleaguered soul sing. This was what he devoted his life to—
His Lord was walking on the earth!

Those ruled by earthly passions will never understand when
Jesus speaks. But servants of God, no matter how desperately
flawed they are or how foolish their questions might seem, can
call on Him and receive an answer. It might be comforting; it
might be challenging. You just have to be prepared to listen.

*Jesus, I cry unto You with my whole heart. Show me what to
do. And please reveal Yourself and Your ways to me. Amen.*

These commandments that I give you today are to be on your hearts. Impress them on your children. Talk about them when you sit at home and when you walk along the road, when you lie down and when you get up.
DEUTERONOMY 6:6–7 NIV

God's words in Deuteronomy were originally delivered to the people of Israel by Moses. These verses (Deuteronomy 6:3–9) later became known as "the Shema," meaning "hear" in Hebrew.

The Shema is one of the central points of the morning and evening Judaic prayer services. For Jews and Christians alike, it serves as a spiritual pledge of allegiance.

In verses 6–7, God gives us the ins and outs of His commandments in regard to our families. Check out God's desired time commitment: it's not what you would call hit or miss! These verses in Deuteronomy remind us that, like breathing, our commitment to God isn't haphazard; rather, it's a minute-to-minute lifeline.

Today, as we get up and lie down, may we also remember to commit to this pledge of allegiance as one nation under God.

God, I dedicate myself anew to You and to Your Word. May the Bible be constantly on my mind and on my lips. In Jesus' name, I pray. Amen.

He replied to him, "Who is my mother, and who are my brothers?"
MATTHEW 12:48 NIV

That sounds a bit harsh. Disrespectful, even.

Jesus' family had heard of the crowds of people looking for healings. They were understandably worried. When someone announced their arrival, He asked this question that seemed to deny them.

Part of the importance we place on family comes from the fear of strangers, but each "stranger" is beloved by God. Jesus wasn't excluding His mother and brothers—He was expanding the definition of family. He goes on to say, "Whoever does the will of my Father in heaven is my brother and sister and mother" (verse 50 NIV). That's a pretty wide net to cast—but it goes further. Even those who haven't done the will of the Father can join the family, if they repent.

The idea of a universal family sounds a little hippy to many people. The "flower power" generation grasped the concept of loving humanity, but they sometimes put more faith in sex and drugs than in God.

The idea of a family in which we are all God's children is like G. K. Chesterton's description of Christianity. It "has not been tried and found wanting, it has been found difficult and not tried." A true family of Christ is still possible. It begins when we lay aside fear and hold out a hand.

*Father, grant me genuine love for all my brothers
and sisters in Christ. Give me abiding love. Amen.*

> *After these things God tested Abraham and said*
> *to him, "Abraham!" And he said, "Here I am."*
> GENESIS 22:1 ESV

The command that follows this verse boggles the mind: God tells Abraham to offer his son Isaac as a sacrifice.

Through Isaac, God had promised to give Abraham descendants as numerous as the stars. Yet at God's word, Abraham prepared to obey, trusting the Lord to raise his son from the dead (Hebrews 11:17–19). Why would God ask Abraham to do something He later condemned (Jeremiah 19:5)? Perhaps the answer lies in the test God was administering to Abraham.

The word *tested* appears almost thirty times in the Bible. Job expected vindication after God's testing (Job 23:10). Solomon said praise tested a man (Proverbs 27:21). Paul told Timothy deacons must be tested (1 Timothy 3:10).

Our confusion may be due to the use of the word *tempt* in some versions, including the King James. In contemporary usage, a temptation invites us to sin; a test proves knowledge we are supposed to possess. God knew the quality of Abraham's faith, but He demonstrated it for future generations.

We can face life's tests with the confidence that God expects us to pass. He only wants to let us—and others—measure our faith by our experiences.

Lord, strengthen me by Your Holy Spirit so that I may pass
all the tests and trials of faith You allow me to face. Amen.

All Scripture is inspired by God and is useful to teach us what is true and to make us realize what is wrong in our lives. It corrects us when we are wrong and teaches us to do what is right.
2 TIMOTHY 3:16 NLT

Many versions of the Bible use the phrase "God-breathed" to translate this version's "inspired by God." We may hear these words and hardly give them another thought. It is as if God breathed this scripture, and then it was there. When we consider the Word of God more deeply, though, we also remember that Hebrews refers to the Bible as being "alive."

God's Word continues to be God-breathed. It is as relevant today as it ever was! Scripture speaks to us in our current situations just as it did to people a few thousand years ago. . .just as it will for eternity. God speaks to us today through His Word and helps us to know right from wrong. It is a powerful teacher.

Situations and cultures and languages and technologies have changed all throughout history, but God has been able to speak to people exactly where they are through His living Word. There is certainly no other book, collection of books, or any other thing in the world that can do that. Only the living Word, which continues to be God-breathed.

God, please breathe life into my spirit with Your Holy Spirit and Your Word. Speak to me though the scriptures, I pray. Change my thoughts and my actions to be more like You. Amen.

> *Precious in the sight of the LORD*
> *is the death of His saints.*
> PSALM 116:15 SKJV

Benjamin Franklin said, "Two things in life are certain, death and taxes."

We can sometimes escape paying a tax, but we cannot escape death. Every one of us will die someday.

In Psalm 116, the psalmist tells of his cries to God for mercy. He cried out to God because he was afraid. "The cords of death entangled me, the anguish of the grave came over me" (verse 3 NIV). Then he goes on to praise God for saving him. We can't know if the psalmist was literally saved from dying, or if his words were a metaphor. But we do know from reading scripture that God saves our souls from dying.

The Twenty-third Psalm holds the familiar words "Yea, though I walk through the valley of the shadow of death, I will fear no evil: for thou art with me" (verse 4 KJV). Through our belief in Jesus Christ, we know that we are saved; we become God's "saints."

Psalm 116:15 assures us that our transition from this world to heaven is precious in God's sight. God paid the price of our eternal life through the sacrifice of His only Son. In death, we have nothing to fear.

Father, thank You that I have eternal life through Your Son, Jesus Christ, and need not fear death. I praise You for that assurance.

In those days there was no king in Israel;
everyone did what was right in his own eyes.
JUDGES 21:25 NASB

Reading through the book of Judges conjures up scenes that rival some horror movies produced by Hollywood.

During the era of the judges, the Israelites bounced from one disaster to another while ignoring God's law, only to be brought back into repentance when oppressed by an enemy. Hearing their cries for help, God would raise up a hero to rescue them.

This hero, or judge, ruled over the people and kept them in line until he died. At that point the Israelites again "did what was right in their own eyes" and the cycle began anew.

This situation is not unlike our own culture. Instead of using God's standard of right and wrong, today's society tells us to determine our own morals. Why? Because it claims there is no lawgiver apart from us, individually.

When each Israelite set his own criterion for right and wrong, tragedy and heartache resulted.

Ignoring God's standards didn't work for the Israelites, and it won't work for us today. It's wise to periodically examine our personal criterion of right and wrong to keep it in line with God's standards laid out in the Bible. Ask yourself, "Whose standards am I following?"

Lord, cause me to love Your Word and use it—not my feelings and reasoning—as the standard for what's right and wrong. Amen.

*Good sense makes a man restrain his anger, and it is
his glory to overlook a transgression or an offense.*
PROVERBS 19:11 AMPC

In 1985, "the Boss" reached number five on the pop charts with
"Glory Days." Bruce Springsteen sang of encountering a high
school classmate, and all the guy could talk about were his long-
ago exploits on the baseball diamond. Glory days, Springsteen
concluded, will "pass you by."

Proverbs, though, offers a way to keep the glory going: by
overlooking the offensive behavior of other people. This kind of
"transgression" is never ending, so you'll have plenty of opportunities for glory.

"Good sense"—or, in other translations, "wisdom"—causes
men to hold back their angry responses. Not responding to
irritations, insults, and imbecility is "glory," a translation of
a Hebrew word connoting bravery and honor. Jesus perfectly
pictured today's scripture in the final hours of His life: "When
He was reviled and insulted, He did not revile or offer insult in
return; [when] He was abused and suffered, He made no threats
[of vengeance]; but he trusted [Himself and everything] to Him
Who judges fairly" (1 Peter 2:23 AMPC).

Nothing could be more lastingly glorious than to imitate
our perfect Savior. Let the world do what it does so well; then
trust God to do what *He* does so well—provide the good sense
to respond like Jesus.

*Lord, when I grow annoyed, speak and act
through me—to Your glory and mine.*

I pray that the eyes of your heart may be enlightened in
order that you may know the hope to which he has called
you, the riches of his glorious inheritance in his holy people,
and his incomparably great power for us who believe.
EPHESIANS 1:18–19 NIV

This verse is part of a letter written by the apostle Paul to the
church in Ephesus. His letter addresses the mystery of God's power,
forethought, and purpose.

Here, Paul prays for the eyes of our hearts to be enlightened.
Could it be Paul was speaking from firsthand experience when
he used the words *eyes* and *heart* simultaneously? Essentially,
God performed spiritual surgery on Paul as he walked the road
to Damascus. Not only did he receive a heart transplant, but his
eyes were literally opened to Jesus (Acts 9:1–19).

Our heart is central when it comes to God. It's not only vital
for our physical life but our spiritual life as well. It's the thinking
apparatus of our soul, containing all our thoughts, passions, and
desires. Why was Paul so anxious for Christians to make heartfelt
spiritual progress? Because of the payoff. God freely offers us His
incomparably great power along with a rich, glorious inheritance.
We just have to see our need for a little surgery.

Father, enlighten my eyes that I may get a glimpse of the riches
of the glorious inheritance to which You have called me. Amen.

"What do you mean by repeating this proverb concerning the land of Israel, 'The fathers have eaten sour grapes, and the children's teeth are set on edge'?"
EZEKIEL 18:2 ESV

The Jews of Ezekiel's day were basically saying, "Our fathers sinned, and we're suffering for their sins." They had it wrong. It wasn't just their fathers that God was punishing for their idol worship and sins and disobedience. It was *them*. They were suffering for their own sins because they were just like their fathers (see also Matthew 23:29–32).

The people of Judah were lamenting that they were innocent but suffering for their ancestors' sins of hating God in fulfillment of Exodus 20:5. They failed to see that by not loving and obeying God, they, too, were part of the "hate God" generation and were being punished for it.

God told them to stop using that proverb and declared that every person would be punished for their disobedience or blessed for their obedience. It didn't matter how bad a man's father had been: if that man broke the bad habits he'd been taught, loved God, and did what was right, he'd be blessed (Ezekiel 18:3–18).

We are the products of our upbringing, too, but we can break free of the negative heritage and love and serve God. We can make the right decisions.

Lord, strengthen my resolve to break the bad, selfish habits I learned growing up. Teach me how to walk in my new life. Amen.

I keep asking that the God of our Lord Jesus Christ, the glorious Father, may give you the Spirit of wisdom and revelation, so that you may know him better. I pray that the eyes of your heart may be enlightened in order that you may know the hope to which he has called you, the riches of his glorious inheritance in his holy people, and his incomparably great power for us who believe.
EPHESIANS 1:17–19 NIV

Praying for physical health needs is good. So are prayers for financial challenges, relationship issues, job situations, and any of a million other practical concerns.

But one category of request goes far deeper than these day-to-day needs, to the very bedrock of our faith. The apostle Paul provides the example in his ongoing prayer for the Ephesians, that they would know God better.

When we receive the requested "Spirit of wisdom and revelation," much of our daily confusion is resolved. When we know God more deeply, as well as "the hope to which he has called" us, our spiritual struggles diminish. When we recognize and trust in God's "incomparably great power," miracles can happen.

This kind of prayer—for ourselves and others—can truly change lives. Certainly, keep praying for all those other needs. But don't forget to address the deepest need of every human being: a living, growing knowledge of the God who made, keeps, and redeems us.

Father, I echo Paul's prayer—for myself and for others.

> *"Look! I am creating new heavens and a new earth,*
> *and no one will even think about the old ones anymore."*
> ISAIAH 65:17 NLT

What are your fondest memories? Of leading (or simply cheering) your team to a championship? Of a certain vacation, a business achievement, the acquisition of some long-desired object? Of meeting your girl, getting married, having kids?

How about your *worst* memories? A bad diagnosis, an accident, a house fire? A breakup, betrayal, or bankruptcy?

Life is an ongoing roller-coaster ride. We exult in the peaks and hold on for dear life as we career into the valleys. But no matter how exciting or depressing our experiences on this earth, a day is coming when none of it will matter.

God's promise through Isaiah indicates that our worst experiences will one day be completely erased from our minds. The Christian's eternity with God will be so good that "no one will even think about" what went before.

On the other hand, even our *best* experiences will pale in comparison. As the apostle Paul wrote, referring to another passage from Isaiah, "That is what the Scriptures mean when they say, 'No eye has seen, no ear has heard, and no mind has imagined what God has prepared for those who love him'" (1 Corinthians 2:9 NLT; see also Isaiah 64:4).

Eternity is coming. And it's all good.

Lord, thank You for the promise of perfect peace and rest. I need it!

Then Peter came to Jesus and asked, "Lord,
how many times shall I forgive my brother or
sister who sins against me? Up to seven times?"
MATTHEW 18:21 NIV

Peter underestimates by some considerable amount in this verse. The Lord's answer is either seventy-seven or seventy times seven, depending on which version of the Bible you read (verse 22). Either way, it seems Peter was looking for an easy way out of the forgiveness question. And don't we all?

Perhaps a better question than "How many times shall I forgive?" would be "How many times would I like to be forgiven?"

If we live the biblical three score and ten years, that's roughly 25,550 days. Now we might be hard-pressed to sin when we are babies, but I'm sure most of us make up for that when we hit the teens. And many of us will live more than seventy years. If we sinned or had a sinful thought only once a day (and many would be glad to get off with that little), then that's an awful lot to be forgiven for—way more than seven, Peter.

So how many times should we forgive our fellow sinners? Until we have forgiven once more than the number of times we will hope for forgiveness ourselves.

God, may I continually forgive others even as I myself would
like to be repeatedly forgiven. Help me to be merciful, I pray.

Yet I will rejoice in the LORD, I will be joyful in God my Savior.
HABAKKUK 3:18 NIV

Habakkuk had grown weary of the tough times he was living in.
He wanted to know how long they would continue. So he took his
complaints to God. When would the injustice stop? Why hadn't
God answered his pleas for help?

God answered Habakkuk's grievance. Yes, He was aware of
what was going on, and yes, there would be justice, and it would
come about in *God's* timing. Habakkuk's complaints switched to
words of praise, which is amazing because nothing had changed.
There still wasn't food in the fields or livestock or even buds on
the fig trees.

Habakkuk wasn't the first person in the Bible to face dire
conditions. Joseph was unjustly tossed into prison (Genesis
39:20); Daniel was carried off to a foreign land (Daniel 1:1–6); and
David was on the run because Saul wanted him dead (1 Samuel
23:7–14). How is it possible that these men could praise God in
the midst of such trying situations?

They must have understood as Habakkuk finally did that
joy is found in Jesus Christ alone. Situations change and people
come in and out of lives, but Jesus is always with us, all the time,
all the way.

Sounds like a great reason to rejoice, doesn't it?

*Father in heaven, I thank You for how You provide and take
care of me, even during tough times. May I always trust You!*

Wherefore I put thee in remembrance that thou
stir up the gift of God, which is in thee.
2 TIMOTHY 1:6 KJV

In his letter to Timothy, Paul exhorted his spiritual son to "stir up the gift of God" within. Literally, this directive meant to blow the coals into a flame as one would stir embers under a fire. A similar metaphor in Latin, *excitare igniculos ingenii,* means to "stir up the sparks of genius."

This passage is a reminder to every believer. It demonstrates that our God-given gifts remain strong only through active use and fostering. Gifts left unattended or unused become stagnant and, like an unattended fire, die. But if we continue to exercise the gifts God gives us, like the parable of the talents, they will increase, strengthen, and even multiply.

Just as wood or coal fuels a fire, faith, prayer, and obedience are the fresh fuels of God's grace that keep our fires burning. But this takes action on our part.

Are you using the gifts God has given you? Can He entrust you with more?

Perhaps today is the day to gather the spiritual tinder necessary to stoke the fire of God within.

God, hear my prayers! I want to be used by You. I want
my life to count. I'm stirring up the gifts You've given me.
Please blow gently on them and cause them to ignite. Amen.

*Brothers and sisters, I do not regard myself as having taken
hold of it yet; but one thing I do: forgetting what lies behind
and reaching forward to what lies ahead, I press on toward the
goal for the prize of the upward call of God in Christ Jesus.*
PHILIPPIANS 3:13–14 NASB

The apostle Paul possessed an extraordinary résumé. A "Hebrew
of Hebrews" (Philippians 3:5 NASB), he traced his lineage back to
Abraham, Isaac, and Jacob through both parents.

Highly educated, Paul belonged to the prestigious Jewish sect
of Pharisees. Careful to keep the law, he refused to adopt pagan
customs from the surrounding Greek culture.

When confronted by the risen Christ, Paul redirected his
religious zeal toward spreading the gospel.

Although burdened with memories of mistreating Christians,
Paul didn't allow his past actions to impede his service for Christ.
Neither did he depend on his ancestry or lifestyle for special
favors from God.

We cannot allow past failures to keep us from moving ahead
with our God-given tasks. Neither can we glide along, resting
on past victories and accomplishments or the laurels of family
endeavors.

We live in the now. The past is gone forever, the future yet to
come. "Press on toward the goal for the prize of the upward call
of God in Christ Jesus" (Philippians 3:14 NASB).

*Lord, help me not to live with regret in the past, or in fear
of the future. Help me live in the present, trusting You!*

*He went away a second time and prayed, "My Father,
if it is not possible for this cup to be taken away
unless I drink it, may your will be done."*
MATTHEW 26:42 NIV

If you have a Bible printed in red and black ink, you probably
know that the red words are those spoken by Jesus. In this verse,
Jesus was in the garden of Gethsemane, just hours away from His
arrest and crucifixion. He prayed, asking God if there was some
different way to accomplish redemption. In fact, Jesus didn't just
ask it once—He made the request three times in Matthew 26.
These red-letter prayers reveal the 100 percent human side of Jesus.

In one of His darkest hours, Jesus was overwhelmed with
trouble and sorrow. He asked God the Father for something that
He would not provide. But Jesus, the perfect and obedient Son,
ended His prayers by saying, "*Your* will be done."

When we face our darkest hours, will we follow Jesus' example?
Can we submit to God's perfect will, focusing on how much He
loves us—even when His will doesn't match ours?

*Father, reveal to me the areas of my life where I need to
yield to You. Shine Your light in the dark corners. Help me
to surrender every part of my heart to You, I pray. Amen.*

*Remember, it is sin to know what you
ought to do and then not do it.*
JAMES 4:17 NLT

"The road to hell is paved with good intentions." Wouldn't it be interesting to know what the context was when this proverb was created? It sure sounds like an adaptation of James 4:17.

We've all heard anecdotes about how numerous people stood by and ignored cries for help as a heinous crime was committed. Stories abound on the shocking apathy of human nature, just when it matters the most. And as we learn of them, we think, *I would never stand idly by and do nothing in a circumstance like that.*

And yet, how many smaller opportunities slip right past us as we fail to make the connection? How many times do we think, *It would be really nice if I did something for this person,* and then proceed to talk ourselves out of it. *They'll think this is silly.* Or, *They won't even notice.* Or maybe, *I don't really have the time.*

James warns us to stay focused on doing what's right. Regardless of our plans, we never know what the future holds. We never know when we will desperately need the intervention of a good deed from someone else.

*God, put some fire in me, that I may have the resolve to
do what I know I should. In Jesus' name, I pray. Amen.*

"The greatest among you will be your servant."
MATTHEW 23:11 NIV

"If I won the lottery," a boy said, "I'd hire a butler. Someone to do everything for me."

Ignoring the little matter of being too young to play the lottery, his father went straight to the more important problem of his son's selfishness.

"Oh!" the boy responded, trying to make his dream sound a little more generous. "Everyone could have one!" After a moment's thought his fantasy expanded even further. "Wouldn't it be cool if everyone in the world had a servant taking care of them?"

"And whose would you be?" The father answered the son's confused look by explaining that if *everyone* had a butler or maid, then that would include the butlers and maids! The only way everyone could be pampered like that would be if all the people *with* servants also *were* servants.

Everyone taking care of everyone else—doesn't that sound like a Christian paradise? It only breaks down when people think they are too important to serve. But Jesus served us unto His death and beyond. And God has already done everything for us by giving us this world, this life, and the next.

We have already been served by the greatest. None of us is more important than that. So, whose servant will you be?

Give me the love and humility to serve others,
Lord. May I never think I'm better than others.

None at all is like You, O Lord; You are great, and Your name is great in might. Who would not fear You, O King of the nations? For it is fitting to You and Your due! For among all the wise [men or gods] of the nations and in all their kingdoms, there is none like You.
JEREMIAH 10:6–7 AMPC

If we accept the Bible's account of origins, we should recognize the absolute supremacy of the God we serve. He predated and created the physical universe we inhabit. His wisdom and power brought matter and life into being where none had existed before. He simply spoke to produce vast, star-filled galaxies and one particular planet, perfectly suited for life, that enjoys His special attention. What other "god" or theory or superstition can even vaguely compete with the I AM?

We as Christian men know this mind-boggling God personally. In a limited way, of course—but He has allowed us to understand enough of His majesty to recognize Him as our source of life and hope. With a God like this for us, who can be against us (Romans 8:31)? Why would we ever fear any person or idea or circumstance that arises in opposition?

Life is difficult. But our God is supreme. When we follow Him by faith, we can trust that He has every situation in hand, for our ultimate benefit and His ultimate glory.

I praise You, Lord, for Your wisdom and power.

*"I sent the hornet ahead of you, which drove
them out before you—also the two Amorite kings.
You did not do it with your own sword and bow."*
JOSHUA 24:12 NIV

Throughout the book of Joshua, Israel's armies fought the
Canaanites in one battle after another. You could certainly get
the impression that their swords and bows had a great deal to do
with the conquest of Canaan. But wait! Almost every battle was
accompanied by a miracle: collapsing walls, divine hailstorms,
prolonged daylight—even God inspiring the soldiers to go on
night marches and launch surprise sunrise attacks.

In addition, just before Israel showed up, God drove the
Canaanites crazy and sent many of them fleeing from Canaan,
driven out by massive plagues of hornets. No surprise. God had
forewarned Moses *twice*, forty years earlier, that He would do
that (Exodus 23:28; Deuteronomy 7:20). So when Israel entered
the promised land, Canaan's armies were already depleted and
weaker.

Why did God do these miracles? He wanted Israel to understand very clearly that only He could give them victory, and that
they should therefore fear and serve Him (Joshua 24:8–14; 2
Chronicles 20:12, 15). God still does miracles to help us to achieve
our goals today. . .and His reasons are the same.

---

*God, thank You that You still do miracles for Your children today.
Help me trust that You're willing to do them for me. Amen.*

*So Jesus, when he began his ministry, was about thirty years old.
He was the son (as was supposed) of Joseph, the son of Heli, the
son of Matthat, the son of Levi, the son of Melchi, the son of Jannai,
the son of Joseph, the son of Mattathias. . .the son of Shem, the
son of Noah, the son of Lamech, the son of Methuselah, the son of
Enoch, the son of Jared, the son of Mahalalel, the son of Kenan, the
son of Enosh, the son of Seth, the son of Adam, the son of God.*
LUKE 3:23–25, 36–38 NET

Have you ever wondered why God included such long and boring
genealogies intertwined with the exciting account of Jesus' birth?
To our western ears they seem so dry and lifeless. But the Bible
isn't just for people in modern democracies. It is a book for all
humankind.

In many developing world cultures, one hasn't been properly
introduced until a person's family lineage is known. It places a
person into the context of both family and people. The genealogies aren't boring to them. Instead, Jesus, Mary, and Joseph are
revealed in their proper family setting.

Isn't it great to find that Jesus is properly introduced?

---

*God, I thank You for every word in the Bible, even the
genealogies. There are many mysteries in the scriptures.
Help me to search them out and find the answers, I pray. Amen.*

*"Heaven and earth will pass away,
but my words will never pass away."*
MATTHEW 24:35 NIV

That's quite a claim for the penniless son of a carpenter. Listeners must have struggled to believe such an outrageous statement.

Since then the world has changed with frightening speed. We live in an age where words zip around the globe in milliseconds, and opinions voiced by ordinary folk can be broadcast to millions via the internet.

So how do the words of a "faith healer" from centuries before the printing press hold up to all that?

It's a safe assumption that if all the Bibles ever printed were still available, there would be one for every human being alive today—with plenty left over. The New Testament has been translated into half of the world's languages, and some 90 percent of the world's population can read those languages. The Bible can be accessed in braille, downloaded from the internet, heard via audiobooks, and carried around in a cell phone. One hundred million copies are sold each year, and the average American home is estimated to contain four Bibles.

Heaven and earth are still around, but with many fearing that "pass away" thing. Meanwhile, Jesus' words go from strength to strength. It's time to accept that Jesus wasn't showing off. It's really time to commit.

*Lord, I'm amazed at how much Your Word has been
published in the world. May it continue to go forth.*

*"We do not make requests of you because we are
righteous, but because of your great mercy."*
DANIEL 9:18 NIV

Many people know that Daniel saw visions of the end times,
writing dramatic prophecies in a Bible book that bears his name.
Few probably realize that Daniel read the earlier writings of a
fellow prophet, trying to understand exactly what was happening
to his homeland.

Daniel lived most of his life in Babylon, having been kidnapped
as a youth from a ransacked Jerusalem. But he faithfully served
Israel's God in a pagan land—for which he was once thrown into
a den of lions. (God, of course, protected Daniel from harm.)

When Daniel "understood from the Scriptures, according
to the word of the LORD given to Jeremiah the prophet, that the
desolation of Jerusalem would last seventy years" (Daniel 9:2
NIV), he prayed a long prayer of confession for his people, who
had sinned so badly and persistently against God that He had
allowed heavy punishment to fall upon them. And in the midst
of that prayer, Daniel uttered one of the great truths of scripture,
the verse we know now as Daniel 9:18.

Let's understand, with Daniel, that we bring absolutely nothing
to God. But let's also know, like Daniel, that in God's great mercy,
He chooses to hear, love, and forgive us.

*God, thank You that my relationship with You doesn't depend
on any righteousness of my own but on Your great mercy.*

Finally two came forward and declared, "This fellow said, 'I am able to destroy the temple of God and rebuild it in three days.'"
MATTHEW 26:60-61 NIV

What an impossible claim! Destroy the temple and rebuild it in three days? Accusations spread like wildfire.

The chief priests and Sanhedrin sought false evidence against the Lord to put Him to death (verse 59). They couldn't find any, so several accusers stepped up and told the assembly that Jesus claimed He could destroy and rebuild the temple in three days. The innuendo was unfair and inaccurate; the men clearly embellished the truth to give their accusations credibility.

The truth is, John 2:19 (NIV) records Jesus saying, "Destroy this temple, and I will raise it again in three days." Jesus spoke of His own death and resurrection. The temple He referred to was His physical body, not the structure of the Jews' worship center (John 2:21). He spoke in response to the moneychangers who refuted Jesus' authority to cleanse the temple. So the Jews took what Jesus said literally (verse 20) and used His words to create unfounded accusations against Him.

Making a few minor modifications, we often take the most holy things or innocent people and build a case against them. But we are to *seek* and *speak* the whole truth, void of personal biases or prejudices. This is possible with prayer:

Lord, may I always speak Your Word in context, not wrestling it into contorted positions to make it say what I want it to say. Amen.

*I love the LORD because he hears
my voice and my prayer for mercy.*
PSALM 116:1 NLT

So many verses in the book of Psalms are songs of lament. Hurting, pain, struggle. . .certainly God understands these things. Some of these verses can be outright depressing if you really consider them for very long.

Psalm 116:1, though, is a wonderful short verse that should not be missed. It is neither lament nor praise, as are many of the other psalms. But it is a strong assurance of hope. Whether we are offering our praise to God or falling at His feet with our struggles, we know from these few words that God hears us. Isn't that amazing? The almighty God of the universe who created and assembled every particle in existence hears us when we come before Him.

Maybe we go to the Lord in song, praising. Maybe we spend some time reading and thinking about God's Word. Maybe we are praying to Him as we reach out for His comfort. Whatever we do, God hears us and is interested in what we have to say. Isn't that a great reason to love the Lord? May we never forget to give thanks to God daily for the opportunity that He provides us simply to be heard.

*Father in heaven, so often I come to You, asking for Your
mercy. I thank You that You've always heard my prayers.*

*Herod feared John and protected him, knowing him to
be a righteous and holy man. When Herod heard John,
he was greatly puzzled; yet he liked to listen to him.*
MARK 6:20 NIV

John the Baptist was at Herod Antipas' mercy. Herodias, Herod's wife, wanted the Baptist dead, so her husband threw the prophet in prison. John shouldn't have lived as long as he did, but Herod "liked to listen to him."

Why? Because there is something in each of us that yearns for God. Our souls came from Him and long to be reunited with Him—even the souls of the "bad guys."

A tiny part of Herod must have hoped John would answer his questions and show him salvation. Sadly, Herod's trust in earthly power meant that would never happen.

John's was a voice "in the wilderness," not in a lush garden (Matthew 3:3 NIV). He didn't talk only to those who wanted to hear; he was compelled to address those who claimed they couldn't care less—people like Herod.

God wants the faithful, but He also wants the "godless." They'll struggle and fight against it, of course—but their souls cry out to be saved. Look around you. Whose wilderness might you speak His love in?

*Lord, help me not to hold back loving words and kind acts
even from my enemies. May Your Spirit use me to touch them.*

Do not be yoked together with unbelievers.
2 CORINTHIANS 6:14 NIV

History doesn't reveal much of the apostle Paul's social life. There is a tradition that claims he'd been married once and that his wife was not sympathetic to the demands of the Christian lifestyle. The Bible is silent on this phase of Paul's personal life.

What Holy Writ is not silent about is the difference between believers and unbelievers. Paul was fully aware of the world. He knew how pernicious worldliness can be. As oil and water do not mix, so, too, the attitudes of the worldly and born-again believers.

The apostle's warning is not necessarily limited to courtship and marriage. He was aware that the Corinthian church was infiltrated with unbelievers and troublemakers. The weekly love feasts and observances of the Lord's Supper were misused, and spurious philosophies were being advocated by not-yet-grounded newbies.

In no uncertain terms, Paul compares believers flirting with life outside of Christ as light to darkness, righteousness to wickedness, and Christ to Belial (6:14–15). His solution is this direct advice: "Come out from them and be separate" (6:17 NIV).

> *God give us believers separate from the crowd!*
> *A time like this demands strong minds, great hearts,*
> *true faith, who need not the approval of the crowd.*
> JOSIAH GILBERT HOLLAND

Dear God, give me wisdom to know which of my relationships amount to me being "unequally yoked" and which don't. Amen.

When the storm has swept by, the wicked are
gone, but the righteous stand firm forever.
PROVERBS 10:25 NIV

We as Christians may wonder why God allows storms in our lives. But today's scripture indicates that everyone—righteous and wicked alike—experiences rough weather. The difference is who's still standing when the tempest is past.

Believers build their lives on the firm foundation of Jesus—and however hard the wind blows, their house is unmoved (Matthew 7:24–25). Through the worst of storms, Jesus goes with us, awaiting the proper moment to calm the wind and waves (Mark 4:35–41). God directs hail- and snowstorms to His own purposes, "for times of trouble, for days of war and battle" (Job 38:23 NIV). Whether literal or figurative, the tempests of life are simply one of God's methods for dealing with humanity.

Since He wants "everyone to come to repentance" (2 Peter 3:9 NIV), God may use the terror of storms to draw the unsaved to Himself. In believers' lives, He might allow a storm for His greater, unseen purposes—as He did with Job. In ultimate terms, God will use the storm to sweep away His enemies, all the while strengthening and protecting His own children.

We won't always understand the storms. But we can be sure that God does and is using every one of them for His wise design.

Lord, help me to accept storms as part of
Your plan—and keep me standing strong.

> *I am Alpha and Omega, the beginning*
> *and the end, the first and the last.*
> REVELATION 22:13 KJV

Who said that Jesus is not deity? Over and over we find that the titles God gave to Himself in the Old Testament are being applied to Jesus Christ as well. In the Old Testament, the Lord God called Himself a shepherd, the Alpha and Omega, the Beginning and the End, and the Almighty. He is called the First and the Last. In the New Testament, we find the same titles given to Jesus. This makes our God unique among the religions of the world.

No other religion has a God whose Son is equal to the Father. The Jews and Muslims reject the idea of God having a Son. Only Christianity has a triune God—three persons in one God.

The Bible is unique because in it God fully reveals who He is. Since Jesus is fully God, let it renew our hope and faith in our Savior. He who created all things out of nothing will re-create this world into a paradise without sin.

Jesus, I worship You as the Son of God, as God the Son,
equal to God the Father. As the Christmas hymn "Hark!
the Herald Angels Sing" declares, "Veiled in flesh,
the Godhead see! Hail the incarnate Deity!"

We love because he first loved us.
1 John 4:19 NIV

Where does love begin? Love—that unselfish and unconditional emotion that drives us to our knees in worship, to forgiveness when broken, and to give to others beyond where common sense ends.

The Bible tells us we love because God loves first. Our love flows from God's bottomless well of devotion for us. He initiates the relationship He wants with us, drenching us with His love as He adopts us as His children.

We worry when we can't love others as He told us in the greatest commandment—to love Him and to love others. We can't do this on our own. But God loves with an everlasting love.

The power of His love within us fuels our love when human love is running on empty. He plants His love within our hearts so we can share Him with others. We draw from His endless supply.

Love starts with God. God continues to provide His love to nourish us. God surrounds us with His love. We live in hope and draw from His strength, all because He first loved us.

Father, I thank You for Your unconditional, endless love that surrounds me, fills me, and upholds me. Your love gives me hope and courage. Help me, in my most discouraged moments, to remember that You never stop loving me.

Beloved, I urge you as sojourners and exiles to abstain from the passions of the flesh, which wage war against your soul.
1 PETER 2:11 ESV

If he were writing today, Peter wouldn't win a popularity contest with the exhortation of today's scripture. "What?" many would say. "Go against my feelings? Tell myself no? I can't do that—this is just who I am!"

Before we lob a morality grenade at the unsaved people around us, note exactly who Peter was addressing: "beloved" fellow Christians. He had just described his readers as "a chosen race, a royal priesthood, a holy nation. . .God's people" (1 Peter 2:9–10 ESV). Clearly, the passions of the flesh affect us as Christian men too.

This war for our souls is fierce and ongoing—and even when the battlefield seems quiet, be sure the enemy is preparing another onslaught. Whether your passions run toward sex or alcohol or drugs or overeating or laziness or any of a thousand other temptations, Peter simply says, "Abstain." And what the Bible tells us to do, we can—with the help of God's Holy Spirit inside us.

It will be challenging. Every war is. But "the LORD is a man of war" (Exodus 15:3 ESV), and He'll be in the foxhole with you. When you obey His commands, God guarantees your safety and ultimate victory.

*Lord God, this world is truly a battlefield.
Strengthen me to abstain from the passions of my flesh.*

A Canaanite woman from that vicinity came to him,
crying out, "Lord, Son of David, have mercy on me!"
MATTHEW 15:22 NIV

One day Jesus and His disciples traveled north out of the borders
of Galilee into the region of Tyre. When a non-Jewish lady, a
Syrophoenician woman, heard that He was there, she repeatedly
cried, "Lord, Son of David"—a common name for the Messiah—
and begged Jesus to drive a demon out of her little daughter.

Many Christians are mystified by how Jesus at first ignored
the woman, finally informed her that He was "sent only to the lost
sheep of Israel," then compared her to a dog—simply because she
was non-Jewish (Matthew 15:24–27 NIV). Matthew clarifies this
by stating the children of Abraham, the Jews, had to eat their fill
first before the dogs could expect to share the food.

Jesus loves Gentiles; He was simply taking the Gospel *first* "to
the lost sheep of Israel" (Matthew 10:5–6 NIV), "first to the Jew,
then to the Gentile" (Romans 1:16 NIV).

The astonishing thing is that this woman was not simply a
Gentile, but a despised *Canaanite*—yet Jesus even had mercy on
her and answered her prayers. This gives hope to all of us.

Lord, help me to be as persistent in my prayers as
that Canaanite woman was, knowing that, in Your
time, You will answer. In Jesus' name. Amen.

*"As soon as you began to pray, a word went out, which I
have come to tell you, for you are highly esteemed."*
DANIEL 9:23 NIV

Daniel was an upright Jewish man, carried off into captivity
as the Babylonians conquered Jerusalem. Enrolled in King
Nebuchadnezzar's indoctrination program, Daniel spent three
years learning the culture of Babylon before becoming one of the
king's most trusted advisers. Living in exile for most of his life,
Daniel nevertheless remained faithful to God, and his heart broke
for the cumulative sins of the people of Israel.

In the middle of pouring out his heart to God one day, Daniel's
prayer is interrupted by the appearance of the angel Gabriel.
Bringing insight and understanding (verse 22), Gabriel's message
contains the interesting concept that in the instant that Daniel
began to pray, the answer was already on its way.

Before Daniel got past his salutation, God knew Daniel's
heart and had already set in motion the response to Daniel's
unfinished prayer.

As He did for Daniel, God knows our needs even before we
give voice to them in prayer. We can rest in the knowledge that
even before the words leave our lips, God has already heard them,
and He has already answered them.

*Thank You, God, that I have been made righteous by the blood of
Jesus Christ Your Son, and because of that, You hear my prayers.*

So Judas threw the money into the temple and left.
Then he went away and hanged himself.
MATTHEW 27:5 NIV

Judas has become known as the arch betrayer, but *two* people betrayed Jesus on the night He was taken. The other was Peter.

Judas identified Jesus in front of His enemies; Peter denied he ever knew Him, not once but three times. In terms of betrayal, they were both horrible—yet Peter went on to do great works while his fellow member of "the Twelve" died in torment and disgrace. What made the difference?

Perhaps Judas sold the Lord for greed, or maybe he wanted to provoke Jesus into defeating Rome's rule over the Jews. Either way, he took matters into his own hands. Even after admitting his mistake, Judas still assumed control of his own life by ending it.

Peter, on the other hand, owned his shame—it appears in all of the Gospels—and stayed with the Twelve. He trusted in the Lord's redemption and was given great responsibility by the risen Jesus.

Judas betrayed the Lord but also himself, as we do when we take our lives into our own hands. There are more loving and capable hands awaiting, as a repentant and saved Peter learned.

Dear Lord, if You forgave Peter's sin—terrible as it was—You will
surely forgive my sins. I thank You for Your great mercies.

At this, Job got up and tore his robe and shaved his head. Then he fell to the ground in worship.
JOB 1:20 NIV

Grief expresses itself in different ways. When troubles come, some people spill copious tears, others burst with fits of anger, and a few simply shut down in silent numbness. In Western cultures, black is the color of grief. People wear white in oriental countries.

How did Job express his grief?

He followed the traditional ways of mourning in his culture by tearing his clothes and shaving his head. But Job also *worshipped*.

Despite the overwhelming darkness of shock and grief, he turned to God. He lay prostrate on the ground in front of the Lord, submitting his entire self. In his time of overwhelming loss and overpowering helplessness, he opened his heart to the only one who fully understood and could help him in his time of deepest need—God.

When everything in life seems gone, lost, or out of reach, God is waiting. God understands our sorrow and stays with us while we grieve. As we turn our hearts to Him in worship, His healing Spirit will provide comfort.

God, help me to worship You during my times of grief, to never forget that You are God and that You are altogether good. Amen.

*The person without the Spirit does not accept the things
that come from the Spirit of God but considers them
foolishness, and cannot understand them because
they are discerned only through the Spirit.*
1 CORINTHIANS 2:14 NIV

In this passage, Paul divides humans into two classes: the natural (the unbeliever, unrenewed through the new birth) and the spiritual (the born-again believer, walking in full communion with God).

The natural man and woman may be extremely intelligent yet fail to understand God's Word because it is spiritually discerned. Consequently, the basic truths of scripture are hidden from them. Natural instincts and worldly desires dictate their hearts, and spiritual things make little sense. So they are unable to comprehend the magnitude of God's love and the power of His promises.

On the other hand, the spiritual person is focused on the thoughts and will of God. The indwelling presence of God's Spirit leads, guides, comforts, and speaks to the believer.

Jesus said, "Very truly I tell you, no one can see the kingdom of God unless they are born again" (John 3:3 NIV). Only through the new birth, can we attain true spirituality. The moment we repent of our sins and accept Jesus into our hearts, we become God's own. And from then on, we begin to understand.

*Thank You, Father, that You redeemed me by the blood of
Jesus and gave me a spiritual birth by Your Spirit.*

Yea doubtless, and I count all things but loss for the excellency of the knowledge of Christ Jesus my Lord: for whom I have suffered the loss of all things, and do count them but dung, that I may win Christ.
PHILIPPIANS 3:8 KJV

Even the most ambitious, aggressive men find that worldly success is elusive or unfulfilling. Average guys often learn that lesson early on.

Scripturally speaking, though, every worldly achievement is nothing—"loss" and "dung" in the language of the old King James Version, "yesterday's garbage" and "a pile of waste" in the modern paraphrase of the Voice Bible.

What truly matters—what rises above all other things in importance—is knowing the Lord Jesus Christ. And, happily, that's achievable by the ambitious and the average alike. Whether you're riding high as the CEO of a Fortune 500 company or you're a retired laborer in an assisted living facility, if you desire and pursue more of the Lord, He will allow you—like the apostle Paul—to "win Christ."

Bible reading, prayer, meditation, church attendance, fellowship, service. . .whatever God the Father allows you to do, to whatever level, will lead you to have more of His Son, Jesus Christ, and the Holy Spirit in your life.

Anything that came earlier, whether good or bad, is history. Only Jesus Christ matters going forward. This is our priority.

Heavenly Father, grant me Your Spirit so I can better know Your Son. May Jesus Himself be my priority.

"For the king knows about these things, and I am speaking freely to him, because I cannot believe that any of these things has escaped his notice, for this was not done in a corner."
ACTS 26:26 NET

Paul could speak boldly, because what had occurred twenty-six years earlier at the crucifixion was widely known, even among non-Christians such as the Jewish historian Josephus. He records in *Antiquities of the Jews*:

> *Now, there was about this time, Jesus, a wise man, if it be lawful to call him a man. . . . He drew over to him both many of the Jews and many of the Gentiles. He was the Christ; and when Pilate, at the suggestion of the principal men amongst us, had condemned him to the cross, those that loved him at the first did not forsake him, for he appeared to them alive again the third day, as the divine prophets had foretold these and ten thousand other wonderful things concerning him; and the tribe of Christians, so named from him, are not extinct at this time.*

Most in the first century accepted the historical fact of Jesus, but then, as now, many refused to accept His lordship. You're a lot wiser than that, right?

Lord, I'm inspired every time I see that You left Yourself witnesses in secular history and archaeology.

*He found a new jawbone of a donkey and stretched out
his hand and took it and slew a thousand men with it.*
JUDGES 15:15 SKJV

God used Samson to provoke and judge the Philistines, who were
ruling harshly over Israel. At one point, Samson set their fields on
fire, and the Philistines responded by burning his wife. His own
people, fearful of further violence, came to arrest Samson and
hand him over to the Philistines. He agreed, but at the moment
of handoff, the Spirit of God came upon Samson. He grabbed a
jawbone of a donkey and wiped out a thousand Philistines.

How could that be? It was certainly the power of God that
allowed one man to take down a legion of others. Sadly, though,
Samson was dismissive of the things of God. He was a man of
the flesh, a womanizer who never rose to his true potential—and
he ended up praising his own strength and a lowly jawbone for
the victory, rather than the empowering Spirit of God.

That's common for human beings. We'll worship something—
either the stuff of this world or the God who gave us this world
by His power.

Which will you choose today?

---

*Father, may I never take the gifts You've given me for granted.
Help me keep my eyes and my hopes on You. In Jesus' name. Amen.*

For we brought nothing into the world,
and we can take nothing out of it.
1 TIMOTHY 6:7 NIV

Paul preached "you can't take it with you" long before those words became a familiar saying.

In this letter, Paul addressed the issue of falling into the trap of believing that riches brought about a contented life. Paul reminded Timothy that one day people would leave their things behind. In addition, Paul warned that spending their time chasing after wealth was going to lead his flock into temptations that would have a domino effect in their lives. Soon they'd be more dedicated to their money than they would be to their faith.

Jesus also preached about the struggle the wealthy face when it comes to thinking about the kingdom of God (Matthew 19:16–30). The book of Ecclesiastes is full of the despair that comes from seeking after the wrong things.

Though we don't take anything out of the world, we do leave things behind—and not just material items. We leave behind the people whose lives we have touched for better or for worse. We leave behind the words we've spoken, which may or may not have been encouraging.

Finally, we leave behind the comments that others say about us, remarks that can show either our love for possessions or our love for God.

God, restrain me from the folly of chasing worldly riches. May I learn to be content in You and focus on leaving a good legacy.

> *"Circumcise yourselves to the LORD, circumcise your hearts,*
> *you people of Judah and inhabitants of Jerusalem."*
> JEREMIAH 4:4 NIV

The ancient people of Egypt, Edom, Ammon, and Moab all practiced circumcision (Jeremiah 9:25–26), but God gave the rite to Abraham as a sign of the covenant between the two of them (Genesis 17:9–14).

Although circumcision is a physical thing, the Bible also speaks of it in metaphorical terms. When God called Moses to confront Pharaoh, he replied that he was "uncircumcised of lips" (Exodus 6:12, alternate NIV reading). Jeremiah accused the Israelites of having uncircumcised ears, incapable of hearing the Lord's message (Jeremiah 6:10, alternate NIV reading).

Moses pointed to a day like Jeremiah's, when the people would need to repent of their uncircumcised hearts (Leviticus 26:40–42). In Deuteronomy, God expanded on the concept of "circumcising hearts" by commanding the people to stop being stiff-necked (10:16) and to love the Lord with all their hearts and souls (30:6).

For Christians, the Holy Spirit circumcises our hearts at the new birth (Romans 2:29). He replaces our hearts of stone with a new heart and a new spirit (Ezekiel 36:26).

Everyone—including us—is prone to a stubborn persistence in our own ways. But if we renew our commitment to love God with all our hearts, souls, minds, and strength, we can "circumcise our hearts" and live.

Dear God, give me a circumcised heart in all things, I pray.

For in him dwelleth all the fulness of the
Godhead bodily. And ye are complete in him.
COLOSSIANS 2:9–10 KJV

Paul wrote the epistle to the Colossians to counter two forms of heresy that were making inroads into their church: On the one hand was an ultrastrict form of Judaism emphasizing tradition, circumcision, and ritualistic ceremonies (Colossians 2:8, 11, 16–17). On the other hand an early branch of Gnostics were promoting philosophy, "secret knowledge," and asceticism (Colossians 2:4, 18, 21, 23).

Paul insisted that both these extremes were missing the point. "Secret wisdom" and philosophical arguments were exalting themselves against the knowledge of God (2 Corinthians 10:5), and an insistence on keeping rituals and traditions was an attempt to say that faith in Christ was not enough.

Paul stated clearly that the fullness of deity lives in bodily form in Christ. He is God the Son, and when you have God in your heart, you are complete. You don't need anything added—whether ceremonies or so-called secret knowledge—to make you *more* complete. If the Spirit of Jesus Christ dwells in your heart and you are connected to God, you've got it all! Don't let anyone persuade you otherwise (Colossians 2:8).

Lord, what a comforting thought: I'm complete in You. Help me to not be moved away from the simplicity that is in Christ. Amen.

"Do you not fear Me? This is the LORD's declaration. Do you not tremble before Me, the One who set the sand as the boundary of the sea, an enduring barrier that it cannot cross? The waves surge, but they cannot prevail. They roar but cannot pass over it."

JEREMIAH 5:22 HCSB

With the exception of the great flood of Genesis, the seas have kept to their God-ordained limits since the third day of creation. That's when the Lord decreed, "Let the water under the sky be gathered into one place, and let the dry land appear" (Genesis 1:9 HCSB). If God sets parameters for His creation, they'll be obeyed.

The physical world follows God's orders without complaint. Only human beings, made in God's image but possessing free will, resist His good and wise direction.

Even at that, God still sets protective limits. "A king's heart is like streams of water in the LORD's hand," the Proverbs say. "He directs it wherever He chooses" (21:1 HCSB). "The nations rage like the raging of many waters," Isaiah wrote. "He rebukes them, and they flee far away" (17:13 HCSB).

When it seems like the world is spinning out of control, it isn't. . .God is completely aware of everything that happens and superintending it. We may not understand or even like what we see. But we can trust that even as circumstances crash like breakers, they will never go beyond God's parameters.

Lord, thank You for protecting me with Your wise and powerful boundaries.

The man measured the gateway entrance, which was 17½ feet wide at the opening and 22¾ feet wide in the gateway passage.
EZEKIEL 40:11 NLT

If you're an architect (or always wanted to be), you'll love Ezekiel 40. If not, this detailed verbal blueprint of the future temple may be daunting.

God gave Ezekiel a vision of the gateways, outer and inner courtyards, and rooms both for priests and the preparing of sacrifices. There are plenty of measurements and explanations: window placement, numbers of steps, even decorations (carved palm trees appear throughout). The level of detail is reminiscent of the plans for the ark of the covenant that God had given Moses (Exodus 25).

So what does it all mean to us?

One takeaway is simply the immense knowledge of God. The One who flung the farthest stars into the universe has also planned three-inch hooks for the temple's foyer walls (Ezekiel 40:43), a level of detail squaring perfectly with Jesus' teaching: "What is the price of five sparrows—two copper coins? Yet God does not forget a single one of them. And the very hairs on your head are all numbered" (Luke 12:6–7 NLT). And God's not just showing off. Jesus went on to say, "So don't be afraid; you are more valuable to God than a whole flock of sparrows."

With a God like this, human worry is utterly unnecessary.

Thank You, Lord, for overseeing all the details. Help me to trust You completely.

*Always learning and never able to come
to the knowledge of the truth.*
2 TIMOTHY 3:7 NASB

Beginning with the year AD 1, it took until 1500 for mankind's knowledge base to double one time. Currently it's been estimated that this base doubles every one or two years, and some claim this happens in less than twelve months.

Today we have 24-7 access to the internet, TV, and radio. Medical breakthroughs have provided us with artificial knees, transplanted organs, and laser surgery. Modern medications treat conditions ranging from an annoying headache to an irregular heartbeat. New technologies unveiled the complexities of the microscopic cell and peered deep into outer space.

Scientific discoveries have revealed the design and order of our world as never before. God's fingerprints are everywhere. Nonetheless, our culture spurns God along with His Son, Jesus.

Learning is good, but knowledge divorced from God is incomplete and leaves us vulnerable to false teachings and intellectual fads. The apostle Paul warns they "will turn their ears away from the truth and will turn aside to myths" (2 Timothy 4:4 NASB).

What are we to do? "Be diligent to present yourself approved to God as a workman who does not need to be ashamed, accurately handling the word of truth" (2 Timothy 2:15 NASB).

*Father, help me not to embrace any teaching
that clashes with Your truth in the Bible.*

As Jesus was getting into the boat, the man who had been demon-possessed begged to go with him.
MARK 5:18 NIV

Almost all the Gerasenes wanted Jesus gone. The only one who thought differently was a man who'd been living in tombs, someone chains couldn't hold, an outcast from whom Jesus had driven a "legion" of demons. This Gerasene had just been handed his life back, and his response was to give that same life back to Jesus.

Jesus said no—and yes.

The man faced an all-too-modern dilemma. Letting Jesus save our lives often involves a separation from the people around us, the people who played such a big part in our "earthly" lives. In this instance, these were people who valued their pigs above the new believer's redemption.

Seems he wanted to turn his back to them, going instead where he knew he was loved. But Jesus sent him back into their midst. It must have been a lonely walk. Faith doesn't always put us where we want to be—it puts us where we are most needed.

Left on his own, among people who didn't want to know Jesus, this redeemed soul spread the word to ten cities—and "all the people were amazed" (Mark 5:20 NIV).

Look around yourself—at your workplace, your friends, your family—and ask, "Who could I amaze today?"

Jesus, help me to follow You and do Your will, wherever You place me, and whatever You call me to do. Amen.

"For I know the plans I have for you," declares
the LORD, "plans to prosper you and not to harm
you, plans to give you hope and a future."
JEREMIAH 29:11 NIV

When God promises something, He is sure to deliver.

Due to their sin and rebellion, the Jews were held hostage by Babylon. At the end of Israel's seventy-year captivity, Jeremiah prophesied that their deliverance was near. God promised that if the people would pray and seek Him with all their heart, He would listen and be found (verses 12–14).

In Jeremiah 29:11, the prophet's reassuring words of hope must have soothed and refreshed like cool water on parched lips. The same is true today.

Sometimes hope comes in the form of a second chance, easing our sense of failure. Other times it's clothed in the words of a doctor who informs his patient that a full recovery is near. Hope thrives in the fertile soil of a heart restored by a loving gesture, a compassionate embrace, or an encouraging word. It is one of God's most precious gifts.

God *wants* to forgive our sins and lead us on the paths of righteousness—just as He did for the Israelites of old. He has great plans for us. That's His promise and our blessed hope.

Lord, I know You have wonderful things planned
for me. May I trust Your goodness, and experience
everything You have for me, I pray. Amen.

Miserable comforters are ye all.
JOB 16:2 KJV

Those familiar with Job's story recognize this plaintive cry.

It was Job's description of three friends—Bildad, Eliphaz, and Zophar—who had originally come to sympathize with him. Days before, Job had lost everything but his wife in a series of freakish "accidents" orchestrated by Satan. The "perfect and upright" Job (1:1 KJV) lost all seven thousand of his sheep, three thousand camels, five hundred yoke of oxen, five hundred female donkeys—and worst of all, ten children—when Satan tried to break his faith. Shortly, again with God's permission, Satan would also take Job's health.

When the friends came to commiserate, they wisely sat in silence for seven days. But then they began to question *why* Job had suffered—ultimately concluding that Job had committed terrible sins. It wasn't long before Job uttered his "miserable comforters" quotation.

Many modern Bible translations have kept the King James Version's phrasing, while the New American Standard uses "sorry comforters" and the New Century Version "painful comforters."

Of course, none of those adjectives—*miserable, sorry,* or *painful*—actually go with the word *comforter.* When our friends are going through trials, let's make sure we're true, loving, and godly comforters.

---

*God, help me to be a comforter to all
those in pain and suffering, I pray.*

"Therefore, in the present case I advise you: Leave these men alone! Let them go! For if their purpose or activity is of human origin, it will fail. But if it is from God, you will not be able to stop these men; you will only find yourselves fighting against God."
ACTS 5:38–39 NIV

Peter and the apostles were preaching Christ. This didn't sit well with the Sadducees, who arrested them. They escaped from jail, were arrested again, and brought before the Sanhedrin. They were sentenced to die after Peter boldly spoke of Christ's resurrection and said he would continue to preach about Christ because "we must obey God rather than human beings" (Acts 5:29 NIV).

Gamaliel, a highly respected Pharisee, addressed the Sanhedrin. He reminded them of the other men who had started movements or preached. Once those men were killed, their followers fell away. Yet, Gamaliel's advice was to set Peter and the others free. Gamaliel believed that if Peter's actions were man inspired they would eventually fail. If, however, what Peter was doing was by God's hand, nothing would stop them. The Sanhedrin, realizing they'd lose in a fight against God, released the men.

When we face obstacles while doing the work God has called us to, we can press on, reassured in the knowledge that God's plan for our lives will always triumph.

Lord, help me to be confident that You're on my side and will keep me safe. In Jesus' name, I pray. Amen.

"See, I have engraved you on the palms of my hands."
ISAIAH 49:16 NIV

Have you ever had a bad day turn into a bad week. . .turn into a bad month. . .turn into a bad year? Judah was in the middle of one of those times. The storm clouds of impending judgment had begun to gather, and God was preparing to hold His people accountable for forsaking Him. Assyria and Babylon were growing in power, and it wouldn't be long before living in exile became the new reality for God's people.

In the middle of tumultuous times, it's tempting to proclaim that God has forgotten us. Both Israel and Judah struggled with the idea that God had abandoned them. But God took steps to contradict this notion. In an image that prefigures Jesus' crucifixion, God boldly proclaimed that His children were engraved on the palms of His hands. The nail-scarred hands that His Son would endure bear the engraved names of all of us who call upon Him as Savior and Lord.

God does not forget us in the midst of our troubles. It is His nail-scarred hand that reaches down and holds our own.

Lord, You've never forgotten me and will never abandon me, no matter how it seems. Your hands strengthen and uphold me, even during my most desperate moments.

Our ancestors in Egypt were not impressed by the LORD's miraculous deeds. They soon forgot his many acts of kindness to them. Instead, they rebelled against him at the Red Sea. Even so, he saved them—to defend the honor of his name and to demonstrate his mighty power.

PSALM 106:7-8 NLT

Have you ever overlooked God's incredible power? Forgotten His kindnesses to you? Even rebelled against Him? We all have.

Even so, God loves you.

If you have accepted His gift of salvation, your mistakes and outright disobedience are covered by Jesus' sacrifice on the cross. Because of Christ, God the Father saves you "to defend the honor of his name and to demonstrate his mighty power." This is how God shows His righteousness, "for he himself is fair and just, and he makes sinners right in his sight when they believe in Jesus" (Romans 3:26 NLT).

We're still human and prone to sinful behavior. Sometimes we'll stay quiet when we should speak up. Sometimes we'll pop off when we should zip our lips. Sometimes we'll let our minds or eyes or feet wander to places they shouldn't go. Even so, God loves us.

Nothing will separate us from His love through Jesus (Romans 8:39). That's not an excuse to live in sin. But when we do sin, it's an invitation to return to God's fellowship in repentance.

Father, I'm grateful for Your steadfast love. May it continually move me to greater obedience and service.

"Anyone who strikes father or mother must be put to death."
EXODUS 21:15 NLT

Many find it difficult to love God after reading of the extreme violence in the Old Testament. The chapter where we find this verse gives us insight behind this violence. Here, we find that God is not sending violence upon His people randomly. Rather, the people have agreed to the consequences outlined in the Mosaic law in the chapters in Exodus and Leviticus. All the consequences of turning away from God and disobeying Him were laid out in advance, and the Israelites had agreed to abide by the contract.

We have a legal system of laws with their consequences too. If we apply for a driver's license, we agree to the laws and legal consequences regarding driving and the rules of the road. If we violate those rules, such as speeding through a stop sign, then we know we will bear the consequences if we get caught.

God was not being unfair when the Israelites suffered extreme hardships. It was all laid out in the law. Let us not be surprised that what we sow, we shall also reap. And don't forget, this rule has a positive side to it as well.

Father, may I love You and trust Your justice when I read harsh laws in the Old Testament. Help me understand their context and Your ultimate goal. Amen.

*"I have prayed for you, Simon, that your faith may not fail. And
when you have turned back, strengthen your brothers." But he
replied, "Lord, I am ready to go with you to prison and to death."*
LUKE 22:32–33 NIV

The ups and downs of Simon Peter's life should give every man
hope. Jesus loved this impetuous apostle and stuck with him
through some bad (sometimes incredibly bad) moments. And
through it all, Peter matured into a tremendous leader, a man
who helped introduce billions of people to his Lord. Think about
it: Where might you be today apart from Peter's Pentecost sermon
that kick-started the church (Acts 2)?

It's easy to judge Peter for his boastful statement above, since
we know what happened next. Jesus said, "I tell you, Peter, before
the rooster crows today, you will deny three times that you know
me" (Luke 22:34 NIV). Jesus was exactly right, validating and
necessitating His words "when you have turned back."

Peter's later compatriot, Paul, warned about overconfidence
in the Christian life. After describing the failures of the ancient
Israelites, Paul said, "These things happened to them as examples
and were written down as warnings for us. . . . So, if you think you
are standing firm, be careful that you don't fall!" (1 Corinthians
10:11–12 NIV).

Peter is probably nodding in agreement, saying, "Don't ever
think you can live the Christian life in your own power."

Lord, please strengthen me by Your Spirit.

Oh, that my people would listen to me,
that Israel would walk in my ways!
PSALM 81:13 ESV

The way God deals with people changes over time. But because He is perfect and eternal, His desire for fellowship with mankind remains the same. It behooves us to endeavor to please God and enjoy His blessing.

As Christians, we know God at a more intimate level than did the ancient Israelites. They were His chosen nation and experienced many benefits from that status—but the work of Jesus Christ was still future and the Holy Spirit did not yet make His home in human hearts. So the Israelites often failed, sometimes spectacularly, as God cried out for them simply to do what He said.

That was God's desire then; it's still His passion now. We who know God the Father through God the Son, who entertain God the Spirit in our deepest inner being, should be even more committed to listening to Him and walking in His ways. Not to be saved—that's purely a work of grace, through our faith in Jesus Christ. But because we are thankful, because we recognize how merciful God has been, because we want to honor our Lord, and because, in the long run, it's by far the best thing for us.

We know God's desires by the Word He's given us. Listen to it, and walk in His ways.

Lord, guide me in Your ways. I want to please You.

For my people have committed two evils; they have forsaken me the fountain of living waters, and hewed them out cisterns, broken cisterns, that can hold no water.

JEREMIAH 2:13 KJV

God's people committed two fundamental sins: they turned away from God, and they sought pleasure in idolatry and idolatrous living.

Through the voice of Jeremiah, God used the illustration of a broken cistern to describe the fruitlessness of idolatry and the sinful life. In ancient times, the people spent much time and effort digging pits into the earth or rock to receive rain. Yet these cisterns cracked with changing temperatures, leaving mud and filthy sediments at best.

Similarly, the world—even some Christians—hew cisterns of wealth, pleasure, and prominence, thinking these elements contain the waters that will sustain and bring them happiness. Instead, their unprofitable efforts leave them void and empty; or as the Lord said, "Hath a nation changed their gods, which are yet no gods? but my people have changed their glory for that which doth not profit" (verse 11 KJV).

Jesus said, "For what is a man profited, if he shall gain the whole world, and lose his own soul?" (Matthew 16:26 KJV). Living waters flow from a personal relationship with Christ, for only He can quench our thirst. Man-made cisterns become cesspools, but God's waters are always pure, sparkling with new life.

God, I choose to drink from Your fountain of life. I forsake my muddy cisterns containing stale water. Amen.

And the word of the LORD came to him:
"What are you doing here, Elijah?"
1 KINGS 19:9 NIV

Isn't it surprising when God, who knows everything, asks *us* a question?

At the time God asked Elijah this question, He already knew what had brought Elijah to the point of such despair that he prayed to God to take his life.

God knew Elijah had just been victorious over the prophets of Baal. He knew, too, that Elijah had been threatened by Jezebel and was running in fear for his life. Despite knowing all this, God still asked Elijah why he was hiding out in a cave.

Elijah isn't the first person God has asked a direct question, knowing the answer. God asked Adam and Eve where they were even though He knew they were trying to conceal themselves from Him (Genesis 3:9). In their case as well as Elijah's, fear and despair had driven them to a place of hiding and shame.

Sometimes we live in a manner that causes God to ask us the question He posed to Elijah. Whether we're in a literal place we shouldn't be or our emotions have lead us to a place of captivity, God wants us to stop and consider where we are.

Aren't you thankful He cares enough to ask?

God, thank You for Your Word that convicts me,
Your questions that spur me to check my heart
and consider my attitudes and actions.

*Jesus, full of the Holy Spirit, left the Jordan
and was led by the Spirit into the wilderness.*
LUKE 4:1 NIV

Jesus had just been baptized and received the ultimate accolade
from His approving Father, God. Then He went into the desert.
But He wasn't just wandering—He was deliberately led there by
the Holy Spirit.

Forty days' worth of temptation! What would have been the
point if there weren't at least a possibility that Jesus' human nature
might have rebelled against His mission? In Luke we read of a few
instances of Jesus resolutely defying Satan during this time, but
He was out there for almost six weeks. Jesus already knew what
awaited Him, and part of Him must have been sorely afraid—so
the Holy Spirit immediately put Him to the test.

Those forty days, when Jesus might have struggled to remain
resolute, give hope to the rest of us. He would have been scared,
perhaps tempted—and there would have been doubts and the
possibility of failure. But because of that experience, the Lord
is able to stand right beside us, empathizing, when we face *our*
testing times.

Turn to Jesus, because He knows what it's like—and He knows
the way out of the desert.

*Jesus, I'm deeply comforted knowing that You were
tempted in all the ways I am. You understand my
fears and desires and still love me. Thank You.*

Your eyes saw my unformed body; all the days ordained for me were written in your book before one of them came to be.
PSALM 139:16 NIV

The psalmist states it in a dozen poetic ways: God knows everything about us. He knows where we are at all times. He knows what we are going to say before we open our mouths. In fact, He knows every one of our days and has since before our conception.

The Bible talks about several people God set apart from birth: Samson, the first candidate for the "world's strongest man"; Jeremiah, prophet to the nations; John the Baptist, called to prepare the way of the Lord.

But God also knows the days of ordinary people. Job said, "A person's days are determined; you have decreed the number of his months" (Job 14:5 NIV). The same knowledge applies to our new birth. He created us anew in Christ Jesus for good works "which God prepared in advance for us to do" (Ephesians 2:10 NIV).

The God who knows everything about us still loves us. Let's declare, with the psalmist, "Such knowledge is too wonderful for me, too lofty for me to attain" (139:6 NIV).

Lord, all these examples of Your vast wisdom and knowledge are beyond my ability to grasp. But they encourage me to trust You.

Our "God is a consuming fire."
HEBREWS 12:29 NIV

Fire signifies the presence, judgment, and holiness of God. Fire is a powerful image throughout the entire Bible, causing worshippers to approach the throne of the Lord with awe and reverence.

An Israelite, ready to make the perfect offering to the Lord, would bring the best lamb to sacrifice on the altar. The holy ritual of spilling blood and burning the fat of the animal in an all-consuming fire symbolized the cleansing of the worshipper's sin.

A consuming fire destroys everything. The massive destruction observed in fierce forest fires at first looks like complete annihilation. But soon signs of rebirth appear with shoots of green growth and the return of life. What was destroyed soon brings forth new life.

God's fire burns away our self-centeredness, ego, and sinful nature when we place our hearts on His altar. His love melts away our selfishness, pride, and anything that blocks His light from shining through our lives. May we permit the passion of God to burn away our old lives, allowing His life to be reborn within us.

Father, purify my heart so Your Spirit can burn brightly within me, and Your light can shine into the lives of all those around me.

He began by saying to them, "Today this
scripture is fulfilled in your hearing."
LUKE 4:21 NIV

At the start of a mission that would change the world, Jesus declared Himself the Anointed One in front of a hometown audience. More than a few jaws would have dropped, but the listeners were quite civil about it—until He wouldn't play the game the way they wanted. Then they tried to throw Him off a cliff.

These folk knew Jesus' parents, and they had known Him as a child. Now He was shaking their world.

People who come to faith later in life or Christians who find themselves in a faithless environment (perhaps in the workplace) face the same dilemma. It's difficult to stand up in front of people who know your shortcomings and say, "I am a child of God." Some will think you've flipped; others will poke fun. Who needs the hassle? It's much easier just to do good works and keep quiet, isn't it?

But that isn't what it's all about. God wants to be heard. Jesus spoke up—now God wants us to do the same.

Face others and tell them who you are. It won't be easy, but God will provide the courage. When you proclaim "the Lord's favor" (verse 19 NIV), the scripture is fulfilled in you.

Lord, strengthen me so that I may speak boldly about You. Put Your
words and wisdom on my lips. In Jesus' name, I pray. Amen.

He will not let your foot slip—he who
watches over you will not slumber.
PSALM 121:3 NIV

Ever stayed up all night studying for a major test, waiting for a loved one to come home, or soothing a sick child? The next day or two your mushy brain barely functions, and your body, drained of all energy, finds it difficult to focus even on the most important decisions.

You'll regain your balance and energy only after a few nights of refreshing sleep. The human body requires regular periods of rest in order to thrive.

The psalms tell us that God does *not* sleep. He watches over us, never once averting His eyes even for a few quick moments of rest. God guards our every moment.

The Lord stays up all night, looking after us as we sleep. He patiently keeps His eyes on us even when we roam. He constantly comforts when fear or illness makes us toss and turn.

Like a caring parent who tiptoes into a sleeping child's room, God surrounds us even when we don't realize it. We can sleep because God never slumbers.

Thank You, Father, that You watch over me at all
times. Nothing happens without Your knowledge.
Guard and keep me safe today, I pray.

*"Very truly I tell you, unless a kernel of wheat falls
to the ground and dies, it remains only a single
seed. But if it dies, it produces many seeds."*
JOHN 12:24 NIV

Jesus compared Himself to a grain of wheat to emphasize the
necessity of His death, the power of His resurrection, and the
incalculable regenerated souls gleaned from His sacrifice.

In nature, before a seed is sown it lies on the barn floor
seemingly lifeless. The corn of wheat is entombed within itself
until—buried in proper soil—chemical agents begin to penetrate
its waterproof coating. Soon, roots emerge downward as tiny
fronds push upward. And before long, the seed blossoms into
towering stalks filled with innumerable grains of wheat.

This parable not only applies to Christ, but to every believer.
The apostle Paul stated, "I die daily" (1 Corinthians 15:31 NASB).
Death to self means life to the spirit. Jesus had to first die in order
for God to raise Him from the dead. Similarly, we must die to self
to experience resurrection life.

If we nurse our selfishness and refuse to deny self and all its
trappings, we will never reach spiritual fruitfulness and maturity
or win souls to Christ. But if we allow God to cultivate the soil of
our hearts and minds, one seed will turn into many.

*God, help me to deny myself, to die to my natural lusts and
desires, so that I can be fruitful for Your kingdom, I pray.*

*"But the one who stands firm
to the end will be saved."*
MATTHEW 24:13 NIV

In Matthew 24, Jesus describes signs of the end times. His comments come just after His triumphal entry into Jerusalem and His condemnation of the scribes and Pharisees.

While the disciples admire Jerusalem's temple and the fine things inside, Jesus is unimpressed. When He tells them that the temple will be completely destroyed, the disciples are shocked. The temple is the center of their universe—its destruction equals the end of the world.

Later, on the Mount of Olives, the disciples ask Jesus when the temple will be destroyed and what signs will indicate the end of the age. Jesus warns them of deceit and wars, famine and earthquakes. Then He says, "You will be handed over to be persecuted and put to death, and you will be hated by all nations because of me" (Matthew 24:9 NIV). Imagine how the disciples felt about that—but in Matthew 24:13, Jesus gave them hope, saying, "But the one who stands firm to the end will be saved."

During troubled times, we, too, can find hope in Matthew 24:13. When we stand firm in Christ, we will certainly receive His promise of eternal life.

*Jesus, help me cling to You, to hold on tightly to my heavenly
hope. I thank You that You have given me eternal life. Amen.*

*The cows took the straight way to Beth-shemesh
and went along the highway, lowing as they went,
and did not turn aside to the right hand or the left.*
1 SAMUEL 6:12 SKJV

In one battle, the Philistines defeated the Israelites and captured the ark of the covenant, which symbolized the very presence of God. Soon multitudes of terrified Philistines were dying from a plague. They reasoned that they must have angered God and decided to send the ark back to Israel.

The Philistines built a new cart and hitched it to two milk cows which had never been yoked or pulled a cart before. They took their calves away and set the cows on the road to Israel. Knowing that normally nursing cows would never leave their calves behind, the Philistines made this a test: if the cows acted contrary to their nature and pulled the cart all the way to Israel, then God was the one who had sent the plagues.

Sure enough, the cows took the ark straight down the road, "lowing as they went." They were distressed at leaving their unweaned calves behind, but still they obeyed God. Sometimes, as Psalm 126:6 says, we, too, go forth weeping to do God's work— but when we return, we will be rejoicing, glad that we obeyed.

---

*God, help me to obey You, even when it involves
personal sacrifice or goes against the grain of
my natural reasoning. I pray this in Jesus' name.*

*If anyone thinks they are something when they
are not, they deceive themselves.*
GALATIANS 6:3 NIV

Constantine the Great probably thought he was something special. As Roman emperor he was the most important man in the world. Much as she loved him, though, his mother, Helena, may have had a different view.

Constantine was the first Christian emperor, but he was often more "emperor" than "Christian." His mother was a powerful influence in his life, and in the 1950 novel *Helena*, Evelyn Waugh portrayed her praying for help for her son. Her request would have surprised many.

"May he, too, before the end," she said, "find kneeling space in the straw. Pray for the great, lest they perish utterly." The "straw" she mentioned was the straw around the manger, and by "perish utterly" she didn't just mean physically. Helena knew that being ruler of the known world didn't guarantee a place in heaven.

Let's not deceive ourselves, thinking that money or position makes us anything in the eyes of God. Some who are "nothing" by the standards of the world might be everything in the heart of the Lord. What matters in the end won't be the time we spent trying to be something special. It will be the times we saw ourselves as nothing without Him, the time we spent "in the straw."

*Lord, keep me from getting an exalted opinion of myself. May I
always know that my true value is found only in You. Amen.*

How lovely is your dwelling place, O LORD of Heaven's Armies.
I long, yes, I faint with longing to enter the courts of the LORD.
With my whole being, body and soul, I will shout joyfully to the
living God. Even the sparrow finds a home, and the swallow
builds her nest and raises her young at a place near your altar,
O LORD of Heaven's Armies, my King and my God! What joy for
those who can live in your house, always singing your praises.
PSALM 84:1-4 NLT

Psalm 84, by some unnamed descendants of Korah, celebrates the
physical place of worship. God's house, the courts, and the altar
where He was honored and praised brought joy and longing to
the psalm writers' hearts. They even envied the little birds that
could build their nests in the nooks and crannies of the temple.

For Christians today, Psalm 84 doesn't really point us to our
church buildings. Since the day of Pentecost recorded in Acts 2,
followers of Jesus are actually God's temple. As the apostle Paul
wrote, "Don't you realize that all of you together are the temple
of God and that the Spirit of God lives in you?" (1 Corinthians
3:16 NLT).

What could be a greater cause for joy? The God of the entire
universe has chosen to make His home in *you.* That's a perfect
reason to always sing His praises.

Lord God, You are awesome. Thank You for living in me.

*There was a disciple named Timothy, the son of a
believing Jewish woman, but his father was a Greek.*
ACTS 16:1 HCSB

Here is Timothy's biblical debut. The man who would become
the apostle Paul's "dearly loved and faithful son in the Lord"
(1 Corinthians 4:17 HCSB), recipient of two letters that became
books of our Bible, is introduced as the child of a believing Jewish
woman. "But his father," the author of Acts tells us, "was a Greek."

Luke may have meant that Timothy's father was non-Jewish,
from Greece, or both. The word *but*, however, seems to indicate
a lack of Christian faith compared to Timothy's mom. That was
no impediment, though, to Timothy's own acceptance of Christ
and his growth in grace. The believers of his hometown of Lystra
"spoke highly of him" (Acts 16:2 HCSB), as did Christians in
Iconium, a day's journey away.

Timothy's experience can (and should) be true of all of us,
whatever "but his father" realities we face: was not a Christian,
worked too much, was abusive, never came to ball games, acted
hypocritically. Even great human dads sometimes disappoint
their sons, if only by causing pain when they die.

As Ezekiel 18 plainly teaches, each of us is responsible for
choosing to obey God. And He will gladly give us that power as
our hearts incline toward Him.

*Lord, I want to be a Timothy—respected for my present
goodness no matter what challenges dot my past.*

*Lot lifted up his eyes and saw all the valley of the Jordan,
that it was well watered everywhere—this was before the LORD
destroyed Sodom and Gomorrah—like the garden of the LORD.*
GENESIS 13:10 NASB

The available pastureland no longer could support the massive
flocks and herds of both Abram and his nephew, Lot. As a solution,
Abram offered Lot first choice of the surrounding areas. Abram
would relocate in the opposite direction.

Eyeing the best land, Lot moved onto the lush and beautiful
plains of the Jordan Valley.

But the inhabitants of this fertile area were "exceedingly
wicked sinners against the LORD" (Genesis 13:13 NASB). When
their evil ways escalated to the point of no return, God destroyed
the place with fire and brimstone. Only Lot and his two daughters
escaped the destruction.

The ashen ruins of ancient cities dot the Jordan Valley. Still-
recognizable city walls and buildings have been transformed into
calcium sulfate and calcium carbonate ash, both byproducts of
intensely burning limestone and sulfur.

Lot took what looked like the best. But he ended up losing
everything except what he and his daughters carried while fleeing
their city.

Sometimes there's wisdom in holding back.

*Father, help me not to always put my needs first—nor to choose
the best for myself—but to consider others' needs also. Amen.*

Then he turned to his disciples and said privately,
"Blessed are the eyes that see what you see."
LUKE 10:23 NIV

What would you give to have been down by the Sea of Galilee when Jesus was calling His disciples? "The Twelve" were blessed, blessed men to have been in the right place at the right time. It wasn't that they were particularly special—not until Jesus chose them—but no man or woman before them or since them has been as blessed.

The disciples were lucky enough to see Jesus in the flesh, to live, eat, and walk with Him as a human being, something none of us will get to do. And they paid dearly for the privilege.

But Jesus' mission wasn't finished once the flesh was left behind. He would appear to the disciples and guide them as they spread the good news in foreign lands, and He had also taught them to look for Him in "the least of these."

We didn't get to be part of the Twelve, but that doesn't mean we don't get to see Jesus. We just have to look in different places. Until we join Him in His eternal kingdom we will see the Lord in the humble, the hungry, the lonely, the destitute—and our eyes will be blessed too.

Jesus, I thank You that one day I shall be blessed to live with You
in Your kingdom and see You in Your eternal resurrected body.

"Look at the nations and watch—and be utterly amazed.
For I am going to do something in your days that
you would not believe, even if you were told."
HABAKKUK 1:5 NIV

The prophet Habakkuk cried out to God, "Our LORD, how long must I beg for your help before you listen? How long before you save us from all this violence? Why do you make me watch such terrible injustice? Why do you allow violence, lawlessness, crime, and cruelty to spread everywhere? Laws cannot be enforced; justice is always the loser, criminals crowd out honest people and twist the laws around" (Habakkuk 1:2–4 CEV).

Do Habakkuk's words sound familiar? They were written about twenty-six hundred years ago, yet they echo the cries of Christians today: "Lord, why won't You do something about the injustice and violence in the world?"

God answered Habakkuk: "If I told you how I'm going to fix this, you wouldn't believe me." Then God allowed an evil army to cause even greater injustice and violence, but He promised to punish them in the end. This was not the answer that Habakkuk expected—or wanted.

When you become discouraged with the state of the world, meditate on Habakkuk 1:5. God is in control. He works all things together for the good of His people (Romans 8:28).

God, You don't impose Your rule now, but I thank You that when
Your kingdom comes, You will bring justice in all the earth.

*The Lord turned and looked straight at Peter. Then Peter
remembered the word the Lord had spoken to him: "Before
the rooster crows today, you will disown me three times."*

LUKE 22:61 NIV

What do you think Peter saw when he looked into the eyes of the
Lord he had just abandoned? Remember, he lived in times when
to betray your king was seen as treason, a crime that almost always
brought a sentence of death.

In His time of greatest need this particular king turned to
His man and heard him lie, heard him put his own safety before
his previously declared loyalty. The expression on His face made
Peter run away. Not to hide or go into voluntary exile, but to weep
bitterly, because, undoubtedly, he would have seen only love and
understanding on Jesus' face.

In a way it is necessary that we fail, necessary that we are
broken down. How else do we come to realize that the things of
this world will not sustain us? How else do we come to the place
where God can build us back up?

Like others who betrayed their king, Peter died. Those bitter
tears signaled the death of the man he thought he was. But the
love of Jesus allowed him to be reborn as the Peter his Lord knew
he could be.

*Lord, I thank You for Your compassion during the times
that I failed You. And thank You for restoring me afterward.*

Whatever your hand finds to do,
do it with all your might.
ECCLESIASTES 9:10 NIV

This verse is a call to excellence. Ecclesiastes 9:10 admonishes us to summon—with unwearied diligence—all of our strength and effort for whatever we have the opportunity or ability to do. Our first and best efforts should be made to turn away from and repent of our sins, to depend on God's wisdom above our own.

But this passage involves far more than spiritual determination. In a similar verse, Paul exhorted Christians to regard all work as a service to the Lord (Colossians 3:23). In essence, we are to think of God—not our earthly boss—as our employer. When we give, we give our best; when we work, we do so as if we were working for God Himself; when we pray, we pray with all of our heart.

Meanwhile, God's eyes are open to our efforts. In biblical times, Paul admonished slaves to obey their masters and respect them, just as they would Christ. In doing so, the Lord promised to reward them for their obedience (Ephesians 6:5–9).

The call to excellence is clear: "So whether you eat or drink or whatever you do, do it all for the glory of God" (1 Corinthians 10:31 NIV). Do your best—and leave the rest to God.

God, help me rise up in response to Your call to excellence. May I
be meticulous, diligent, and hardworking in all that I do. Amen.

To the weak I became weak, to win the weak.
I have become all things to all people so that
by all possible means I might save some.
1 CORINTHIANS 9:22 NIV

Jesus is for everyone. There is plenty of room in the kingdom of heaven for everyone ever born, and to say that Jesus went out of His way to reach people wherever they were is an understatement. Jesus did everything that could have been done to offer hope. He performed miracles one after another. He healed the sick. He made the blind see and the lame walk. His teaching caused enormous crowds to gather as word of who Jesus was spread from region to region. He showed compassion to people, whether or not there were others around to witness it. Certainly Jesus knew how to reach people!

It may seem difficult to imagine that anyone could relate to the Son of God. How amazing it is to consider that while He was so far above everyone else, He humbled Himself and was able to relate to all people on a level that no one else in history ever could. Today as representatives of our Lord, let us never forget to be at peace with everyone so that they can see that love of Jesus shine through us.

Jesus, inspire and strengthen me by Your Spirit as I strive to walk
as You walked and to love and help others as You did. Amen.

Show me your unfailing love in wonderful ways.
By your mighty power you rescue those who
seek refuge from their enemies.
PSALM 17:7 NLT

David certainly wasn't feeling love and adoration from humanity as he penned these words—he was on the run. His prayer cries out to God for vindication and protection. And yet, in the midst of fleeing his enemies, David calls out to his God of unfailing love. Giving in to despair and frustration must have been tempting, but David kept his focus on God in the midst of a dangerous situation.

We may never find ourselves running from murderous enemies, but all of us have moments where the cards seem to be stacked against us. Sometimes the situation is a direct result of our actions, and other times we are left to struggle with the injustice of circumstances beyond our control. Whatever the scenario, we have a choice—like David—to remember God's unfailing love.

Today, look for the ways God reveals His love for you. It may be in a sunrise that takes your breath away, the scenery you encounter on your commute to work, or an unexpected comment by a stranger. God's unfailing love is at work in your life in wonderful ways.

Father, keep me from succumbing to despair. I trust in Your
unfailing love. I keep my eyes on You, for You will help me.

*Gracious words are a honeycomb, sweet to
the soul and healing to the bones.*
PROVERBS 16:24 NIV

Remember this old nursery rhyme? "Sticks and stones may break my bones, but words will never hurt me."

It may be a classic, but it's simply not true. Harsh words spoken by another person do hurt, cutting deep into our spirits. They churn in the pit of our stomachs like undigested food.

But how sweet the taste of pleasant words. Encouraging and loving remarks give renewing energy that revitalizes the whole person.

Honey is a symbol of delight and health in the Bible. This proverb contradicts the old nursery rhyme—words coated with honey bring health throughout the body and soul. They provide healing to our wounds.

We often forget the immense power of our words in soothing another person's spirit—or in injuring with deep cuts. Passing on an overheard compliment, saying, "I love you," or writing that long-overdue note of appreciation transmits God's love through our words.

Choose your words carefully—and coat them with honey.

*Dear God, help my words to encourage and inspire others. May they
always be gracious, kind, and loving. In Jesus' name, I pray. Amen.*

*"Be strong, and let us fight bravely for our
people and the cities of our God. The LORD
will do what is good in his sight."*
1 CHRONICLES 19:13 NIV

The unsaved world often describes Christianity as a crutch. . .in
their view, faith is simply something that weak people use as a prop.

There is truth in the claim, since we as Christians *are* weak
and need all the support we can get. (This is even more true of
unbelievers, though that's a topic for another time.)

As followers of Jesus, we have come to believe in an all-
knowing, all-powerful God who has our best interests at heart.
Having reached that point of belief, we can live our lives according to His Word, then say as King David's military commander
Joab did, "The LORD will do what is good in his sight." We don't
need to stress over every potential outcome, since we know it is
in our God's supremely capable hands.

Human as we are, we'll sometimes struggle with this off-
loading of responsibility. As men, we're wired to figure things
out and fix whatever's wrong. But many things are truly beyond
our ability. Absolutely nothing is beyond God's. He'll do whatever is good in His sight, and we can rest easy.

If that's a crutch, so be it.

*Lord, life throws many challenges at me.
I'm grateful for Your knowledge and power
and the fact that You will do whatever is good.*

Take away the dross from the silver, and there
shall come out a vessel for the silversmith.
PROVERBS 25:4 SKJV

Silver is rarely found in the earth in a pure state. Generally when silver is dug out of the rocks it's mixed with the sulfide ore of lead or other less valuable minerals. It then must be put through a refining process to remove the dross, the cheaper or worthless alloys.

There are a number of ways of doing this, but one ancient method was to melt the ore containing the silver in a furnace and add lead to the mix; the lead oxidized and worked as a flux to draw out the cheap alloys. The result was pure silver, which could then go to the silversmith to be made into articles of beauty and value.

The Bible describes God's people as silver and the Lord as a "purifier of silver" who puts them through the refiner's fire to remove the impurities (Malachi 3:2–3 NIV). If we endure the fire and allow God to purify us, we will be vessels fit for the Master to use (2 Timothy 2:20–21). If we resist the process, then the refining process is in vain, and we will be "rejected silver" (Jeremiah 6:27–30 NIV).

The choice is up to us.

Lord, purify my heart, even though this means
the heat of fiery trials. Help me to be willing to
endure Your purification process. Amen.

*Jesus said, "Father, forgive them, for they do
not know what they are doing." And they
divided up his clothes by casting lots.*
LUKE 23:34 NIV

They never accepted Christ; they worshipped pagan gods; they
weren't even very nice guys. There were many reasons why the
soldiers who drove nails through Christ's hands and feet then
hoisted His cross high should never have met God personally. But
Jesus asked His Father to forgive them, even as they killed Him. If
ever anyone felt the full force of forgiveness, it would be those guys.

We will never be as forgiving as Jesus. That's a given. But we
are called on to try.

Take a few minutes to recall the people who've hurt you or
betrayed your trust. . .the ones you refuse to talk to, whose hands
you determinedly refuse to shake. Then ask how their sins stack
up against those of the men with the hammer and nails.

Forgiveness is one of the biggest tests we face in this life—and
one of the blessings we need the most. Can't bring yourself to do
it? Try imagining the faces of those arriving up above—like those
soldiers—to find your prayers have preceded them, and they're
already forgiven! Aren't those expressions worth the effort?

---

*God, forgiveness isn't easy for me, especially when it
comes to certain people. But help me to forgive, I pray.*

> *"The LORD, the God of Israel, chose me from my whole family to*
> *be king over Israel forever. He chose Judah as leader, and from*
> *the tribe of Judah he chose my family, and from my father's sons*
> *he was pleased to make me king over all Israel. Of all my sons—*
> *and the LORD has given me many—he has chosen my son Solomon*
> *to sit on the throne of the kingdom of the LORD over Israel."*
> 1 CHRONICLES 28:4-5 NIV

Here's a little Bible quiz for you: What is unusual about all of the leaders David mentions in today's scripture?

Answer: None of them were firstborn sons, breaking the custom of their time and place.

David himself was the last of the eight sons of Jesse, yet he was the one God chose to be king of Israel (1 Samuel 16). David's tribe was God's choice for prominence in Israel, yet Judah had been the fourth of Jacob's twelve sons (Genesis 29). And David's God-ordained successor, Solomon, was at least the seventh of the king's sons (1 Chronicles 3).

God is never bound by conventional wisdom—He often turns human expectation on its head, choosing "the weak things of the world to shame the strong" (1 Corinthians 1:27 NIV). If you're not the most talented, smartest, wealthiest, best-looking—or even "most spiritual"—guy you know, that's okay. If you're simply willing, God can use you for good.

Lord, here I am. Live Your life through me!

*Then went king David in, and sat before the LORD,
and he said, Who am I, O Lord GOD? and what is
my house, that thou hast brought me hitherto?*
2 SAMUEL 7:18 KJV

David has undeniable importance in the biblical record. His name
appears nearly 900 times in the King James Version, second only
to Jesus' 942. David was good-looking, musically talented, and
physically courageous, a leader of men and hero to women. He
reunited a nation fractured by King Saul's folly, guiding Israel to
military victories and a golden age under the leadership of his
handpicked successor, Solomon.

This all began when David was just an overlooked kid brother
tending his family's sheep (1 Samuel 16).

The same God who provided the physical and intellectual
gifts also chose David to be king of Israel. And this man, who
made many mistakes in his forty-year rule, was wise enough to
see God's hand in all his success. "Who am I, O Lord GOD," he
wondered, "that thou hast brought me hitherto?"

David recognized that all his abilities and achievements came
from God's generosity. He was personally undeserving. But in the
often-paradoxical way in which God works, that acknowledg-
ment is what opens the door to even greater blessing. "Humble
yourselves therefore under the mighty hand of God," the apostle
Peter wrote, "that he may exalt you in due time" (1 Peter 5:6 KJV).

---

*Lord God, I don't deserve Your blessings.
But I appreciate them, and I welcome more.*

Some of them said, "Could not he who opened the eyes
of the blind man have kept this man from dying?"
JOHN 11:37 NIV

Jesus enjoyed a special friendship with three siblings in the town of Bethany, near Jerusalem. The Lord "loved" Martha, Mary, and Lazarus (John 11:5). When Lazarus became seriously ill, the sisters quickly called on Jesus—who waited two full days before leaving His place "across the Jordan" (John 10:40 NIV). His delay and the journey meant He didn't reach Bethany until Lazarus had been four days in a tomb.

When He arrived, Jesus found "many Jews had come to Martha and Mary to comfort them in the loss of their brother" (John 11:19 NIV). The Lord spoke personally with both sisters then wept publicly upon approaching the grave (John 11:35). And some of the people who'd come to support the women began wondering: "Could not he who opened the eyes of the blind man have kept this man from dying?"

Unlike the troublemaking queries Jewish leaders often posed to Jesus, this was an honest question. And the Lord's miraculous raising of Lazarus answered it. John 11:45 says many came to believe in Jesus.

God can handle our honest questions—He's heard them from psalmists, prophets, and plenty of other people through time. You can feel free to ask Him anything. Just be ready to accept and believe in whatever answer He sends.

Lord, I have questions. Please help me to accept Your perfect answers.

When he had said this, he showed them his hands and feet.
LUKE 24:40 NIV

Promises are easy to make—and to break. If you don't manage to keep one (and you don't care about your word), you can retroactively change the conditions to make it seem that wasn't what you meant in the first place. There's always "wiggle room," right?

Think about Jesus, though. He could have summoned legions of angels to His defense, but instead He walked to a humiliating, awful death. After the resurrection, He could have slipped the bonds of human flesh and returned in all His glory. But He didn't come to terrify or overwhelm—He came to keep a promise. Jesus was the embodiment of a promise of redemption foretold by prophets of bygone times. He was the promise that God would never forsake His creation, that He loved us all despite our failings.

The torn flesh of His hands and feet spoke without words. "Do you see how much I love you?" they asked.

Let's live the promise of our faith in such a way that when we get to heaven, God will say, "I saw how much you loved Me." Remember, when it came to keeping the most important promise of all, Jesus may have writhed, despaired, and cried out. . .but He never wiggled.

Father, strengthen my resolve to keep my promises.
Help me to be a man of my word. Amen.

A voice of one calling: "In the wilderness prepare the way for the LORD; make straight in the desert a highway for our God."
ISAIAH 40:3 NIV

An ancient custom in the Near East required that a representative be sent ahead of a dignitary to prepare the road. He removed obstacles like rocks and boulders and filled in the potholes. Travel was easier when the crooked road became straight and even.

People wanted to get through the hot, parched desert quickly. Travelers were prone to injury while walking on the rocky ruts in the road. If they found the straightest route, they arrived quicker at their destination, often an oasis. Here they found cool refreshing water and much-needed rest to regain their strength to complete their journey.

Our journey in life often veers into the valleys of spiritual dryness. We crave God's living water to quench our thirst yet feel we are alone on a long, winding highway. We want to do what is right but stumble over the uneven terrain.

God prepares our way for us and, through Jesus' death and resurrection, removes the obstacles and makes straight our paths. We may still have dry times, but we journey onward, relying on God's strength.

"Teach me thy way, O LORD, and lead me in a plain path"
(Psalm 27:11 KJV). Show me where I should go, I pray. Amen.

Be anxious for nothing, but in everything,
by prayer and supplication with thanksgiving,
let your requests be made known to God.
PHILIPPIANS 4:6 SKJV

The verse above is a clear echo of Christ's teachings. In the Sermon on the Mount, Jesus told us, "Do not worry about your life," and went on to explain that we shouldn't worry about where our food and drink is coming from or where we'll get the money to buy new clothes. Jesus concluded with "Don't worry about tomorrow" (Matthew 6:25–34 SKJV).

"Be anxious for nothing" sounds like great advice, but at times most of us have the feeling that it only works for highly mature saints and is not practical for the average Christian, who is, frankly, quite *often* anxious about today's problems and worried about today's troubles, such as bills coming due and looming deadlines.

Yet the key to making it work is found in the same verse: we can "be anxious for nothing" if we are continually taking those problems to God in prayer, thanking Him for solving past problems, and trusting Him to work the current situation out. Praying about things, of course, shouldn't keep us from doing what God inspires us to do to solve the problems. But we should trust and pray instead of fretting and worrying.

Father, I thank You for solving problems in the past. I ask You
now to resolve today's problems. In Jesus' name, I ask. Amen.

*Yet it pleased the LORD to bruise Him. He has
put Him to grief. When You make His soul an
offering for sin, He shall see His offspring.*
ISAIAH 53:10 SKJV

Your salvation is as solid as the Rock of Gibraltar. Even more so, coming from the God who created the Rock of Gibraltar.

When Isaiah prophesied of God's "righteous Servant" (53:11 SKJV), he knew only a fraction of what we do today. By inspiration, the great prophet described a Messiah who would suffer terribly before enjoying the fruit of His work. We look back on the birth, life, death, and resurrection of Jesus Christ and understand exactly what Isaiah saw only in a distant vision: God the Father "bruised" His own Son on the cross. Jesus was "put. . .to grief" to pay the penalty for sin. His soul was an "offering," the perfect and final example of the old sacrificial system. But Jesus would return to life and "see His offspring," the hundreds of millions, if not billions, of people who would put their faith in Him for salvation.

All of this was by God's plan, His "determinate counsel and foreknowledge," to quote Peter's sermon at Pentecost (Acts 2:23 SKJV). Nothing could have kept Jesus from going to the cross. Nothing will stop Him from seeing your salvation through eternity. This pleases the all-knowing, all-powerful creator God we serve.

*Heavenly Father, I'm so glad for Your pleasure
in my salvation. May I please You in return.*

*Does not wisdom call out? Does not
understanding raise her voice?*
PROVERBS 8:1 NIV

Proverbs 8 personifies Wisdom, describing a woman who stands
in public places, shouting for attention, offering instruction,
promising a better life to anyone who will listen.

It's a compelling image. But in today's world, we see countless
people completely missing her. Faces buried in screens, they never
look up to notice her beckoning. Ear buds filling their heads with
noise, they never hear her cries.

"Choose my instruction instead of silver, knowledge rather
than choice gold," she calls out, "for wisdom is more precious than
rubies, and nothing you desire can compare with her" (Proverbs
8:10–11 NIV). Christian men, though prone to the distractions
of this world, know that Wisdom's call is true. We are taught by
God's Spirit within us that she is a genuine friend.

And real friends always point us to God. "The LORD brought
me forth as the first of his works, before his deeds of old. I was
formed long ages ago, at the very beginning, when the world came
to be," she says. "I was constantly at his side. I was filled with
delight day after day, rejoicing always in his presence, rejoicing in
his whole world and delighting in mankind" (Proverbs 8:22–23,
30–31 NIV).

This knowledge of God, this true delight, is ours for the taking.
Wisdom is calling. Heed her words in your own Bible.

Lord, please grant me Your wisdom today.

He went there to register with Mary, who was pledged
to be married to him and was expecting a child.
LUKE 2:5 NIV

You probably recognize Luke 2:5 from the story of Jesus' birth. It's
an unassuming verse, one we might read without much thought.

Caesar Augustus decreed that a census be taken of the entire
Roman world, and everyone went to his own town to register.
Joseph and Mary traveled from Nazareth to Bethlehem, where
she gave birth to Jesus (Luke 2:1–7). Those are the simple facts.

The Bible doesn't tell us that the journey from Nazareth to
Bethlehem was almost a hundred miles. The route would take
the couple through rugged terrain, up and down steep hills. That
must have been a concern for the two, since Mary was nearing
the end of her pregnancy. The trip would take a minimum of
five days on foot, and at night, Joseph and Mary would need safe
places to camp. That Mary completed the trip is in itself a miracle.

Mary and Joseph aren't the only ones who face life's ups and
downs. Most people—spouses, friends, coworkers—experience
"rugged terrain" in their relationships. God understands! This
entire life is a journey of faith. When we're tired and face steep
hills to climb, He'll give us strength to persevere.

Father, thank You for being with me, especially on the most difficult
parts of my life's journey. I couldn't have made it without You.

*Though an army besiege me, my heart will
not fear; though war break out against me,
even then I will be confident.*
PSALM 27:3 NIV

Although King David was a man of many faults, his love for and
confidence in the Lord was undeniable. His assurance and faith
were birthed from an intimate and ongoing relationship with God.

In Psalm 27, the psalmist-king bemoaned the actions of those
who hated and tried to kill him. Yet in the same pass of the pen,
he acknowledged God's presence and power at work in his life.
Undaunted, David pledged that no matter the circumstances, he
would trust God—because he knew it was safe and wise to do so.

Overconfidence can be a problem, but godly confidence is
essential in our walk with God. Without it, our faith falters.
Trusting God with heartfelt assurance is an expression of that
faith, and indispensable to persevering despite the odds.

The more we seek God, the more our faith grows. We can be
confident of that.

---

*Lord, keep me from being overconfident in my strength or
intelligence or social skills. Help me be ever more confident
in Your ability to do miracles in my life. Amen.*

The temptations in your life are no different from what others experience. And God is faithful. He will not allow the temptation to be more than you can stand. When you are tempted, he will show you a way out so that you can endure.

1 CORINTHIANS 10:13 NLT

There have been times that we have looked around and wondered if anyone else has struggled with a particular temptation. The Bible says that Satan is the father of lies. He wants us to believe that we have extraordinary temptations, or maybe extraordinary weakness against certain temptations. But God's Word paints a different picture.

Sometimes we may be incredibly tempted to give in to sin. We may have weaknesses, and we may feel as if we fall flat on our faces in front of God way too often. But the Word of God assures us that there is nothing extraordinary about what tempts us.

Satan works very hard on God's children. All of us! But we know from 1 Corinthians 10:13 that God has stepped in on our behalf and drawn a line that cannot be crossed. No matter how weak we may feel, with God on our side we can endure anything. It is so reassuring to know that God is there for us.

God, I praise You for Your promise that puts my many temptations in perspective. Thank You that You always provide a way out for me.

*We always thank God for all of you and continually mention
you in our prayers. We remember before our God and Father
your work produced by faith, your labor prompted by love,
and your endurance inspired by hope in our Lord Jesus Christ.*
1 THESSALONIANS 1:2–3 NIV

Imagine being on the apostle Paul's prayer list—and not only his,
but those of other early church leaders like Silas and Timothy.

Today's scripture shows Paul and Company praying specifically
for the believers of first-century Thessalonica. Perhaps they even
looked forward from that time and place, praying for yet unborn
people to be blessed by the Thessalonians' faith. Looking backward from the early 1900s, Scottish evangelist Oswald Chambers
thought his ministry might be "the answer to someone's prayer,
prayed perhaps centuries ago."

One great figure of Christian history *definitely* prayed for you—
and those prayers were undoubtedly heard by God the Father.
In John 17, Jesus Himself looked ahead to your life, praying for
your spiritual well-being as a beneficiary of His disciples' work:
". . .that all of them may be one, Father, just as you are in me and
I am in you. May they also be in us so that the world may believe
that you have sent me" (verse 21 NIV).

Be encouraged: you've been prayed over by the best. And
according to Romans 8:34, He's still interceding today.

Lord Jesus, I appreciate Your prayers—I need them!

*"We have come to believe and to know that
you are the Holy One of God."*
JOHN 6:69 NIV

Jesus had just been deserted by many followers who found His teachings difficult. And though He already knew their answer, He asked the disciples where *they* stood. Simon Peter gave this simple but profound statement of faith.

The disciples were rough, realistic, working men, guys like Peter the fisherman and Matthew the tax collector, who would otherwise have had little in common. They had earned a hard living in a hard land then walked away from those jobs to follow Jesus.

In doing so, they set themselves against their society's rulers— and made themselves enemies of the greatest military empire the world had yet known. They left their homes and families, and in many cases, walked willingly down a road that would lead to execution.

These were ordinary men, like those you might find on a construction site, in an office building, or on a farm. What would cause them to walk away from all that they knew? What would make any twelve people you know do that? Only something very convincing.

Belief will take you only so far. But *knowing* will take you all the way. The disciples *knew*—and through this verse we know they knew. That certainty is something to hold on to in moments of doubt.

*Jesus, please help me to pin all my hopes on You. Help me
trust You till the end, for You are worthy of my trust. Amen.*

🌲 DAY 226

*"Yet a time is coming and has now come when the true
worshipers will worship the Father in the Spirit and in truth,
for they are the kind of worshipers the Father seeks."*
JOHN 4:23 NIV

Our Christian culture has created catchphrases with the word
worship. "Worship form," "worship function," and "worship songs"
have permeated our vocabulary. We seem always to be looking for
the next best thing in our quest to worship God.

Straight out of His encounter with the woman at the well,
Jesus focused the discussion on the kind of worshipper God
desires. Isn't that an interesting idea: God has a specific concept of what true worship should look like, and He has already
defined it. There is a certain kind of worshipper who captures
God's heart.

True worshippers worship in spirit and in truth. We know
that Jesus *is* truth (John 14:6), and we know that the Holy Spirit
lives in us when we accept Christ as the Truth (Ephesians 1:13).
Worship fulfills God's design as it acknowledges the "worth-ship"
of God, as revealed by Jesus and prompted by the Holy Spirit. This
worship captures His attention. No doubt it makes Him smile.

Does your own worship reflect spirit and truth? How have
you experienced God's smiling approval during your times
of worship?

*Dear Lord, help me to push beyond my church's rituals and outward
forms of worship and truly worship You in the Spirit. Amen.*

*And ye now therefore have sorrow: but I will
see you again, and your heart shall rejoice,
and your joy no man taketh from you.*
JOHN 16:22 KJV

Knowing that Jesus is your Savior, do you ever get sad? With
the promise of heaven ahead of you, do you ever get down and
depressed?

Of course you do—and nonbelievers will use that as a weapon
against you. "If you really believed you were saved," they say, "you
would be singing and dancing all the time!" Churchgoers, while
avoiding addressing their own failings in the matter, will tell you
that joy comes—if only you believe harder.

One of the devil's most effective weapons is to make you believe
your lack of joy is due to your own shortcomings.

But we are sad because we are broken. The fall separated us
from Love, and ever since then, in many and various ways, that
sadness has been seeping through.

Here Jesus makes the beautiful promise, "I will see you again,
and your heart shall rejoice." Our hearts will rejoice because Jesus
is the Physician who will heal our wound. He is the Counselor
who will restore us to Love.

Until then, if you feel a bit down, don't beat yourself up.
Remember, there's a good reason for it—and it's all going to get
much better soon.

*Lord, I often feel sad or down. I pray that You fill me with
Your supernatural joy. I need this gift of Your Spirit. Amen.*

*After the king burned the scroll containing the words
that Baruch had written at Jeremiah's dictation, the word
of the LORD came to Jeremiah: "Take another scroll and
write on it all the words that were on the first scroll."*
JEREMIAH 36:27–28 NIV

No wonder the southern Jewish kingdom of Judah was in trouble.
Its king was burning God's Word.

Judah's northern neighbor, Israel, had already fallen to Assyria.
Now Jeremiah warned Judah of a looming Babylonian threat.
"Perhaps when the people of Judah hear about every disaster I
plan to inflict on them," God told His prophet, "they will each
turn from their wicked ways" (Jeremiah 36:3 NIV).

King Jehoiakim, however, resented Jeremiah's message. "Why
did you write on it," he asked, "that the king of Babylon would
certainly come and destroy this land?" (Jeremiah 36:29 NIV).
As the prophet's scroll was read, the king cut off strips that he
tossed into the fire.

Jehoiakim got rid of Jeremiah's scroll, but he could never
destroy God's Word. Nor could any other king or nation. Why?
Because the Word of God is "alive and active" (Hebrews 4:12 NIV).
Though people are like withering grass, God's Word "endures
forever" (Isaiah 40:8 NIV). In the words of an old hymn, "The
Bible stands though the hills may tumble / It will firmly stand
when the earth shall crumble; / I will plant my feet on its firm
foundation, / For the Bible stands."

Lord, thank You for Your enduring Word.

*"For David, after he had served God's purpose in his own
generation, fell asleep, and was buried among his fathers."*
ACTS 13:36 NASB

The youngest of eight sons, David began life as the annoying baby
brother to his siblings and the underrated child to his dad.

When the prophet Samuel invited Jesse and his sons to a
special sacrifice, Jesse didn't think to include David until Samuel
asked if there were other sons.

While delivering food to his brothers on the battlefield, David
became incensed when he heard Goliath's boasting. His oldest
brother chided him, telling David to get back to his few sheep,
a real put-down.

But God had a divine purpose for this boy's life.

God designed him with a natural talent for music and poetry,
which David used to write many of the psalms. His God-given
leadership abilities gave him success on the battlefield and later
as king of Israel.

David desired to obey God but failed miserably at times. Yet
God looked deep within David's soul and saw "a man after My
heart, who will do all My will" (Acts 13:22 NASB). Despite the ups
and downs, David accomplished God's plan for his life.

God has a tailor-made purpose for each of us, too, and He's
designed us with the talents and abilities needed to complete it.
Isn't that exciting?

*God, help me to be a "man after Your heart" also.
Help me to complete Your purpose for my life. Amen.*

Then the disciple whom Jesus loved said to Peter,
"It is the Lord!" As soon as Simon Peter heard him say,
"It is the Lord," he wrapped his outer garment around
him (for he had taken it off) and jumped into the water.
JOHN 21:7 NIV

"As soon as Simon Peter heard"—in other words he hadn't actually recognized Jesus at that point. But he didn't need the evidence of his eyes. He only needed the merest possibility.

Peter had been stripped down for work, but he grabbed his coat or robe before launching himself into the water. Why? It wasn't going to help him swim faster. In fact, a heavy woolen garment was more likely to drag him down. So why did he take it with him? Because, there and then, Simon Peter had no notion of ever returning to the boat. He was all about getting to his Lord.

After the resurrection the disciples never knew when or where they might meet Jesus—and that's pretty much the situation today. The question of how we respond is still an important one. Will we be hesitant, asking for all kinds of assurances and looking around to see who is watching? Or will we follow Simon Peter's example, casting our so-called dignity to the wind, grabbing our coats, and diving in headfirst?

Lord, show me where You're walking today. Give me
the faith to believe I'll find You and the courage
to follow You. In Jesus' name. Amen.

The LORD said to him, "Who gave human beings their mouths? Who makes them deaf or mute? Who gives them sight or makes them blind? Is it not I, the LORD?"
EXODUS 4:11 NIV

In Exodus, God asked Moses to complete some pretty heavy-duty jobs. Throughout chapter 4, we repeatedly hear Moses tell God why God's plan won't work, finally stating, "Uh, Lord, You've picked the wrong guy for the job. . .you see, I'm not eloquent enough" (see Exodus 4:10).

Did Moses really think this was news to God? God's response in Exodus 4:11 is fairly chastising.

Likewise, when God asks us to do something, we have a similar response. We doubt, ignore, get angry, or even laugh (like Sarah in Genesis 18:10–14). In our attempts to tell God why He's wrong, God's response would surely be something like "I know you, better than you know you, so get on with it. . . . Oh, and don't forget. This isn't a solo mission" (see Exodus 3:12).

Ironically, what we label impossible and imperfect is often God's perfect way to execute His plans. It's up to us to make ourselves available, remembering we're not alone.

Lord God, forgive me for all the times I've tried explaining to You why Your plan won't work. Help me simply trust You. Amen.

What is more, I consider everything a loss because of the surpassing worth of knowing Christ Jesus my Lord, for whose sake I have lost all things. I consider them garbage, that I may gain Christ and be found in him, not having a righteousness of my own. . .but that which is through faith in Christ.
PHILIPPIANS 3:8-9 NIV

Paul had room to boast. His Jewish heritage was unequaled. He was a Pharisee and son of a Pharisee, raised under Gamaliel, the renowned teacher of the law (Acts 22:2–5). He was a zealous and devout "Hebrew of Hebrews" (Philippians 3:5 NIV), yet he surrendered his very birthright for the sake of Christ's kingdom.

This passage reveals the apostle's heart and the heartbeat of Christianity. Namely, when we surrender what we once treasured, admired, and highly esteemed for the sake of the kingdom, we gain far more. In verse 7 (NIV), Paul explained, "But whatever were gains to me I now consider loss for the sake of Christ."

When the things of this world lose their luster and no longer compete for the throne of our hearts, we will attain all the privileges and blessings of a child of the King. But to know Christ's resurrection, we must first die to self. To gain the righteousness through faith in Christ Jesus, we must first consider our own righteousness worthless.

Father, I forsake any right to boast in my own strength and credentials. I'm only a sinner saved by grace. Thank You for saving me.

> *Don't let anyone look down on you because you are*
> *young, but set an example for the believers in speech,*
> *in conduct, in love, in faith and in purity.*
> 1 TIMOTHY 4:12 NIV

In almost every other aspect of life, age has its privileges. If we have any intelligence at all we can't help but accumulate wisdom as we pass through this world. An older person will not necessarily be better educated than a young person but certainly ought to be wiser.

It doesn't work that way with faith. How did Jesus ask us to come to Him? Like little children! A long life can provide a longer walk with God, but we could live to be 150 and still not understand Him the way a child instinctively does. Much of the wisdom we gain comes through experiences we try to shed in an effort to get back to a purer, more innocent state. The poet Thomas Hood wrote, "I'm farther off from heaven than when I was a boy."

Young believers can be a reminder to the older generation of the joy and enthusiasm a pure faith can generate. And they have another important task; after all, "peer pressure" doesn't always have to be negative. The young are best positioned to bring other young folk to God, and that is work fully deserving of respect.

Dear Lord, grant that I may have the wisdom and experience
of the aged, but the faith and innocence of a child. Amen.

When Jesus heard this, he was amazed at him, and
turning to the crowd following him, he said, "I tell you,
I have not found such great faith even in Israel."
LUKE 7:9 NIV

It's hard imagining Jesus being amazed. Yet in the Gospel of Luke that's exactly what happened.

A centurion had sent for Jesus to come to his house and heal his dying servant. Before Jesus could arrive, however, the centurion sent another message. He told Jesus he wasn't worthy to have Jesus come to his home and that he believed Jesus had the power to heal his servant from where He was. Jesus was moved by the centurion's faith. He was moved so much, in fact, that He spoke of it to the crowd gathered around Him.

The centurion wasn't the only one whose faith Jesus commended. There was the Canaanite woman who begged Jesus to heal her daughter (Matthew 15:22–28); the four men who tore through the roof of a house in order to get their paralyzed friend inside to see Jesus (Mark 2:1–5); a woman who'd been bleeding for twelve years, who believed that by touching Jesus' cloak she'd be healed (Matthew 9:20–22).

Each one approached Jesus in a different manner, but all came to Him with a faith that He applauded.

Could Jesus praise our faith?

God, increase my faith, I pray. I choose to believe You, even though I'm inclined to doubt. So help my faith grow. In Jesus' name, I ask. Amen.

When I am afraid, I put my trust in you. In God, whose word I praise—in God I trust and am not afraid.
PSALM 56:3–4 NIV

King David was forced to fight many wars. First, King Saul's armies hunted him. Then he was arrested by the Philistines. After David became king, his land was attacked, first by the Philistines, then by the Ammonites, then by the Arameans. In his later years, after David had conquered all his outside enemies, his land was troubled by civil war—think of Absalom and Sheba's rebellions—and other conspirators were eager to end his life (Psalm 56:5–6).

David had many powerful enemies, and he was often tempted to despair. David didn't say that he was never afraid, because that wasn't true. There were times, when war loomed and his armies were vastly outnumbered, when he *was* afraid. But David's key to success was this: "When I am afraid, I put my trust in you." When he trusted that God would be with him, David's courage returned and he could declare: "I will not be afraid."

Most of us today don't have enemies out to kill us, but the principle that helped David survive decades of opposition three thousand years ago works just as well for us today.

Father in heaven, lead me to put my trust in You when danger surrounds me and fear begins to fill me. I know You won't fail me. Amen.

When they saw the courage of Peter and John and realized
that they were unschooled, ordinary men, they were astonished
and they took note that these men had been with Jesus.
ACTS 4:13 NIV

The priests and the Sadducees were among the most educated
men around and probably thought themselves the wisest. Yet here
were two "unschooled, ordinary men" leaving them lost for words.
Faced with the disciples' simple truth, the priests abandoned their
supposed wisdom and resorted to threats.

How did Peter and John come to have such an impact? Well,
codes have their cipher, treasure maps have their X, and every
lock has a key—somewhere. God created the universe and all the
wisdom these learned men hoped to attain. They studied ancient
scrolls to gain knowledge, but Peter and John had stood in the
presence of God's living key. Jesus opened their minds to what
was real in the world.

We don't get to stand in His physical presence, but we do get to
invite Him into our lives, and with Him comes the key to understanding. So, when you are faced with a worldly dilemma, step
back from conventional wisdom, forget about what others think
you ought to do. Consult with the Lord. The world won't always
like it, but they will take note that you, too, have been with Jesus.

Lord, You promised, "Draw near to God and He will draw near
to you" (James 4:8 SKJV). So draw near to me, I pray.

"He must become greater; I must become less."
JOHN 3:30 NIV

John the Baptist knew exactly who he was and what role he was called to play.

When John's disciples complained that a new preacher, Jesus, was drawing followers from their group, John set his ego aside and said, "Jesus must become greater; I must become less."

John understood his call as the forerunner. His job was to prepare the way for the Messiah. He played second fiddle to the first chair.

Every orchestra needs a second fiddle (or trumpet, or clarinet) for the music to be complete. The lead in a play needs a supporting actor for the story to come across correctly. John prepared the path for Jesus then stepped out of the limelight.

Maybe we're feeling our call to serve Christ isn't good enough. Not everyone can teach or preach—but perhaps we can make coffee on Sunday or hand out bulletins before the service. Physical limitations may prevent us even from getting to church, but we can pray daily for others. Each role serves a purpose in sharing God's story.

John models the right attitude for serving God: we set our own agendas and egos aside. God's light shines through us more brilliantly when we become less.

Father, thank You that You accept what little I am able to do for You. Help me not to despise my own efforts, I pray. Amen.

But the Israelites said, "We have sinned. Deal with us as You see fit; only deliver us today!" So they got rid of the foreign gods among them and worshiped the LORD, and He became weary of Israel's misery.
JUDGES 10:15-16 HCSB

Creating and maintaining the universe is no challenge to our infinite, almighty God. A familiar passage from Isaiah emphasizes the Lord's strength and stamina: "Do you not know? Have you not heard? Yahweh is the everlasting God, the Creator of the whole earth. He never grows faint or weary" (Isaiah 40:28 HCSB).

So why does the book of Judges say God *can* be wearied?

Reread today's scripture and watch carefully for what wearies the Lord: it's the misery of His people. In the time of the judges, that misery was self-inflicted, due entirely to Israel's idolatry and rebellion. But as soon as the people admitted their guilt and changed their ways, God admitted His pain and changed His people's fortunes.

If you are in Christ, God the Father loves you with an everlasting love (Jeremiah 31:3). Even when you sin, He longs for you to return to His side. And as soon as you make the first move, He rushes to welcome you back. God is never weary to forgive and restore.

Heavenly Father, it's amazing to realize that my misery wearies You. May I always avoid sin so that neither of us needs to suffer.

The day is Yours; the night also is Yours.
You have prepared the light and the sun.
PSALM 74:16 SKJV

Most of us, at some point in childhood, are afraid of the dark. Part of "growing up" is shedding that particular fear.

But even men can dread the nighttime—not for presumed monsters under the bed but for the frightening things that inhabit our own minds. Minus the distractions of the day's activity, we might worry over career and finances, our marriage or kids, the state of the world, or any of a million other topics that disrupt sleep. What's a guy to do?

Psalm 74 offers both sympathy and hope. Clearly referencing the Babylonian destruction of Jerusalem, the psalm writer spends the first eleven verses bemoaning God's anger and seeming rejection of His people. Bad people were oppressing God's people, and the Lord was allowing it to happen.

But then the psalm writer changed his mindset entirely. "God is my King of old, working salvation in the midst of the earth," he wrote (verse 12 SKJV). The Lord possessed enough power to divide seas, dry up rivers, and break open fountains, all to help His people. There would be times of darkness, as today's scripture indicates. . .but God is always preparing light and sun to follow.

Every night gives way to day. This is God's plan, in both the natural and spiritual realm.

Father, allay my fears and remind me that Your day is coming.

I have fought the good fight, I have
finished the race, I have kept the faith.
2 TIMOTHY 4:7 NIV

It's an ideal we would all aim for—but finishing the race isn't always easy. In 1992, Derek Redmond was determined to win the Olympic 400-meter dash. But less than halfway around the track, his hamstring tore, and Redmond collapsed in agony. Thousands of spectators—and a worldwide television audience—watched the other runners leave Redmond in their dust. But he picked himself up and hobbled after them.

The runner's tears and suffering were too much for his father, who ran out of the stands onto the track to help his son complete the journey.

We'll never know if Derek Redmond could have finished that Olympic race on his own. In his moment of direst need he didn't have to depend on his own strength.

It's the same in the race for heaven. We might set out with our eyes on the prize, convinced our belief is unshakable. But there are attacks, traps, and diversions along the way. Our faith will take a beating—and might be in tatters as we approach the last lap. We might have to hobble, hop, and crawl just to glimpse the prize in the distance. Let's face it—alone, we might fail.

Leaning on our Father is the guarantee of crossing the finish line.

Father, thank You that I don't have to finish this race in
my own power. You will be there with me. Amen.

I will utterly consume all things from off the land, saith the LORD. I will consume man and beast; I will consume the fowls of the heaven, and the fishes of the sea.
ZEPHANIAH 1:2–3 KJV

"Doom and gloom" is an apt phrase for the prophet Zephaniah's message. After briefly introducing himself as the son of Cushi, prophesying during the reign of Judah's godly king Josiah (verse 1), Zephaniah launches into a message of looming destruction at the hand of God.

Though Josiah, who became king at age eight, led a revival in Judah, there was still trouble on the horizon. Within a half century, invaders from Babylon would wreck Jerusalem and essentially wipe Judah off the world map.

Zephaniah's message—which may have hinted at that Babylonian invasion, the end of time, or both—is intriguing for its mirror-image deconstruction of creation. The prophet's order of God's "consuming"—man, animals, birds, then fish—is exactly the opposite of His creation of life in Genesis 1.

God can do whatever He pleases—whether creating an orderly universe out of nothing or consuming what He's made in a similarly logical order. But what God really pleases is for "everyone to come to repentance" (2 Peter 3:9 NIV).

Lord, You created this world and will judge it. Then You'll create a new heaven and earth. You do all things well. Amen.

I think of God, and I moan, overwhelmed with longing for his
help. You don't let me sleep. I am too distressed even to pray!
PSALM 77:3–4 NLT

Have you ever been so upset, depressed, angry, or overwhelmed
that you couldn't even pray? If so, you're in good company.

Even Bible writers struggled like that, as Psalm 77 proves.
Asaph, a Levite assigned by King David to lead music when the
ark of the covenant was moved to Jerusalem (1 Chronicles 15),
came to prominence in a time of joy. How different his outlook
when he penned today's psalm.

"I cry out to God; yes, I shout," Asaph began. "Oh, that God
would listen to me! When I was in deep trouble, I searched for
the Lord. All night long I prayed, with hands lifted toward
heaven, but my soul was not comforted" (Psalm 77:1–2 NLT).
And then Asaph wrote the words of today's scripture, record-
ing his moaning, longing, and sleeplessness. He found it impossible even to pray.

Happily for Asaph—and instructively for us—he discovered a
way out of his morass. By verse 11 (NLT), this talented musician
had decided to "recall all you have done, O Lord; I remember
your wonderful deeds of long ago." And that proved to be enough.
Today, let's follow Asaph's example, praying as he did:

"You are the God of great wonders! You demonstrate your
awesome power among the nations" (Psalm 77:14 NLT).

"We cannot help speaking about what we have seen and heard."
ACTS 4:20 NIV

Anyone who doubts the resurrection happened or the power of the Holy Spirit ought to give some thought to this verse from Acts.

One of the men speaking here is Simon Peter. He is addressing the Sanhedrin in the same temple where, a short time before, he cowered like a whipped dog, protesting he had no idea who this Jesus fellow was. Now he stands there as a miracle worker, having accused the priests of nothing less than the murder of his Lord. He isn't scared, and he isn't backing down. It's the Sanhedrin's turn to be afraid.

Peter's personal courage doesn't come into it, though. He literally can't help but speak because he has seen and heard things that put the powers and policies of the worldly rulers firmly in their place. And that place is an insignificant one.

The Peter who denied Christ would never have spoken like this if he didn't know he had a mighty ally behind, around, and inside him.

If you face it alone, this world can be overwhelming. You might cower, like Peter. But if you believe what he saw and if you claim the Holy Spirit as your constant companion, you can stand up to anyone—in Jesus' name.

Lord, please give me boldness like You gave to Peter. May I be unafraid of people's opinions. In Jesus' name. Amen.

"Be strong and courageous. Do not be afraid or terrified because of them, for the LORD your God goes with you; he will never leave you nor forsake you."
DEUTERONOMY 31:6 NIV

We find Deuteronomy 31:6 in a speech that Moses delivered to the Israelites just before they entered the promised land. Moses told them that he would not be traveling with them into Canaan. God had chosen to replace Moses with a new leader, Joshua. The Lord Himself would go on ahead with Joshua to take possession of the land (Deuteronomy 31:1–7).

The Israelites worried that fighting might occur with the Canaanites. In Deuteronomy 31:6, Moses encourages them to be strong and trust that the Lord will be with and protect them. Many times, Moses reminded the Israelites that they needed to trust in God. These words are echoed in the New Testament in Hebrews 13:5 (NIV): "God has said, 'Never will I leave you; never will I forsake you.' "

It is interesting to note that conflict still exists in what was once the promised land. As we face troubled times in the world, we can find comfort in Deuteronomy 31:6.

God, I thank You that You are always with me, even in the midst of danger and conflict. Help me to never stop trusting in You. In Jesus' name, I pray. Amen.

Then Ananias went to the house and entered it. Placing his hands on Saul, he said, "Brother Saul, the Lord—Jesus, who appeared to you on the road as you were coming here—has sent me so that you may see again and be filled with the Holy Spirit."
ACTS 9:17 NIV

Ananias was a disciple of the Lord. This kind and faithful man had heard of Saul of Tarsus and feared to meet him.

Saul (later known as Paul) murdered Christians—that is, until Jesus met him on the road to Damascus. The event left Paul blinded and traumatized. He hid in the dark of someone's spare room and didn't eat or drink for three days.

To Ananias, Saul must have seemed a wild and genuinely dangerous man, very different from himself. But because Jesus was now in this man's heart the first word Ananias spoke was "Brother." Paul must have wept.

It's a problem we still have. How can people so different from us ever be like us? There are different rituals, languages, and interpretations. And then there are those outside the church but who still believe. It's confusing, and easier just to keep a safe distance sometimes. No doubt Ananias felt the same. But if Jesus is there in the hearts of these strangers, He expects us to call them brother or sister—and mean it.

Dear Lord, help me to love all those who love You.
Give me a deep and enduring love for them. Amen.

And so the Lord says, "These people say they are mine. They honor me with their lips, but their hearts are far from me. And their worship of me is nothing but man-made rules learned by rote."
ISAIAH 29:13 NLT

Think of one of the Christian creeds or prayers that you have committed to memory. Perhaps it's the Lord's Prayer; maybe you learned the Apostles' Creed in a catechism class. Now, consider the last time you were invited to recite it. Did you savor each word as it was spoken, reflecting anew on its meaning, or was the experience more of a rote recitation?

From God's perspective, the actions of our hearts speak louder than our words. And if our worship consists of mindlessly repeating words and going with the flow, we are missing out on connecting with a God who fiercely loves us and desires to be in an unscripted relationship with us.

This verse carries a sobering reminder that God looks beyond the words of our mouths and considers the heart that utters them. Creeds and prayers are familiar ways to connect with God and serve as wonderful reminders of His steadfast character. The next time an opportunity arises to recite from memory, consider how to bring the well-known words to life in a new and fresh understanding—spoken from the heart.

I love You, Father. I worship You. May I truly mean the words I say, not merely repeat memorized text.

When you arise, O Lord, you will laugh at their silly ideas
as a person laughs at dreams in the morning.
PSALM 73:20 NLT

"Cheaters never win." Yeah, right.

These days, playing by the rules seems like a quaint, old-fashioned notion. Watch the news—or observe neighbors and coworkers—and you may conclude that living honorably just holds you back.

But that's nothing new. The author of Psalm 73 grappled with the same frustration centuries before Jesus' birth. "I envied the proud when I saw them prosper despite their wickedness," the psalmist complained. "They seem to live such painless lives; their bodies are so healthy and strong. They don't have troubles like other people; they're not plagued with problems like everyone else. They wear pride like a jeweled necklace and clothe themselves with cruelty" (verses 3–6 NLT).

Of course, that's not the whole story. The psalm writer had an epiphany in the temple when he realized the destiny of the proud oppressors (verse 17). Though they could hurt their fellow man seemingly with impunity, they would not escape God's justice (verse 19). In fact, the Lord would chuckle at their ridiculous bluster, turned so quickly into terror.

As Christians, we are called to love and pray for our enemies, not gloat over their demise. But those who steadfastly refuse God's mercy will face justice. We can be sure that God will make proper retribution and vindicate His own.

Lord, help me to trust in Your perfect justice.

*The LORD is slow to anger but great in power; the LORD will
not leave the guilty unpunished. His way is in the whirlwind
and the storm, and clouds are the dust of his feet.*
NAHUM 1:3 NIV

Clouds always point to God's power. He created the clouds. God
resides within and beyond the heavens. As this verse tells us, the
Lord is so huge, the clouds are merely the dust of His feet.

By watching clouds, we see hints of God's presence. We see
God as Creator when we imagine the different shapes of clouds
to resemble animals, funny faces, and flocks of sheep.

Storm clouds remind us that God is also powerful. During
the raging winds, crashing thunder, and startling lightning, our
fear grows. The devastating violence of a storm can obliterate
everything in its path. Is this the same God we remember on
fair-weather days?

But God is very patient. He waits in His unhurried way for
us to acknowledge Him as our King and Savior. He welcomes
us back into His arms. He invites us to look up at the clouds in
His heaven and understand His many sides—powerful, creative,
and loving.

*Father in heaven, I praise You because of Your wonder,
Your majesty, and Your imagination that are daily on
display in the clouds. I marvel at Your creation. Amen.*

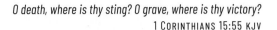

O death, where is thy sting? O grave, where is thy victory?
1 CORINTHIANS 15:55 KJV

This verse personifies both death and the grave. In ancient paintings, death is sometimes depicted as a crowned skeleton with a dart in his hand. Like an ox goad, the dart's sharp point continually irritates and taunts.

The apostle Paul explains that the sting of death is sin, and sin is the parent of death. Yet through the death and resurrection of Christ, we have atonement for our sins. So Christians no longer need to fear death and the grave. Or as Paul said, "But thanks be to God, which giveth us the victory through our Lord Jesus Christ" (verse 57 KJV).

Earlier in this passage, Paul declared that when Jesus returns, all believers—alive and dead—will receive new, glorified bodies that are imperishable and immortal (verses 50–54).

So the question in 1 Corinthians 15:55 is rhetorical. Because of Christ, the deadly darts of sin no longer hold sway over us. Sin has lost its power, death has no sting, and our shackles are loosed. We have nothing to fear and everything to gain.

Jesus, thank You that Your sacrifice on the cross paid the price for my sins. I thank You that death need hold no fear for me, for angels will then usher me into Your loving presence. Amen!

I do not understand what I do. For what I
want to do I do not do, but what I hate I do.
ROMANS 7:15 NIV

Who is this weak-willed, indecisive wimp? Has he no faith, no moral fiber?

Actually, he was the worldwide leader of the early church, and this verse comes from his letter to Christians in Rome. So what kind of impression was he giving them?

He was laying out the harsh reality that faith does not make us perfect. Paul lived, suffered, and died for his adoration of the Lord, but in day-to-day life he frequently and consistently failed to live up to his own ideal. That's because his ideal life was Christ's, and no one could live up to that example.

Still he tried, because, while his body belonged to sin, his soul belonged to the Lord—and his mind was the general directing the battle between the two.

It can be disheartening to fail. Some people fall away from faith because of it. But here is the remedy to that situation. In your struggle you are no better or worse than Saint Paul. Thankfully, your ultimate success won't be measured by the number of times you fall; it will depend entirely on the number of times you reach for Jesus to help you back up.

Lord, I acknowledge my sin. I come to You, knowing that in You is
forgiveness and the courage to keep on going. I love You, Lord.

The heavens declare the glory of God;
the skies proclaim the work of his hands.
PSALM 19:1 NIV

The cosmos, the universe, outer space. . .called by any name it's a place of awe and enchantment, filled with stars, comets, quasars, and our home planet, Earth.

Though the first verse of the Bible clearly states that God created our world, the belief in an infinite, eternal universe held sway with scientists for generations.

But in 1915, Einstein's general theory of relativity challenged that assumption. Over the ensuing decades, scientific observations indicated that our universe did indeed have a beginning, just as the Bible says.

But science goes much deeper than the birth of the universe. It shows an Earth fine-tuned for intelligent life, an amazingly rare possibility even in the vastness of space. The evidence points to a planet designed by a Creator.

With the heavens displaying the Creator's glory, it shouldn't surprise us that scientists also discovered that the conditions that make life possible on Earth provide a perfect setting to study our universe as well.

Stand outside on a clear night, gazing into the sky. Drink in the glory and majesty of creation. Only a mighty and powerful God could fashion all the wonders we see.

God, how powerful You are, and how wonderful is this vast,
amazing universe You created. And thank You for creating Earth!

How long, Yahweh? Will You be angry forever? Will Your jealousy keep burning like fire? Pour out Your wrath on the nations that don't acknowledge You, on the kingdoms that don't call on Your name.
PSALM 79:5–6 HCSB

We could complain that complaining is so easy, but that doesn't seem right. Scripture clearly denounces our human tendency to murmur and grumble: "Jesus answered them, 'Stop complaining among yourselves'" (John 6:43 HCSB); "Nor should we complain" (1 Corinthians 10:10 HCSB); "Be hospitable to one another without complaining" (1 Peter 4:9 HCSB).

And yet. . .

Today's passage is one of many in the Psalms that contains a complaint (or series of complaints) addressed directly to God. Psalm 142:2 (HCSB) even says, "I pour out my complaint before Him." How can we resolve this tension?

Clearly, our world and the human beings in it are broken. Bad things have happened, are happening, and will continue to happen. We will struggle with the unfairness of life, whether it personally affects us or other people. And sometimes, like the writers of the Psalms, we'll find ourselves venting even to God. He doesn't like humanity's sinful, hurtful ways any more than we do.

Just don't stop at the complaint. Like the writer of Psalm 79, ask God to fix the problem. Then praise Him in advance for His ultimate response.

"We. . .will thank You forever; we will declare Your praise to generation after generation" (Psalm 79:13 HCSB).

> *For I am convinced that neither death nor life,
> neither angels nor demons, neither the present nor the
> future, nor any powers, neither height nor depth,
> nor anything else in all creation, will be able to separate
> us from the love of God that is in Christ Jesus our Lord.*
> ROMANS 8:38-39 NIV

Isn't that an encouraging thought?

Of course, the flip side is that lots of things will *try* to separate us from God—way more things than you can put down to mere coincidence. The mockery of loved ones, ill health, loneliness, financial stress, depression, just the sheer scale of an unbelieving world seemingly antagonistic to faith. . .any of these things, or some others specifically targeted to your situation, will try to separate you from the love of God.

Why? Because God's love is a great prize. Otherwise no one on this earth (or below it) would care. The struggles you experience for your faith are a measure of the reality and importance of what you are going to achieve in the end. It's a real battle, but Paul is telling you that you are on the stronger side. If you'll only hold on to Jesus, He'll wrap His arms—and His love—around you.

Earthquakes, meteor strikes, and superheroes couldn't break that embrace. You'll be home to stay.

---

*God, I thank You that absolutely nothing
can separate me from Your vast love for me.
Thank You that You love me so much! Amen.*

I have hidden your word in my heart,
that I might not sin against you.
PSALM 119:11 NLT

When Jesus was tempted by Satan, He did not yield, because He remembered the Word of God.

It must have been difficult. The Bible says that Jesus had been in the wilderness for a long time. He hadn't eaten for forty days and nights and, being fully human, must have been in a weakened state. It is difficult for anyone to function well after experiencing that kind of hunger.

But Jesus knew the Word of God very well. Each time He was tempted, He was able to ward off trouble by using God's Word as a weapon.

This same weapon is available to us. By reading and meditating on God's Word, we become much stronger in our faith. It becomes easier to battle temptation. The Bible says that we will never be tempted beyond that which we are able to handle (1 Corinthians 10:13). And Psalm 119:11 indicates we can find victory by filling our hearts and minds with God's Word.

Lord, thank You for Your powerful Word. Help me to constantly
read it and meditate on it so that I may have strength to
resist temptation also. In Jesus' name, I pray. Amen.

He broke up the bronze serpent that Moses had made, because
the people of Israel had been offering sacrifices to it.
2 KINGS 18:4 NLT

One day the Israelites complained bitterly against Moses and God,
so God sent poisonous snakes that bit many of them. When the
people repented, God told Moses to hammer out a bronze snake
and hold it up on a pole, and "anyone who was bitten by a snake
could look at the bronze snake and be healed" (Numbers 21:9 NLT).

You can understand why the Israelites would hang on to
such a symbol of God's power for hundreds of years. It was like
a national heritage. You could even understand why they might
think it still had healing powers many years later. But somewhere
during the centuries the Israelites began to worship the bronze
snake and burn incense to it.

When King Hezekiah was destroying idols in Judah, he sarcas-
tically named the snake *Nehushtan*. That sounds like the Hebrew
words for "bronze" and "serpent" but means "unclean thing."
Then he smashed it into pieces.

God gives us many helpful things, good things, but if we begin
to worship those things instead of God Himself—or give them
too much of our attention—then they become idols and must be
destroyed. Let's never push Him to that point.

God, You've given me many good things—including money and
possessions. Help them to never become idols to me. Amen.

Now we see only a reflection as in a mirror;
then we shall see face to face. Now I know in part;
then I shall know fully, even as I am fully known.
1 CORINTHIANS 13:12 NIV

"Dark matter," "dark energy," "dark flow". . .the scientific model of the universe depends on all of these. The expression *dark* means, "We think something ought to be there, but we can't find it."

Cosmologists face the unenviable task of trying to understand creation while they themselves are a part of it. They envisage a necessarily restricted model and call the bits beyond their comprehension "dark."

In that, they're not so different from people of faith. Not even the greatest Bible scholars fully understood God's grand plan. His ways have been mysterious since the beginning. And because of that there are things we don't understand, things we would have difficulty explaining to anyone else, things, if we are honest, that might sometimes cause us to doubt the validity of our faith. But hold on.

Paul addresses those "dark" spots in this verse. He knew those worries. He also knew there was an answer.

The scientific community invests billions in solving its mysteries. Paul advises the rest of us to invest a little faith and a little time. Then we "shall know fully," and there will be no dark.

Lord, thank You for the mysteries of Your doings in my life.
Help me to believe You for the things I can't see. Amen.

*The Lord said to Moses, "Speak to the Israelites and say to them:
'These are my appointed festivals, the appointed festivals of
the Lord, which you are to proclaim as sacred assemblies.'"*
LEVITICUS 23:1-2 NIV

Holidays in Israel combined festive celebrations along with worship to commemorate God's amazing blessings on the nation.

The weekly Sabbath, although a day for rest and worship, served as a time to "remember that you were slaves in Egypt and that the Lord your God brought you out of there with a mighty hand and an outstretched arm" (Deuteronomy 5:15 NIV).

The feast of harvest, or Pentecost, occurred fifty days after the Passover observance. Loaves of bread were presented to the Lord as an offering from the wheat harvest, along with sacrificial animals. Jewish tradition also links this feast to the day God gave Moses the Law on Mount Sinai.

During the feast of booths, the Israelites camped out in fragile shelters for seven days as a remembrance of God's care and protection following their escape from Egypt. This joyous feast took place at the end of the harvest season and included a time of thanksgiving to God for the year's crops.

Like the Israelites, let's use all our holidays to celebrate God's goodness, reflecting on the blessings He has given us personally and as a nation.

*Father, thank You for our holidays which give me a chance
to relax, to think of You, and to be thankful. Amen.*

The god of this age has blinded the minds of unbelievers,
so that they cannot see the light of the gospel that
displays the glory of Christ, who is the image of God.
2 CORINTHIANS 4:4 NIV

The "god of this age" is undoubtedly Satan. The "unbelievers" are people who think themselves too wise for faith. Their master gave them powerful weapons when he blinded them to their fate and armed them with scorn.

After all, no one likes to be laughed at. A little public humiliation might dampen a strong faith and kill a weak one. So many of us just keep quiet in front of people like that.

As a result they go happily to their fate, and the Lord's heart is twice broken.

How did Jesus deal with the blinded? He got in their faces. His actions might be described as a little scornful. He spat in their eyes, rubbed mud in their eyes, then commanded them to see!

If we can stand a little humiliation for the sake of those who mock us; if we can weather their scorn, knowing they are pawns of Satan but beloved of God; if we get in their faces, they will have to look. And if we do all that in God's name, then the blind will have no option but to see.

God, help me to brave the thorns to pluck the beautiful
rose. Help me endure the scorn and the doubt of
the unsaved to win a soul for You. Amen.

And because the Israelites forsook the LORD and no
longer served him, he became angry with them.
JUDGES 10:6–7 NIV

This verse raises an important question: Is anger sin? If so, how can a loving, sinless God express anger?

To explore these questions, we need to understand the moral attributes of God. He is good, loving, compassionate, patient, truthful, faithful, just, and slow to anger. But He does become angry—not in an imperfect human manner, but with a righteous indignation against evil.

It was righteous indignation that moved Jesus to drive the greedy and ungodly out of God's temple. In the same way, after the Israelites returned to idol worship, they suffered the consequences of their sin; God allowed neighboring nations to oppress them for eighteen years (Judges 10:8).

From the beginning of time, God has revealed His wrath against all forms of wickedness and idolatry. But His disdain toward evil is also an expression of love for goodness and righteousness.

The apostle Paul taught New Testament believers, " 'In your anger do not sin'. . .do not give the devil a foothold" (Ephesians 4:26–27 NIV). For us as Christians, it's right to express anger against sin and injustice. It's wrong to let that anger lead us to sin.

Not all anger is sin. But it's an emotion best left to God's control.

Lord, help me to be slow to anger. May I only
be angry over things that anger You. Amen.

*The apostles left the high council rejoicing that God had counted
them worthy to suffer disgrace for the name of Jesus.*
ACTS 5:41 NLT

The apostles performed "many miraculous signs and wonders
among the people" and "more and more people believed and were
brought to the Lord" (Acts 5:12, 14 NLT).

Filled with jealousy, the Jewish council arrested the apostles.
After much debate, the council released the men, forbidding
them to speak about Jesus and punishing each with a flogging.

As the apostles limped away in pain, with sliced and bleeding
backs, they rejoiced that God had allowed them to suffer for Him.

How could suffering persecution be cause for celebration?

Years later, the apostle Peter penned, "If you have suffered
physically for Christ. . .you won't spend the rest of your lives
chasing your own desires, but you will be anxious to do the
will of God" (1 Peter 4:1–2 NLT). Persecution keeps us on track
with Christ.

It also offers future blessings. "If you suffer for doing what
is right, God will reward you for it" (1 Peter 3:14 NLT). However,
we are to suffer persecution "in a gentle and respectful
way. . . . Then if people speak against you, they will be ashamed"
(1 Peter 3:16 NLT).

Are you experiencing difficulties because of your Christian
beliefs? Stand strong. Eternal blessings are yours.

Dear God, help me to patiently endure persecution for Your sake. Amen.

And he said unto me, My grace is sufficient for thee:
for my strength is made perfect in weakness. Most
gladly therefore will I rather glory in my infirmities,
that the power of Christ may rest upon me.
2 CORINTHIANS 12:9 KJV

Eric Liddell, the Scottish missionary to China from 1925–45, once wrote a prayer asking "that no circumstances, however bitter, may cause me to break thy law, the law of love to thee and my neighbor." No matter what, he promised to maintain "a heart full of gratitude."

Liddell didn't mention that he was, at the time, captive in a Japanese internment camp. He didn't know if his family was safe. And he was dying of a brain tumor.

But Eric Liddell's certainty that God loved him—and that Christ had died for him—was enough to prove that his blessings still outweighed his problems. He was able to do work that left others in the camp thinking of him as something akin to a saint.

Our down moments need not be hopeless times. When we are at our least, God can fill the space we used to occupy and do marvelous things. When you think you have nothing else going for you, if you have God to lean on, you have more than enough.

Someday you can ask Eric Liddell about that.

God, I don't see how I can keep dealing with the
situations in my life. Give me strength, please.
May I patiently endure. In Jesus' name, I ask.

He was sorry that he had made them.
GENESIS 6:6 CEV

Because of the flood, God has often been painted as the bad guy. "I can't trust a God who got angry and wiped everyone out!" people say. Yet this verse tells us God was *sorry*, not angry.

God did everything possible to avoid the flood. He gave humanity several generations to turn from its wickedness. His long-suffering was so great that He waited until there was only one righteous man left—Noah. And God didn't send the flood without warning. Noah and Enoch were preachers of righteousness. Though they warned the world for a hundred years (the time it took the ark to be built), no one believed them. By the time the rains began, the world reeked of sin. Genesis 4:23–24 indicates there was murder without guilt. A world of killers received the death penalty.

Considering the details of an event, we see a whole new story—and the righteousness of God. Don't be quick to put God down, but carefully research those questions you find disturbing. The Bible has given us every reason to put our whole life into His hands, today and forever.

Lord, You love people and yearn for them to change.
You long for them to repent, and grieve when they don't.
Help me to trust in Your justice and righteousness. Amen.

Don't be selfish; don't try to impress others. Be humble,
thinking of others as better than yourselves.
PHILIPPIANS 2:3 NLT

Another great verse along these lines is "Your love for one another
will prove to the world that you are my disciples," found in John
13:35 (NLT).

The way in which we conduct ourselves says volumes about
what is most important to us. Isaiah 53:2 tells us that there was
nothing beautiful about how Jesus physically looked that would
attract anyone to Him, yet with one look people could see that
He was full of love.

Imagine being able to see the love people have just by how
they look at you. Perhaps you could know this in the way they
speak to you. Maybe it is just in the way they say your name. That
is what Jesus had. Those fortunate enough to be in His presence
during that short time He was on the earth must have truly been
filled with His love.

Today, we are the disciples of Jesus. If we are to be that, we
must conduct ourselves according to Philippians 2:3 and many
other verses that were written to guide us. It is now we who need
to display this love toward others. With each person we encounter,
may we shine with the love of Jesus.

Father, help me to esteem others very highly in love.
Help me especially to love my brothers and sisters
in Christ. In Jesus' name, I pray. Amen.

*"Call to me and I will answer you and tell you great
and unsearchable things you do not know."*
JEREMIAH 33:3 NIV

In this verse, God is speaking directly to the prophet Jeremiah.

For forty years, Jeremiah had been warning that Judah and Jerusalem would be destroyed for their sins. Now, his predictions were coming true: the Babylonian army was poised to attack. King Zedekiah commanded that Jeremiah be thrown into prison for speaking the words of God. While Jeremiah was there, God commanded him to pray. "Call to Me," He said, "and I will answer you" (Jeremiah 33:3 NASB).

Jeremiah 33:3 teaches that if we pray to God, He will answer us with wisdom. In the King James Version of the Bible, the word *pray* is listed more than five hundred times. God wants us to pray. When we call on Him in prayer, we know that He hears us (1 John 5:15).

Proverbs 2:6 (NASB) says, "For the LORD gives wisdom; from His mouth come knowledge and understanding." God knows us fully, and He is able to direct us in wisdom and guide us through the works of His Holy Spirit.

Just as God gave Jeremiah wisdom when he prayed, He will do the same for you. Just call on Him in faith (James 1:5–6).

*God, I claim this promise. I'm calling to You now for the
wisdom I need, and am expecting You to answer.*

> *Teach me good judgment and knowledge: for I have*
> *believed thy commandments. Before I was afflicted I*
> *went astray: but now have I kept thy word. Thou art*
> *good, and doest good; teach me thy statutes.*
> PSALM 119:66–68 KJV

Affliction in this life is an opportunity to move closer to God.

Sometimes we bring affliction upon ourselves, as did the prodigal son. After squandering his inheritance, he became so hungry that he "longed to fill his stomach with the pods that the pigs were eating" (Luke 15:16 NIV). This young man's own choices had caused his hardship, and yet his difficulties became an opportunity once "he came to his senses" (Luke 15:17 NIV) and repented. Affliction had brought about obedience from the heart.

Other times, affliction comes from the hand of the Father. Jesus Himself experienced this: "Son though he was, he learned obedience from what he suffered" (Hebrews 5:8 NIV). We are God's beloved children too, and so "God disciplines us for our good, in order that we may share in his holiness" (Hebrews 12:10 NIV).

And finally, affliction comes simply from being in this dying world. Jesus reminded His followers, "You will have suffering in this world" but in the same breath added this promise: "Be courageous! I have conquered the world" (John 16:33 HCSB). Be patient in all affliction, and believe in God's goodness through it.

Father, thank You for anything that draws me closer to You.

DAY 266

As Jesus went on from there, he saw a man named
Matthew sitting at the tax collector's booth. "Follow me,"
he told him, and Matthew got up and followed him.
MATTHEW 9:9 NIV

In New Testament times, the Roman tax structure provided ample opportunity for lucrative kickbacks and payoffs to officials working in the system. These underhanded operations reached down to the lowest level of the tax hierarchy—the publicans or tax collectors.

Utilizing common practices of the day, Matthew's superiors encouraged him to overcharge the general populace, to falsely accuse merchants of smuggling in hopes of extracting hush money, and to impose arbitrary duty taxes on all imports and exports. These and other cunning schemes provided dishonest wealth for tax officials throughout the agency.

Many Jews believed it unlawful to pay tribute in any form to Rome and regarded Jewish tax collectors as traitors. Already despised, a Jewish publican had frequent interaction with pagan Gentiles, rendering him defiled in the eyes of most Jews.

Yet Jesus asked Matthew, a detested publican, to "follow Me," and Matthew immediately complied. He became one of Jesus' twelve disciples and penned the Gospel bearing his name.

Do you have family members, friends, or coworkers living far from God? There is hope. Keep them in your prayers and let Jesus work in their hearts.

Lord, please work in my loved ones' hearts. Cause them
to be sick of their sin and draw them to Yourself. Amen.

Delayed hope makes the heart sick.
PROVERBS 13:12 HCSB

A guy wants his career to be exciting and lucrative. . .his favorite team to win it all. . .his wife to be strong, capable, and gorgeous. . .his muscles firm and his joints flexible. . .his kids to be successful. . .his car to go from zero to sixty in three seconds.

But jobs can disappear. Favorite teams fall short. Marriages struggle and sometimes implode. Bodies age and ache. Kids may jump the rails. Some cars hit sixty only if they go over a cliff.

Disappointment is common. But that's not a bad thing.

Consider: If you always got what you wanted, how much would you pray? Think God might use disappointments to draw you closer to Himself?

The psalm-writing sons of Korah recognized these truths—even when the disappointment included God's silence. "My tears have been my food day and night," they wrote. "I say to God my Rock, 'Why have you forgotten me?' " (Psalm 42:3, 9 NIV).

But Psalm 42 also suggests a practical solution: the conscious recognition of God's worth. "Why, my soul, are you downcast? Why so disturbed within me? Put your hope in God, for I will yet praise him, my Savior and my God" (verses 5, 11 NIV).

Let today's disappointments push you to God, who promises a perfect forever.

Father, many of my hopes have been frustrated.
May I find true satisfaction in You.

*And he said to me, "Son of man, eat what is before you,
eat this scroll; then go and speak to the people of Israel."*
EZEKIEL 3:1 NIV

Why would the Lord instruct Ezekiel to eat a scroll? Simply put,
the scroll contained God's words for the defiant Israelites. Its con-
tents were harsh judgment sweetened with blessed redemption.
But before Ezekiel could preach the Word of God, he had to first
ingest and commit himself to it.

When Satan tempted Jesus in the wilderness to turn stones
into bread, Jesus replied, "Man shall not live on bread alone, but
on every word that comes from the mouth of God" (Matthew 4:4
NIV). God's Word nourishes and sustains every believer; it is our
meat and potatoes. However, we must first digest it and imprint
it on our hearts and minds before we can become effective for
the kingdom.

The prophet Jeremiah said, "When your words came, I ate
them; they were my joy and my heart's delight, for I bear your
name" (Jeremiah 15:16 NIV). So it is with every Christian. The
scriptures bring joy, life, hope, peace, comfort, encouragement,
and all the spiritual nutrients we need to fortify our hearts and
minds. It empowers us to preach the Good News of Jesus Christ.
Have you had your serving today?

---

*God, give me a hunger for Your Word. Help me to chew it
thoroughly—read it slowly and carefully. And help me to
digest it—think deeply upon it and absorb it, I pray. Amen.*

"Produce fruit in keeping with repentance. And do not begin to say to yourselves, 'We have Abraham as our father.' For I tell you that out of these stones God can raise up children for Abraham."

LUKE 3:8 NIV

Being one of the faithful isn't an inherited position, much as some people might like to think so. We aren't automatically saved because our parents were.

Thinking of themselves as the chosen race had made some of the folk of Jesus' day lazy about their faith. John pointed out that the choice was God's—and nobody should give Him cause to regret it.

Imagine God as an employer. He's hiring, but He doesn't want people who think they're owed a job. He doesn't "do" nepotism—you won't get the job because your old man worked for the company way back. God has no place for "seat warmers" in His business. He seeks people who want to be there, people who will "produce fruit" from the raw materials He provides.

God, Inc., is a thriving business that's really going somewhere. There are always vacancies for those willing to work. It's a lifelong, recession-proof position with a wonderful retirement package.

It's too good an opportunity to risk losing through complacency. You can bet those stones would jump at the chance—if stones could jump.

Father, thank You for making me Your child.
Help me to walk daily in my new life. Amen.

All God's people here send you greetings,
especially those who belong to Caesar's household.
PHILIPPIANS 4:22 NIV

The apostle Paul wrote his letter to the Philippians three centuries before the Roman empire officially adopted Christianity. But the faith was already planted in "Caesar's household."

Rome, with its pagan beliefs and emperor worship, was no friend—and often a powerful enemy—of Christianity. Paul wrote Philippians while imprisoned in the city, awaiting trial before the emperor. Many believe that was the infamous Nero, who ultimately had the apostle beheaded.

But during his stay in Rome, "what has happened to me has actually served to advance the gospel," Paul wrote. "As a result, it has become clear throughout the whole palace guard and to everyone else that I am in chains for Christ" (Philippians 1:12–13 NIV). By his cheerful submission to unfair treatment from Jesus' enemies, Paul had a powerful effect behind enemy lines.

The same can be true of us. In a world so clearly darkened by Satan, the light of Christ in our lives should shine all the brighter. If we're "always giving thanks to God the Father for everything, in the name of our Lord Jesus Christ" (Ephesians 5:20 NIV), we'll have opportunities—like Paul—to point a member of Caesar's household or a Philippian jailer (Acts 16) to the Lord.

God is working in all times and places. Let's be sure we join Him.

Here I am, Lord. . .use me behind enemy lines.

> "No one can serve two masters. Either you will hate the one and love the other, or you will be devoted to the one and despise the other. You cannot serve both God and money."
> MATTHEW 6:24 NIV

A master rules with complete control and authority. In this verse, *money* also translates as "mammon," which means all manner of earthly possessions.

Mammon cannot be our master. We can use our possessions and money for God's purpose, but we can't let these things rule our lives. When mammon controls hearts, we have no time or space for God.

We may try to juggle two masters for a while—and we may even look successful—but Jesus warns us that this is not the way to live. Just as the juggler handles only one ball at a time, we must let go of one to cling to the other.

Today we are easily seduced into thinking we can have it all. But when we try to cling both to our possessions and to God, we eventually have to let go of something.

God is our master. Some things we cling to—our home, job, family—are good things, but we place them out of order in our priorities. What distracts from God is our mammon. He wants to be number one in our hearts.

God, may I always give You first place in my heart. I need material things, but help me keep them in their place—serving You. Amen.

For you were once darkness,
but now you are light in the Lord.
EPHESIANS 5:8 HCSB

It's a paradox of the Christian life: the more we grow in our relationship with God, the more we recognize our own sinfulness.

That's not all bad. We should be amazed at God's grace, His willingness to save rebellious human beings through faith in Jesus. But once we are saved—once we're much-loved sons of God by the work of *the* Son of God—let's not obsess over our failings. When we sin, let's just confess to God, ask His forgiveness, and move on in His grace. The backward look is a poor use of our time and energy.

Famed nineteenth-century preacher Charles Spurgeon found encouragement in the fifth verse of Genesis (HCSB): "God called the light 'day,' and He called the darkness 'night.' Evening came and then morning: the first day." Both darkness and light, Spurgeon noted, were called "by the name that is given to the light alone!" Though we find both darkness and light in ourselves, we shouldn't think of ourselves as sinners but as saints—because we possess some degree of God's holiness.

Saints on earth still have darkness inside, but the day will come when we are completely light in God's presence. Until that time, emphasize the grace He's given you. Call yourself by the right name: "Light in the Lord."

Thank You for saving me, Lord.
Increase Your light in my life every day.

> *But people are counted as righteous,*
> *not because of their work, but because*
> *of their faith in God who forgives sinners.*
> ROMANS 4:5 NLT

Have you ever played the Opposite Game? When the leader tells you to step forward, you step back. When he calls out the color green, then you call out, "Red." It's challenging to the very young because they have to think before they act.

Well, many of us have played the Opposite Game with God. Today's scripture tells us that God will not count us righteous based on our works. So what do many of us do? We try to please God by what we do! "I've worked hard at being a good person. I hope God will let me into heaven." "No matter how hard I try to do good, I still feel that God doesn't accept anything I do."

Abraham is given as a good example. God told Abraham that his seed would be as numerous as the stars, and Abraham believed God. God then counted him righteous—and Abraham had not lifted a finger.

Our faith is what pleases God. Then, because God has saved and empowered us, we can perform good works to honor Him. Let's be careful to keep our priorities straight.

Lord, I praise You for sending Your Holy Spirit into my
heart and making me righteous. Thank You it wasn't
by my own efforts or works. I need Your Spirit, Lord.

*My flesh and my heart may fail, but God is the
strength of my heart and my portion forever.*
PSALM 73:26 NIV

Have you heard of Asaph? He's the man who wrote Psalm 73. Asaph
was David's music director and author of twelve of the psalms.

In Psalm 73, Asaph wonders, *If God is good, then why do the
righteous suffer and the wicked prosper?* He says, "Did I keep my
heart pure for nothing? Did I keep myself innocent for no reason?
I get nothing but trouble all day long; every morning brings me
pain" (verses 13–14 NLT). Asaph confesses that he sometimes
feels like giving up and joining the wicked (verses 2–3).

In desperation, Asaph seeks God in His sanctuary. There he
realizes that while the wicked might prosper for a season, God
will defeat them in His own way and in His own time. Asaph
ends up with praise: "But as for me, how good it is to be near
God! I have made the Sovereign LORD my shelter, and I will tell
everyone about the wonderful things you do" (Psalm 73:28 NLT).

When our bodies are tired and sick, when we feel as if we can't
go on, Psalm 73 reminds us that God is our everything.

*God, I'm sick at times, discouraged, and weak. But help
me keep my mind on You. May I not choose the easy way
out. Help me to know that it's worth it to serve You.*

Examine yourselves to see whether you are in the faith;
test yourselves. Do you not realize that Christ Jesus
is in you—unless, of course, you fail the test?
2 CORINTHIANS 13:5 NIV

When we are in church or a Bible group, we know we are among kindred spirits. We can relax a little, knowing we won't be upsetting anyone with our faith and knowing the others will help keep us on track. Christ Jesus will be in us. But much of His work isn't done among the faithful. We need to venture out of our comfort zone, and that's when it gets dangerous.

The world is a trap for the spiritually unwary. There are countless diversions and it's easy to get lost, which is why fellowship with other Christians is so important. But if you don't have that opportunity, if you are a "voice in the desert," it is vitally important that you regularly ask, "Am I doing this for the love of God? Would He approve?" When you can no longer answer, "Yes," to those questions then you know you have strayed.

But here's the good news. If you have failed the test, you are far from alone. Simon Peter failed it in spectacular style. But you can revisit that test anytime. Simply open your heart and invite Him back in. He will come.

Father, I praise You that You have mercy on me when
I fail. You don't cast me away. Help me return to You,
knowing that You always have mercy. Amen.

Don't let anyone fool you by using senseless
arguments. These arguments may sound wise,
but they are only human teachings. They come
from the powers of this world and not from Christ.
COLOSSIANS 2:8 CEV

"There is no such thing as absolute truth." Ever heard an argument like this? It sounds good on the surface—until you take a step back and start to ponder its meaning. The trouble with this statement is that it declares an absolute truth while maintaining that there is no such thing.

Adam and Eve were deceived in the garden, as the serpent manipulated truth and logic into something that seemingly justified evading God's established guidelines. This legacy of deception continues in our modern world. Positions and viewpoints that appear intellectually solid at first glance break down upon further examination of their components and consequences.

Human logic falls apart in the face of divine wisdom. Worldly philosophy captures and enslaves; the all-knowing, omniscient presence of God radiates both truth and grace. What arguments have you heard lately that have their origins in the roots of this world, rather than the fullness of Christ?

Jesus, help me look to You and Your wisdom and not be moved and led astray by the seemingly wise arguments that people raise. Amen.

*"Where then are the gods you made for yourselves? Let
them come if they can save you when you are in trouble!
For you, Judah, have as many gods as you have towns."*

JEREMIAH 2:28 NIV

The Lord made His intentions clear at Sinai: He forbade the making and worshipping of idols (Exodus 20:4–5).

In spite of that command, Israel fell into cycles of idolatry, judgment, repentance, and restoration (Judges 2:11–19). Solomon, the king who built God's temple in Jerusalem, formalized idol worship, building altars to the gods of Moab and Ammon for two of his wives. Later, "he did the same for *all* his foreign wives" (1 Kings 11:8 NIV, italics added). Since he had three hundred wives and seven hundred concubines, that's the potential for a thousand idols to false gods.

Centuries later, King Manasseh committed a final, awful sacrilege: he brought idol worship into the temple courts (2 Chronicles 33:5–6).

Jeremiah began prophesying during the reign of Manasseh's grandson. Idolatry had so pervaded the land that every town had its own god, and Jeremiah warned, pleaded, wept—to no avail. Jerusalem fell, and her people went into captivity.

What about us? Have we let the false gods of the world—money, things, celebrity worship—take root in our lives? There's only one God, and He demands our attention.

*Lord, help me to avoid exalting some thing or person as
an object of worship. May I worship only You. Amen.*

"I baptize with water," John replied, "but among you stands
one you do not know. He is the one who comes after me,
the straps of whose sandals I am not worthy to untie."
JOHN 1:26–27 NIV

Do you remember how Jesus viewed His relative and forerunner John? The Lord said, "Among those born of women there has not risen anyone greater than John the Baptist" (Matthew 11:11 NIV). Yet in today's scripture, see how John judged himself: the pinnacle of "those born of women" said he wasn't worthy of untying Jesus' shoes.

That's the attitude God wants in His children. "Humility is the fear of the LORD," Proverbs 22:4 says; "its wages are riches and honor and life." "With humility comes wisdom," Proverbs 11:2 adds, and "humility comes before honor" (Proverbs 18:12). "Do nothing out of selfish ambition or vain conceit," the apostle Paul taught. "Rather, in humility value others above yourselves" (Philippians 2:3, all quotations NIV). Encapsulating all, famed Bible teacher Oswald Chambers said, "Humility is the one stamp of a saint."

No matter how impressive you are, someone is always more so. And even if you happen to be this generation's John the Baptist, you're still unworthy of loosening Jesus' sandals. That's just fine. Remember, if we don't come to Jesus as little children, we don't get into His kingdom (Matthew 18:3).

Lord Jesus, my life is all about You. May I always
view myself with appropriate humility.

*In the morning, LORD, you hear my voice; in the morning
I lay my requests before you and wait expectantly.*
PSALM 5:3 NIV

"Lay my request" originates from the Hebrew word *arak*, which means to arrange or to set up as in a legal contract.

We act as lawyers preparing our case. We plead our claims before the Lord: *Lord, here is what I want, or need. I know You love me and have promised to hear me.*

But as in any legal contract, both parties have duties or responsibilities. God listens. We wait in expectation.

Often we forget our side of the legal contract. God fulfills His side of the bargain to hear our prayers. We take off on our merry way, trying to solve our dilemma without Him.

We leave His presence without lingering with the Lord to listen and to worship Him in the silence of our heart. Then the next morning we return with more demands and *gimmes*.

God knows our human hearts and understands. He gently waits to hear from us—and He delights when we keep our end of the bargain and linger in His light with hearts full of anticipation and hope.

*Father, I present my petitions before You. Help me trust that
You hear me and will answer—either by supplying my need
or giving me wisdom. In Jesus' name, I pray. Amen.*

*Wash away all my iniquity and cleanse me from my sin. For I
know my transgressions, and my sin is always before me.*
PSALM 51:2-3 NIV

The eleventh and twelfth chapters of the book of 2 Samuel recount
a series of shameful actions by King David—lust, adultery, and
an attempted cover-up of his sins that included arranging for the
death of one of his top military men.

What a mess David made—for himself, for his family, and
for his kingdom.

Despite these horrendous sins, God still loved David and still
had a plan for him, so He sent the prophet Nathan to confront
the wayward king. David immediately acknowledged that he
had sinned against God, and that led to him writing Psalm 51,
which begins, "Have mercy on me, O God, according to your
unfailing love; according to your great compassion blot out my
transgressions" (verse 1 NIV).

David understood something the apostle John wrote centuries
later: "If we confess our sins, he is faithful and just to forgive us our
sins, and to cleanse us from all unrighteousness" (1 John 1:9 KJV).

God forgives repentant sinners. So when you mess up, don't
try to rationalize, hide your sin, or hide from God. Instead,
run to Him and confess from your heart, knowing that He promises to forgive and cleanse you.

*Lord, when I sin, don't let me hide from You. Instead, bring
me close so that I can confess my sin from my heart.*

Jesus Christ is the same yesterday and today and forever.
HEBREWS 13:8 NIV

Although the writer of Hebrews is disputed, clearly the letter is written for Jewish converts who were tempted to revert to Judaism. The writer encourages them to hold fast and persevere based on the surety of Jesus' death on the cross for eternal life.

To understand the context of today's scripture, however, look at 13:7 (NIV): "Remember your leaders, who spoke the word of God to you. Consider the outcome of their way of life and imitate their faith."

Two thousand years later, we're reminded to remember those who walked the earth with Jesus Christ, obediently taking the first steps toward making disciples of all nations (Matthew 28:19). They were the ones whose eyes were fixed on the changeless Christ, and their faith reflected it. They're the ones who passed the faith to us.

So, as we remember our Christian role models of the past, the disciples, a Sunday school teacher, a parent who led us to Christ, we, too, are asked to imitate their faith, which was built on Jesus Christ, our only absolute that was, is, and forever will be.

Father God, I thank You for Your Son, who is eternally able to save. Thank You for the men and women who passed on to me their faith in Him.

Godly sorrow brings repentance that leads to salvation and leaves no regret, but worldly sorrow brings death.
2 Corinthians 7:10 niv

Here, the apostle Paul identifies two types of sorrow with totally different results. One is from God, the other from the world; one brings life, the other death.

Paul's previous letter of admonishment to the Corinthian church caused the new believers grief. The apostle explained that although he hated to hurt them, he didn't regret writing those words, adding, "For you became sorrowful as God intended" (2 Corinthians 7:9 niv).

Before accepting Christ, each individual experiences varying degrees of conviction—an intense sense of shame and reproof. The guilt associated with realizing our sins and our need for repentance is uncomfortable and troubling temporarily. Yet it is that sorrow that produces humility, a contrite heart, and a change of mind that leads to liberating salvation. Paul wrote, "See what this godly sorrow has produced in you: what earnestness, what eagerness to clear yourselves. . .what readiness to see justice done" (2 Corinthians 7:11 niv).

On the other hand, worldly sorrow destroys and creates inner turmoil. Deep sorrow for lost possessions, jobs, or relatives often produces illness or leads people to pursue desperate means.

The Lord wills for us to experience godly sorrow and—as we trust Him—He helps us overcome all worldly sorrows through His grace and mercy.

Lord, thank You for godly sorrow. Thank You for convicting me of my sin, leading me to Christ, and saving me.

*Great is our Lord and mighty in power;
his understanding has no limit.*
PSALM 147:5 NIV

God has phenomenally *great* power. Genesis 1:16 tells us that
He created all the billions upon billions of stars, and in Psalm
147:4, David tells us that God knows the exact number of stars
in the entire universe. What's more, He calls every one of them by
name—as if they were His pets! Remember this astonishing fact
the next time you need an answer to prayer and wonder if God is
big enough to perform it.

But there's more: Psalm 147:5 says God's "understanding
has no limit." When you're praying for wisdom in a complex or
desperate situation, fix this thought firmly in your mind. You
may have no clue as to the right answer, but God certainly does.
His understanding is without end.

At times, we don't understand why God allows us to go through
troubling times, but He certainly knows—and He cares deeply
for each one of us. He not only knows every star by name, but
He knows *your* name too.

Psalm 147:5 is one of the most powerful scriptures in the
Bible. When we meditate deeply on its words, they can fill our
minds with peace and assurance.

*God, I praise You for Your infinite power and unparalleled wisdom.
You can redeem any situation and resolve any problem.*

*What does "he ascended" mean except that he
also descended to the lower, earthly regions?*
EPHESIANS 4:9 NIV

Paratroopers who led the Normandy invasion jumped, in the dark
of night, into enemy territory. They took every weapon and as much
ammunition as they could carry. Then they loaded kit bags with
more weapons and equipment, tied them onto their ankles, and
threw them out of the plane before they jumped. Honor them as
heroes, knowingly cutting their already-slim chances of survival.

Now imagine yourself making the same jump. Your greatest
enemy controls the region below. But over the drop zone, the
jumpmaster unties your kit bag, taking away all your weapons.
He says there are some good folks below who *might* help—though
they don't have many resources themselves. Oh, and there won't
be a pickup point, because you will definitely die down there.

Would you make the descent?

Jesus' crucifixion and ascension get glory and attention,
appropriately. But a key part of any venture is the beginning. He
had to descend to earth—"enemy territory"—before He could
complete God's plan of salvation.

God isn't asking anything nearly as scary of us. The next time
you think it would be good to help somebody, *but*. . .remember
that without taking that first step in faith, people continue in need.
Jesus weighed risks against love. Love won—and down He came!

*Jesus, thank You for Your great love that motivated
You to come down to earth to die for my sins. Amen.*

Then they got up early the next morning and went to the top of the range of hills. "Let's go," they said. "We realize that we have sinned, but now we are ready to enter the land the LORD has promised us."
NUMBERS 14:40 NLT

Before entering the land God promised to Israel, Moses sent out twelve scouts to explore the region.

After forty days, the men returned and reported, "It is indeed a bountiful country.... But the people living there are powerful" (Numbers 13:27–28 NLT).

Two scouts, Caleb and Joshua, urged the people to go at once and take possession of the land. But the other ten spread fear, saying, "We can't go up against them! They are stronger than we are!" (Numbers 13:31 NLT). Hearing this, the Israelites revolted against Moses and wanted to stone Caleb and Joshua.

During the riot, God's presence appeared above the tabernacle.

For their unbelief, God sentenced the Israelites to wander forty years in the desert. Those twenty years and older—except Caleb and Joshua—would never live to enter the promised land.

Ignoring God's verdict, the men prepared for battle and went up to take the land, but the inhabitants attacked and soundly defeated the Israelites.

Rebuffed opportunities often disappear, never to return. Let's be sure to tune into God's gentle prodding and act on whatever He says.

*God, please give me the faith to obey Your call
when You present a unique opportunity. Amen.*

*The Lord is my Strength and my Song, and He has
become my Salvation; this is my God, and I will
praise Him, my father's God, and I will exalt Him.
The Lord is a Man of War; the Lord is His name.*
EXODUS 15:2-3 AMPC

There's a word that describes someone who is able to turn rivers to
blood, send death on the firstborn of every family, and destroy an
army of battle-tested charioteers with the pent-up force of billions
of gallons of water: *terrifying.*

When God brought the Israelites out of Egypt, His chosen
people must have been both elated to have Him on their side
and scared witless at the thought of being His subjects. This God,
who had promised land and prosperity to their forefathers, had
allowed them to become an Egyptian slave force. Then, after long
years of whispered retellings of His promises, God showed up in
force to set His people free.

Thousands of years later, God is still fighting to free His
people from slavery. This time, from sin itself. We would do well
to remember the joy—and the terror—of being called His people
and praise Him from our hearts accordingly. Remember: "The
Lord is a Man of War; the Lord is His name."

---

*Lord, You are more than a loving Father; You are a Warrior who
fights for His people. Keep me from trying to fight battles by myself
when You are eminently more equipped to fight on my behalf.*

"And everyone who has left houses or brothers or sisters or father or mother or wife or children or fields for my sake will receive a hundred times as much and will inherit eternal life."
MATTHEW 19:29 NIV

Ready for the paradox of Christian living? Salvation is a free gift that will cost you everything.

The Bible is pretty clear about how people can earn God's grace. They can't: "For it is by grace you have been saved, through faith—and this is not from yourselves, it is the gift of God—not by works, so that no one can boast" (Ephesians 2:8–9 NIV).

Because grace cannot be earned, we describe salvation as a gift. At the same time, it is a gift that comes with a cost: "Then Jesus said to his disciples, 'Whoever wants to be my disciple must deny themselves and take up their cross and follow me' " (Matthew 16:24 NIV).

We give up everything—our lives, relationships, family connections, and claims to property—when we choose to accept God's call to follow Him. But in giving up everything, God will give us even more. We will receive far more than whatever we give up, *and* we'll inherit eternal life.

Stop counting the cost of following God, and start counting your blessings.

Father, may I have a heart that is willing to give up everything, knowing that You have offered me far more than what I sacrifice.

"And he shall make a strong covenant with many for one week, and for half of the week he shall put an end to sacrifice and offering."
DANIEL 9:27 ESV

In this prophecy, the angel Gabriel tells Daniel what will happen in the future. After the Messiah dies and shortly before His return, a man will make a seven-year peace treaty with Israel. Sacrifices and offerings will be allowed in Israel, and then in the middle of the treaty he will stop them.

Now, who could have known more than two thousand years ago that Israel would still be around? Most ancient civilizations have been buried under the sands. Furthermore, how could anyone have known that Israel would be in need of a treaty? If you pay attention to the news at all, you'll find trouble between Israel and the Middle East mentioned repeatedly. Many United States presidents have tried unsuccessfully to broker peace in the region.

God is pretty amazing to tell us in minute detail what will happen thousands of years in the future. It's even more amazing to find this important messianic prophecy on the brink of fulfillment in our lifetime.

God, I thank You that Your Word foretold long ago what would happen in the final days. Bring it to pass soon, I pray. Amen.

When he had seen the vision, we immediately
sought to leave for Macedonia, concluding that
God had called us to preach the gospel to them.
ACTS 16:10 NASB

With the blessing of the Antioch brethren, Paul teamed up with Silas and embarked on a second missionary journey. Leaving Antioch, they traveled northward through Syria and into the southern provinces of Asia Minor.

Forbidden by God to speak the word in Asia, Paul and Silas traveled through Phrygia and Galatia to Mysia. At Mysia, "they were trying to go into Bithynia, and the Spirit of Jesus did not permit them" (Acts 16:7 NASB).

A bit perplexed, they proceeded to the seaport town of Troas. There, in a nighttime vision, a Macedonian man appeared to Paul saying, "Come over to Macedonia and help us" (Acts 16:9 NASB). Without delay, Paul and Silas sailed from Troas to the region of Macedonia.

Although Paul and Silas set specific goals for the mission trip, they continued to seek God's direction and changed their itinerary as necessary. These changes gave the men a fruitful European ministry.

Are you listening for Christ's direction in all areas of your life or simply pushing ahead with your own agenda? Seek His guidance and make adjustments to stay on track with Him. Don't miss out on God's best for you.

God, help me to be sensitive to Your Spirit, and may I hurry
to obey even Your slightest bidding. In Jesus' name.

Greet Mary, who has worked very hard for you.
ROMANS 16:6 NET

Mary is the New Testament equivalent of *Miriam*, the name of Moses' sister. There are at least five different women named Mary and possibly as many as seven. There are Mary, the mother of Jesus; Mary Magdalene; the sister of Martha and Lazarus (perhaps the same woman as Mary Magdalene); the mother of James and John; the wife of Clopas; the mother of John Mark; and the unidentified Mary of Romans 16:6.

One strong indication that the Bible is a record of true-life events is how many people carry the same name: five to seven are called Mary, three or four James, three John, and two Judas—wouldn't that be an awful name to be stuck with! There are even three people named Jesus.

When was the last time you read a novel with two characters with the same name? No one writing fiction would create people with the same name. It's far too confusing.

One proof of the Bible's extraordinary character is its internal structure. Read it and judge for yourself: Does this read like a novel or a biography?

Lord, the Bible truly is Your Word, and it contains much evidence that it's divinely inspired and not made up by men. Thank You for that. Amen.

> *"Those who are wise will shine like the brightness
> of the heavens, and those who lead many to
> righteousness, like the stars for ever and ever."*
> DANIEL 12:3 NIV

In the verses immediately preceding this one, God told Daniel about the resurrection of the dead, when the righteous would be raised back to life to discover that they were now immortal (Daniel 12:2). Not only that, but if they had led others to live righteous lives as well, both by word and example, they would shine like stars forever.

In the Bible, stars symbolize angels (Job 38:7), and Daniel had already seen an angel whose face blazed like lightning and whose supernatural body gleamed with light (Daniel 10:5–6). He had a good idea how beautiful and powerful our resurrected bodies would be.

Several hundred years later the apostle Paul described our resurrected bodies in greater detail. Though our bodies are now perishable, dishonorable, and weak, they will be raised imperishable, glorious, and powerful (1 Corinthians 15:42–43). Not everyone will shine with the same level of brilliance and glory, since "star differs from star in splendor" (1 Corinthians 15:41 NIV).

Shine brightly for Christ now, and He'll see to it that you shine brightly for all eternity.

Father, thank You for this message about my future glorified body. Thank You that I have such things to look forward to. Amen.

If anyone is in Christ, this person is a new creature; the old
things passed away; behold, new things have come.
2 CORINTHIANS 5:17 NASB

It's safe to say that the science pages of the *Corinth Daily* never
carried a story about the discovery of any "new creature" that the
apostle Paul described. It didn't report any paleontologist's find
of new-creature bones.

Of course not—Paul's new creature was a creative description
of what happens to any person who enters into a relationship with
God's Son, Jesus the Christ. It's his answer to those who snipe,
"How can you call him a Christian? Why I remember when he. . ."

As in any large metropolis, the Corinthian population had
more than its share of disreputables. The church of that city was
busy with outreach evangelism. As men and women accepted
Christ, it was necessary to make assurance that the new believer
was a new creature in Christ. His old ways were ancient history.
He was encouraged to make amends and share how everything
about him was new.

There is more than one message from this verse: (1) Accept
a new child of God with open arms; (2) Don't let Satan beat you
down for your past life; (3) Newness is how God sees you; your
job is to make amends and share the new life.

God, I praise You for giving me new life. Show me if
there is anyone I need to make amends to. Amen.

> *"Though it is the smallest of all seeds, yet when it grows,*
> *it is the largest of garden plants and becomes a tree,*
> *so that the birds come and perch in its branches."*
> MATTHEW 13:32 NIV

Insignificant beginnings can lead to magnificent finishes. Jesus picked up the tiniest of seeds—a mustard seed—to show the disciples. This seed is about the size of the point of a sharpened pencil tip.

Once planted, the seed grows slowly in a gradual process. The seedling takes days or even weeks before it gives any sign of breaking through the ground. Why does growth drag on slowly?

The mustard seed requires deep roots. The plant grows its roots three times faster than the stalk in order to be well grounded. Mustard trees grow up to twenty-one feet tall with the roots reaching down to sixty-three feet in the ground.

God planted mustard seed–sized faith within each of us. Our faith may seem inadequate and so small we no longer think it exists. But often during these times we are not aware of the deep transformation occurring within our souls.

God is pushing our roots deeper. We can help nourish this growth through prayer and studying His Word.

Miraculous growth from a very small seed is only possible through the work of our God, who creates, sustains, and enhances life.

Lord, I'm in awe of the marvelous things You have created.
I marvel at the mustard seed and what You cause it to grow into.

Eye for eye, tooth for tooth, hand for hand, foot for foot.
EXODUS 21:24 KJV

The movie thug straightened up, wiping his mouth with the back of his hand. Seeing blood, he started forward with menace. "I'll get you for that. An eye for an eye, buddy."

How often have we heard the phrase "eye for an eye," taking it to mean retaliation and revenge? The words have their origin in the second book of the Bible, where, in context, they're not about revenge but fairness in judgment. God told the people of Israel that when two fighters came before the court, a judge was to render a punishment that fit the crime. If the victim lost an eye, for example, the judge was not to take the life of the other man. In modern terms, there was to be no "cruel and unusual punishment."

How do we deal with wrongs against us? God holds us to a higher standard than the rest of the world. Jesus was severely treated on the cross, yet He prayed, "Father, forgive them." That is God's standard for us: forgiveness, not revenge. And we attain it not through the law but by grace.

Father in heaven, I thank You that You call me to walk in love and forgiveness, not vengeance. Help me to show mercy to others even as I would want mercy to be shown to me. Amen.

*They are darkened in their understanding and separated
from the life of God because of the ignorance that is
in them due to the hardening of their hearts.*
EPHESIANS 4:18 NIV

Stubbornness is a terrible thing. How many of us *haven't* let stubbornness harden our hearts against something we would really rather be doing? Perhaps we feel awkward, afraid, or unwanted, so we stand back and pretend we never wanted to take part in the first place. Wild horses couldn't make us admit we care.

But this isn't a high school dance or a club or a wedding reception. Hardening your heart against God's Word isn't something that's going to spoil your weekend then quickly pass. The consequences are too awful to think about, so the hard hearts don't think about them. The question is, Should we think about it for them?

Most of the hard hearts we meet will be normal folk—just stubborn about the wrong things. Does that mean we should leave them behind, saying it serves them right? God doesn't want that. The hard hearts have no idea what they are walking stubbornly toward. The Christian does. Do we allow their fears to separate them from the Lord forever, or do we make sure they know they are wanted?

Hard hearts are a challenge to men of faith. Let's try to soften some.

*Lord, please use me to help hard, stubborn hearts to soften.
Reach into their spirits with Your love, I pray. Amen.*

*"Sacrifice thank offerings to God, fulfill your vows to
the Most High, and call on me in the day of trouble;
I will deliver you, and you will honor me."*
PSALM 50:14–15 NIV

Luke 17:11–19 tells the wonderful, sad story of Jesus healing ten
men afflicted with leprosy, a terrible skin disease.

"Jesus, Master, have pity on us!" they cried out. When they
got Jesus' attention, He told them, "Go, show yourselves to the
priests." Just like that, each man was healed. That's the wonderful,
beautiful part of this account.

Now the sad part.

Jesus had healed ten men that day, but only one of them came
back to Him to express his gratitude. He ran to Jesus, praising
God as loudly as he could and threw himself at Jesus' feet (verses
15–16). The other nine, however, just went on their way, seemingly
unaware that they had just been the beneficiaries of an authentic,
amazing miracle by God in the flesh Himself.

That one grateful man, now healed and cleansed of a disease
that would terribly disfigure him and make him a social outcast,
shows us something about the effect of true thankfulness, and
it's this: it draws us closer to God.

*Father, help me never to forget to "sacrifice thank
offerings" to You. Help me to be like that one grateful
leper who came back to Jesus to say, "Thank You!"*

Whatever you do, work at it with all your heart,
as working for the Lord, not for human masters.
COLOSSIANS 3:23 NIV

There are moments, as when we're watching a beautiful sunset or when a loved one strokes an arm in passing, which we don't hesitate to think of as gifts from God. Then there are the times we choose to see as tedious, like when work is unappreciated or when we are stuck in the company of someone we might think is boring. Those times are no less gifts from God. He is beside us always. The only difference is in how we behave, in how grateful we are.

Brother Lawrence, a seventeenth-century lay brother in a Carmelite monastery, practiced "the presence of God." Believing God was always with him, Lawrence turned the washing of the dishes and the repairing of sandals into acts of worship—simple things he would give his best to as a thank-you to the Lord.

It's easy to think you are working for the Lord when you are on some great quest. It's much more difficult to find a purpose in menial chores or to find a child of God in a self-centered bore.

But believe in the presence of God, and there is nothing you can do that can't also be an opportunity to raise a smile upon high.

Father, I believe You are here, present with me. Help me in
all I do to do it as an act of worship to You, I pray. Amen.

For as he thinketh in his heart, so is he.
PROVERBS 23:7 KJV

Some Christians become so desperate for financial success and relief from economic uncertainty that they subscribe to the magical thinking sweeping society today. The "secret" to prosperity is said to be simple: think about the things that you want God (or the Universe) to give you, focus on them, repeat to yourself, "They're already mine," and they will be yours.

A verse often quoted by such teachers is "For as he thinketh in his heart, so is he"—as if you only need to think about something to bring it into existence. However, this verse is *actually* talking about dining with a stingy man who says, "Eat and drink. . ." but "his heart is not with you." He pretends to be generous, but he's actually cringing as you down his food. In his heart he's stingy, and as he thinks in his heart, so is he.

Certainly God has promised to answer our prayers, and Jesus said, "Everything is possible for one who believes" (Mark 9:23 NIV). So yes, we should have more faith. . .but faith alone is not enough. God's promises are conditional on His will for us and our obedience (1 John 5:14–15; Isaiah 59:1–2). After all, God is God, not our servant.

Dear God, forgive me for the times I've treated You as a servant who is mine to command. You are almighty God. I am Your servant. Please help me to never forget that. Amen.

"Heaven and earth will disappear,
but my words will never disappear."
MARK 13:31 NLT

If there is anything we can be sure of in this world, it is that what God says is true. Jesus said that even the earth will eventually be no more, but His words will continue to be as true as they ever had been.

As humans, we often change our minds as we navigate through life. As we mature in our thought processes, our point of view changes. Sometimes we reach an age where our reasoning has evolved to include different ways of seeing any particular issue. Perhaps it is that we learn more information than before and can make more informed choices with how we feel about things. This is not how it works with God.

Our Lord has been consistent since before there were people on the earth. And because of His infinite wisdom, His Word will never change. Perhaps it would be wise for us not to trust in other people, who may well have an entirely new set of ideas later. Instead, let us invest all of our faith in our God, whose Word will never change.

We can be assured, as Mark 13:31 shows us, that what God says will still be true tomorrow, next week, next year, and forever.

Thank You, Lord, that You know every matter
inside out, from beginning to end. Your Word is
eternally true. I love and worship You, Lord!

*In God, whose word I praise, in the LORD, whose word I praise—
in God I trust and am not afraid. What can man do to me?*
PSALM 56:10–11 NIV

David wrote Psalm 56 in a time of great fear, loneliness, and desperation. He had been on the run from Saul, who intended to kill him, and ended up in a place called Gath (see 1 Samuel 21:10–15).

While David no doubt felt the same emotions any man would when his life is in danger, he focused on his conviction that God was with him and for him (Psalm 56:9). This wasn't just David's hope or plea; it was his trust in what God had already said.

In today's world, very few men will ever face the kinds of threats David faced. But that doesn't mean they won't face situations that leave them feeling bewildered, confused, even afraid. But God is bigger than any*thing* or any*one* we could ever fear in this life. And not only that, this all-powerful, all-wise, all-loving God is unwaveringly for those of us He calls His children.

Knowing all this, what do you have to fear?

---

*Lord, life has a way of bringing fear into my heart
at times. Help me to look past my fears and focus
fully on Your greatness and Your plans for me.*

Anyone who listens to the word but does not do
what it says is like someone who looks at his face
in a mirror and, after looking at himself, goes away
and immediately forgets what he looks like.
JAMES 1:23-24 NIV

Imagine there was a magic mirror that showed your true nature. Would you look? Would you expect to like what you saw there?

James tells his readers there is such a mirror. The Word of God as he had it then, the Bible we have now.

Some folk have a love-hate relationship with mirrors. They don't look too closely because they are scared of what they might see, but from a distance they think they look fine. Some Christians have a similar attitude to the Bible. They can quote it at length and know where all the books are, but they pretend not to see what it asks of them.

A closer inspection of the Bible does more than show up our faults; it shows the beings God created us to be. It's up to us to remember that image when we are away from the "mirror." And how better to remember than by actually living the Word every day?

Being wonderful, being a servant of the Most High, isn't easy. But it's who you were meant to be. And don't you forget it.

Dear God, I yield to You today. Change me, I pray, ever more
into the image of Jesus, who obeyed You in all things. Amen.

See, I set before you today life and prosperity, death and destruction.
DEUTERONOMY 30:15 NIV

When God created humanity, He gave us the power, responsibility, and privilege of free choice. Every person is accountable for his or her individual actions.

Moses told the Israelites, "I command you today to love the LORD your God, to walk in obedience to him, and to keep his commands, decrees and laws; then you will live and increase, and the LORD your God will bless you in the land you are entering to possess" (Deuteronomy 30:16 NIV). In previous chapters, Moses had underscored the blessings of obedience and the horrible curses of disobedience. In Deuteronomy 30:15 he urges the Israelites to choose.

The choice was, and still is, clear: life and prosperity or death and destruction. Without question, we reap the benefits or consequences of whatever choices we make. Obedience leads to present and future blessings, while disobedience leads to present and future miseries. To obey God's Word brings great rewards, but to turn away from God to worship the gods of this world ultimately brings ruin.

The choice is ours to make. As Moses taught, choose wisely.

God, thank You for saving me and making me
Your child. Help me to be obedient. May my
choices be pleasing in Your sight. Amen.

> *"This is to be a lasting ordinance for the generations*
> *to come, wherever you live. It is a day of sabbath*
> *rest for you, and you must deny yourselves."*
> LEVITICUS 23:31–32 NIV

When you finish a project, you step back and admire a job well done. But you also know that you're shifting roles from creator to manager—now you have to take care of the work you've done. That's the idea behind the Sabbath—not stepping away from working as much as stepping into a new role.

God made humans to be stewards of His creation. By ordaining a day of rest from the week's labors, He wasn't telling us to check out but to enjoy Him. Rest isn't relaxation in this sense but recommitment to knowing God. A sabbath is meant to help us manage our trust, to set aside daily labors and believe that God will hold things together.

It's not a legalistic warning to avoid anything that might be construed as work. Resting in God—acknowledging His good care and provision—is part of how He restores us to His original plans in the garden. God wants fellowship with you, and the Sabbath is part of how He meant for that to happen.

Lord God, thank You for all the ways You take care of me each day. You are worth the effort it takes to set aside time to enjoy You and remember who You are and all You've done.

"I will place shepherds over them who will tend
them, and they will no longer be afraid or terrified,
nor will any be missing," declares the LORD.
JEREMIAH 23:4 NIV

Quite a few people see disaster and trouble around the world and wonder why God does not do anything. This verse gives us an insight into how God works in the world. He works through people.

Repeatedly in the Old and New Testaments we find God using people to reach out to a hurting world. He has used shepherds and kings, men and women, old and young to move in the affairs of this life.

In the book of Acts we see men and women of the church moved by the Spirit to minister to vast numbers of people. God is not silent. He is not far off. He is still moving in the churches, hospitals, soup kitchens, disaster-relief workers, and people of ordinary occupations to touch the lives of others.

To those who say that God does nothing, we may tell them that God has always moved through people. Let's stop thinking that God isn't working and instead volunteer to serve. Then we'll find God moving through us.

God, may I rejoice in every opportunity You give me
to serve You. Use me to reach out to the hurting
and needy world around me, I pray.

*But you, man of God, flee from all this,
and pursue righteousness, godliness,
faith, love, endurance and gentleness.*
1 TIMOTHY 6:11 NIV

Paul loved Timothy as a son, calling him his "true son in the faith" (1 Timothy 1:2 NIV). The apostle had a vested interest in helping the younger man succeed in life and ministry and wrote him two letters full of advice.

In the sixth chapter of 1 Timothy, Paul discussed the danger of the love of money (1 Timothy 6:10). The word *but* in verse 11 changes focus. Unlike people who had wandered from the faith, Timothy was a true man of God. Paul advised him to run away from the love of money and to run toward the right things. He repeats his command in 2 Timothy 2:22.

Two of those good things, godliness and righteousness, are closely connected. Godliness is vertical—our reverence toward God; while righteousness is horizontal—how our right relationship with God impacts our relationships with others. Put together with faith, love, endurance, and gentleness, it's a powerful mix.

Flee the bad. Pursue the good. That was Paul's formula for a godly life.

*Lord, may I follow this advice passionately. May I
flee from materialism and greed and run toward
godliness and righteousness. Amen.*

Thus says the LORD to his anointed, to Cyrus, whose right
hand I have grasped, to subdue nations before him.
ISAIAH 45:1 ESV

Who will be president of the United States in 2080? What will be
the name of a child born to one of your neighbors in ten years?
Why don't you know?

Today's scripture shows God telling people in advance the
name of the person who would liberate Israel from Babylonian
oppression—150 years before his birth! Much of Bible prophecy
is literal, especially in cases where God provides names (such as
Cyrus the Great), times (such as seventy years before Israel is
released from captivity), and places (such as Bethlehem, where
the Christ child was to be born).

So when we read Matthew chapter 24 and other places where
end-times prophecies are recorded, we can be sure of their literal
fulfillment. For instance, we do not look for Christ to come out
of a nation, but out of the sky when the sun has turned dark
(Revelation 6:12–14). Prophecy confirms the presence of God
and keeps us from being deceived.

God, thank You for warning us about what the future holds.
Give me a clear understanding of end-times prophecy
so I won't be deceived by the things that are coming
upon the earth. I ask this in Jesus' name.

There is only one Lawgiver and Judge, the one
who is able to save and destroy. But you—
who are you to judge your neighbor?
JAMES 4:12 NIV

Have you ever "gotten even" with someone? Have you ever reacted unkindly to another person's unkindness?

We've all done it. It's our way of passing judgment on others. This is what we think they deserve, so we give it to them.

Does that kind of judgment make us better people? No, never.

So, what's the alternative? Love.

Often, we dismiss love as the soft option, the one that gets us taken advantage of, the one that makes us look foolish to others. But how foolish do we look when we lower all our personal standards to get even, when we make ourselves as bad as our enemies because they "deserve it." That's just a win-win situation for Satan.

Jesus wasn't vague when He told us to love God and one another. It's the answer to every problem, and anyone who dismisses it as foolish obviously hasn't tried it.

Judging others usually only makes us deserving of a harsh judgment in return. Don't judge—love. Then, when it comes our time to face the Lawgiver, His judgment on us will be a love we didn't deserve either.

Father, give me the courage to love others instead of
judging them. I leave judging in Your hands. Amen.

Seven times a day I praise you for your righteous laws.
PSALM 119:164 NIV

In the Bible, the number seven symbolizes completeness. God created the world in seven days. Seven days complete a week. Major festivals such as the Passover and Tabernacles and wedding feasts lasted seven days. In Pharaoh's dream, the seven good years followed by seven years of famine represented a complete cycle. In the New Testament, seven churches are mentioned in Revelation.

The psalmist prayed seven times a day. He lifted up praises to God throughout the entire day. He filled the minutes of his life with gratitude and paying attention to God.

The Bible tells us to pray without ceasing. A fixed-hour prayer ritual is called "praying the hours" or the "daily office." Hearts and minds turn toward God at set times. We make an effort to create a space in our busy lives to praise God and express our gratitude throughout the day.

We can create any kind of prayer schedule. Each stoplight we pass, the ring of the alarm on our watches, or a pause during television commercials can all serve as simple reminders to pray. We can be alert during the day for ways God protects and guides us.

Seven moments a day—to thank the Lord for all the moments of our lives.

*Lord, help me to take advantage of moments all day
long to seek You and to commune with You. Amen.*

Confess your faults to one another and pray for one another, that you may be healed. The effective fervent prayer of a righteous man avails much.
JAMES 5:16 SKJV

The exact authorship of the book of James is uncertain. While this New Testament letter is often attributed to James the half brother of Jesus, the author identifies himself only as "James, a servant of God and of the Lord Jesus Christ" (James 1:1 NIV).

Whoever he was exactly, James encourages us to admit our faults to other trusted Christians. Why? So that we can support and pray for each other that we might be healed. The healing mentioned in this verse isn't limited to physical healing. More often, it means healing the heart of its sinfulness. James adds that the earnest prayers offered by Christians bring results. The results might not always be what we expect, but we can be assured that they are God's results—His will for our lives.

Are you carrying the burden of your faults all by yourself? Why not have a heart-to-heart talk with a Christian friend?

Dear God, there's something that's troubling me. I ask You to lead me to just the right person to share the burdens of my heart with. May I receive good, heartfelt counsel and wisdom, I pray.

"Now then, do away with the foreign gods which are in your
midst, and incline your hearts to the LORD, the God of Israel."
JOSHUA 24:23 NASB

Although Abraham, Isaac, and Jacob worshipped the true God,
this didn't always hold true with their wives. Jacob's wife Rachel
"stole her father's household idols and took them with her" (Genesis
31:19 NLT). Worship of these idols passed on to future generations.

While slaves, the Israelites added Egyptian gods to their other
pagan deities and brought them along when fleeing out of Egypt.

The Israelites knew God performed miraculous feats like divid-
ing the Red Sea, providing manna in the wilderness, and destroying Jericho's walls. Nevertheless, many worshipped pagan deities
as they prepared to receive their inheritance in the promised land.

In an electrifying speech, Joshua challenged the Israelites to
"choose for yourselves today whom you will serve," and the people
answered, "Far be it from us that we should forsake the LORD to
serve other gods" (Joshua 24:15–16 NASB).

Joshua ordered the people to demonstrate their allegiance to
God by destroying their idols. That generation of Israelites abandoned the false deities and followed God to the end of their lives.

Is anything hindering your relationship with God? Perhaps
there are things you need to throw out or stay away from, in a
renewed commitment to Him. Choose today whom you will serve.

Lord, help me to worship You alone and not adore materialism,
people's opinions, or my accomplishments. Amen.

*Jesus said to the people who believed in him, "You are truly
my disciples if you remain faithful to my teachings."*
JOHN 8:31 NLT

Jesus taught us how to live in two ways. He spoke words of wisdom,
making very clear what God expected of us. But even more impor-
tantly, He taught by example. It seems that people say, "Jesus did
this" or "Jesus did that" more often than "Jesus told us to do this."
We remember things best by being shown.

We can say anything we want. We can tell everyone we are
followers of Jesus, and we can put on quite a show for those around
us. All of us have probably known people who attend church and
pretend to be Christians on Sunday but seem to be anything but
Christians during the rest of the week.

Jesus said, though, that we are truly His followers if we are
faithful. That means we continue to be Christians outside the
church. We live the Word of God every day, and although we may
have failures, we strive to live as closely to Jesus' teachings as we
can. As it is so well said in John 8:31, we must remain faithful.
The Lord is certainly faithful to us.

*Father in heaven, may I live every moment of every day for You.
Help me to be faithful and consistent, always seeking to obey Your
words and follow Your example. In Jesus' name, I pray. Amen.*

Discipline me, LORD, but only in due measure—
not in your anger, or you will reduce me to nothing.
JEREMIAH 10:24 NIV

Jeremiah struggled with his constant messages of gloom and doom to the people of Israel. The ending verses of chapter 10 record his personal plea for compassion in the midst of discipline: correct me with justice, not anger. His prayer echoes that of the psalmist, who twice asked God, "Do not rebuke me in your anger" (Psalm 6:1; 38:1 NIV).

Since the Bible teaches that there is none righteous, a cry for justice and not anger seems pointless. Wouldn't justice demand punishment? The ultimate punishment for sin is death (Romans 6:23).

Isaiah tells us that justice is the "measuring line" (28:17 NIV). The American justice system metes punishment to lawbreakers; but the civil courts seek to restore what is lost to those who have been wronged.

If human judges offer justice to the oppressed, how much more so will God! Isaiah said, "The LORD longs to be gracious to you; therefore he will rise up to show you compassion. For the LORD is a God of justice" (30:18 NIV). Grace and compassion are justice's companions.

God's anger may diminish us (the literal translation of Jeremiah 10:24); but His just discipline produces "a harvest of righteousness and peace" (Hebrews 12:11 NIV).

Lord, rain down Your justice upon us. We need
Your righteousness and peace. Amen.

Jesus told him, "Because you have seen me, you have believed;
blessed are those who have not seen and yet have believed."
JOHN 20:29 NIV

Before His ascension into heaven, Jesus appeared to several people, including some of the disciples. One of them, Thomas, had not experienced the initial sightings of Jesus. When others told him, he refused to believe—saying he needed direct proof to be convinced of the Lord's resurrection.

One week later, Thomas got his proof when Jesus walked through the locked doors of a room where the disciples were staying. The Lord invited Thomas to feel His hands and touch His side. In their exchange, Jesus mildly scolded Thomas for his skepticism, saying, "Stop doubting and believe" (John 20:27 NIV).

If we let them, these words Jesus spoke to Thomas can hit us all right between the eyes. Aren't we all like "Doubting Thomas" at times? Don't we often want everything in black and white—or for God to appear in a burning bush (Exodus 3), a miraculous cloud (Exodus 13:21–22), or through the words of a talking donkey (Numbers 22:28–33)?

But the fact is that God does appear to us—through His Word, His Son, and His Spirit. Jesus says to all of us, "Blessed are those who have not seen and yet believe. Stop your doubting."

God, please open my eyes so that I can know that You're present
with me, revealing Yourself to me in the Spirit. Amen.

He who sits in the heavens shall laugh.
PSALM 2:4 SKJV

Ever wonder whether God has a sense of humor? It shouldn't surprise us to find that we who were made in His image laugh as He does. But it's important to read this verse carefully to find out what gives God the chuckles.

Psalm 2 provides a telescope to focus on details in the future. We can see what will happen after Jesus returns to earth: He will set up His kingdom and dole out territories for His faithful servants to rule the world with Him. After a while, though, some people will refuse His rule and plot against Him. Therein lies the humor.

God laughs at the ludicrous. The people secretly plot against a God who reads their very thoughts. They send their strongest to fight the Lord who holds the universe together single-handedly. They think they can outwit the Creator, whose wisdom and power generated the billions of cells that make up their arrogant beings. It is funny, when you think about it.

No one can outsmart God or outwit His plans for our lives. There's comfort in that thought—and that's no joke.

Lord, You're incomparably greater than all Your foolish enemies. Help me never to seek to resist Your will or think that I can outsmart You. In Jesus' name, I pray. Amen.

We are hard pressed on every side, but not crushed;
perplexed, but not in despair; persecuted, but not
abandoned; struck down, but not destroyed.
2 CORINTHIANS 4:8–9 NIV

Throughout his epistles, the apostle Paul alluded to the Grecian games of biblical times—this verse is one such instance. Just as Jesus used contemporary parables to drive His messages home, Paul used familiar references to encourage and help the early Christians.

Interestingly, three expressions of 2 Corinthians 4:8–9 refer to the customs of wrestling, the fourth to running in a race. To the wrestler, "hard pressed" meant having no way of resistance. Puzzled by his antagonist's skill, a wrestler could be "perplexed," not knowing what move to attempt. The grappler who "struck down" his opponent first was deemed the conqueror. "Persecuted," meanwhile, refers to one being pursued in a footrace. In each of the four clauses, the first part refers to the outward experience of our earthly experience, the latter the excellence of the power we have in Christ.

Paul and the disciples were no strangers to hardships, persecution, and trials. So he penned these words encouraging the early Christians that absolutely no problem, tragedy, or sickness could defeat the believer.

That still holds true today. When the outward man suffers and our human resources are exhausted, the Christian spirit soars.

Lord, when my body suffers and my resources are exhausted,
renew me by the power of Your Holy Spirit, I pray. Amen.

Give your burdens to the LORD, and he will take care
of you. He will not permit the godly to slip and fall.
PSALM 55:22 NLT

Few wounds cut more deeply than a friend's betrayal. Psalm 55
addresses such a betrayal—a friend become foe, smooth words
masking surprising hatred, a stunning turn that cut David to the
quick. And so, he turned to God.

The psalms remind us that God cares about every detail
of our lives, that He is worthy of our praise in all the ups and
downs. If you haven't yet suffered a blow that you think you
might never get up from, you will. This world is hard and cruel,
but with God, there is always hope—even if you would rather
die than take another breath.

Never forget that Jesus understands everything you go
through. He knows sorrow and loss, emotional and physical
agony, and the deepest betrayals and rejection. Because He
overcame them, you will too. Life will shake you, but He won't
let you be knocked off your post at His side. If all you can do
is rasp out a single-word prayer—*help* or *please* or *Father*—He
hears and He is there. You're going to be okay.

Father, the pain from old wounds feels like it might
kill me. Heal me, please, and let me know You're still
there and that You'll never cast me away.

*Balak said to Balaam, "What have you done to me?
I brought you to curse my enemies, but you have
done nothing but bless them!" He answered, "Must I
not speak what the LORD puts in my mouth?"*
NUMBERS 23:11–12 NIV

Balaam was a hired prophet, engaged by Balak to curse Israel and drive them from his territory. Balaam took the gig but soon found himself in a pickle: He could only say what God told him to say. Three times he attempted to curse Israel; three times God compelled him to speak blessing over them instead.

When even a mercenary, whose livelihood is based on getting the job done and getting paid, can't go against God's blessing, it's safe to say God's people are secure. Safe in Christ, we're protected not from every hardship but from the ultimate adversity of separation from our Maker. He is with us and watching over us, and He will see us through anything or anyone that comes against us.

Furthermore, there's a reminder for us about speaking God's truth. Our culture demands compliance with its views, but we can't water down God's Word. Love without truth isn't love, and vice versa. When you're loyal to God, He's got your back.

*Lord God, Your truth and love are shaping me into the image
of Jesus. Give me courage to share Your good news and not
to back down from speaking Your truth with Your heart.*

Rejoice greatly, O daughter of Zion! Shout aloud,
O daughter of Jerusalem! Behold, your king is coming
to you; righteous and having salvation is he, humble and
mounted on a donkey, on a colt, the foal of a donkey.
ZECHARIAH 9:9 ESV

Jesus' triumphal entry into Jerusalem is among a handful of events mentioned in all four Gospels (Matthew 21:1–11, Mark 11:1–10, Luke 19:28–40, and John 12:12–15). In each account, Jesus sends His disciples to bring back a colt—a young male donkey—for Him to ride into town on. But why a donkey? Why not a horse?

First, Jesus fulfilled Zechariah's prophecy from today's verse by choosing a donkey to ride into town on. Second, the reason Zechariah spoke about a donkey instead of a horse is because of the message it sent.

A king or military leader who conquers a town through force would ride his warhorse into the defeated city to project an image of strength and to enforce compliance through fear. But a king who enters on a donkey does so because he comes in peace. He humbles himself and invites others to follow him of their own free will rather than demanding their compliance.

How do you bring others to Jesus? Get off your warhorse and find yourself a donkey. With a humble heart, lead others to the King of kings who comes in peace.

Jesus, help me follow Your example by leading
with humility over strong-arm tactics.

Therefore, since we are surrounded by such a great
cloud of witnesses, let us throw off everything that
hinders and the sin that so easily entangles. And let us
run with perseverance the race marked out for us.
HEBREWS 12:1 NIV

The first Olympic competition, in 776 BC, was a running race. When this letter to the Hebrews was sent to Jewish Christians, the ancient Olympics were still being conducted. The recipients were familiar with the race.

Runners often ran naked, not wanting their clothing to interfere with their movement. They knew the route of the race, as it was marked out for them well in advance.

As they completed the race in an amphitheater, crowds cheered the runners on to the finish line. The arena was full of spectators, many of them veteran athletes who had run the race in the past and knew how hard it was to finish well.

The Christian life is like a marathon, a race in which God is our aim. As we run, a huge crowd cheers us on. They encourage us to throw off anything that hinders our pace and may keep us from finishing. This great cloud of witnesses urges us onward, living the Christian life by faith as they did.

Never give up, no matter how hard the race may seem. Heaven awaits.

Lord Jesus, help me to race for Your glory,
living out Your truth every day. May I be inspired
by You and run in the power of Your Spirit. Amen.

*"Do not be afraid of them or their words. Do not
be afraid, though briers and thorns are all
around you and you live among scorpions."*
EZEKIEL 2:6 NIV

Ezekiel's call was a difficult one. He was to preach judgment to
the rebellious, obstinate, and stubborn Israelites (verses 3–4).
Whether they would receive the message was questionable, but
for certain they would seek to kill the messenger. Yet God's sum-
mons to the prophet was delivered with words of encouragement:
"Don't be afraid."

Have you ever sensed God prompting you to speak when you
preferred to remain silent? As Christians we are called to exhort,
encourage, and occasionally, rebuke in the spirit of God's love.

Living for Christ is far from a popularity contest. In fact, we
are often misunderstood or ridiculed for our spiritual convictions,
until we feel as if we are embedded in a field of briers and thorns
while venomous scorpions surround every side. But God's mandate
is the same as it was in Ezekiel's day, namely, communicate the
truth of God's Word with love and without fear.

Just like the prophet of old, we are called to simply speak and
leave the rest to God.

*Lord, give me the courage to speak the truth to those
who need to hear it. Help me to speak in love. And help
them to receive it. In Jesus' name, I pray. Amen.*

Be on your guard; stand firm in the faith;
be courageous; be strong.
1 CORINTHIANS 16:13 NIV

The apostle Paul's letters often included commands to fellow believers, instructions for living the Christian life. When he wrote, Paul chose his words wisely.

"Be on your guard; stand firm." These words invoke the image of an army facing its enemy. Instead of running, it stands and fights against its oppressor. Its soldiers are strong and courageous. This is the image that Paul wanted to impress on the Christians at Corinth. They should be vigilant, stand instead of run, and be courageous and strong. When they were persecuted for their Christian beliefs, they were to react as soldiers in the army of God.

Being firm in our faith is not something that comes easily. We are tempted by evil every day. We forget that we must always be vigilant. When someone treats us unfairly or when we face obstacles that seem insurmountable, we can remember Paul's words in 1 Corinthians 16:13. Face evil with courage and strength. Stand firm as a soldier in the body of Christ.

Lord, this is easier said than done, but I pray You
help me to do just that—to stand my ground
and fight rather than running. Amen.

"I am as strong now as I was when Moses sent me on that journey, and I can still travel and fight as well as I could then."
JOSHUA 14:11 NLT

Caleb was descended from the Kenizzites, a people residing in Canaan during Abraham's time. At some point before the Exodus, members of the Kenizzites turned to God and joined the Israelite tribe of Judah.

Unlike many Israelites, who simply mimicked the religion of their birth, the Kenizzites possessed a deep trust and faith in God.

Caleb demonstrated these convictions when Moses sent him and eleven other men to scout out the promised land. Only Caleb and Joshua returned with a favorable report.

For his faithfulness, God promised, "I will bring him into the land he explored. His descendants will possess their full share of that land" (Numbers 14:24 NLT).

When the time came to distribute the land, Caleb requested Hebron, a city that had terrified ten of the scouts years before. At eighty-five years of age, Caleb prepared to battle the Anakites still living in Hebron and take the town as his inheritance.

Caleb's life reflected his trust in God. Along with an allotment of the promised land, he left the priceless legacy of faith to his family. Like him, let's endeavor to leave a heritage of faith in God to those we love.

Dear God, may I love You sincerely and leave a heritage of faith to my family. Amen.

*Then he showed me another vision. I saw the Lord standing
beside a wall that had been built using a plumb line. He
was using a plumb line to see if it was still straight.*
AMOS 7:7 NLT

Straight walls need a solid foundation to stay upright, but walls
built on solid foundations are not always straight. Plumb lines—a
weight tied to a string that uses gravity to make sure walls are
structurally sound—can reveal whether the wall has tilted since
being built. A wall that leans will eventually fall.

Amos's vision in today's verse shows God checking on the
people of Israel. Were they still standing as straight and tall as the
foundation on which they were built? What God found with His
plumb line was a wall destined to crumble: "The pagan shrines
of your ancestors will be ruined, and the temples of Israel will be
destroyed; I will bring the dynasty of King Jeroboam to a sudden
end" (Amos 7:9 NLT).

When the wall has fallen, God can rebuild it (see Amos 9:11).

Our lives in Christ are built on a solid foundation, but are
we living upright for Him? Ask Him to test your life and your
heart with His plumb line. If your life leans toward the things of
this world, allow God to rebuild it for you lest it crumble when
a strong wind comes along.

*Lord, repair my life to be as solid as
the foundation You laid on the cross.*

*And the sun stood still, and the moon stayed, until the
people had avenged themselves upon their enemies.*
JOSHUA 10:13 KJV

Ever have one of those days when you don't seem to have enough
time to do what you need to do? Well, in today's passage, the fully
armed forces of five kings had come against the city of Gibeah,
which Joshua had agreed to protect. As Joshua prepared his men
to fight, God promised him that He had already delivered them
into Israel's hand and that none of the enemy would stand before
the Israelites (verse 8). After they had smashed the overwhelming
foe in battle and watched God drop bombs of hailstones on them,
Joshua asked God to stop the clock. The sun and moon paused,
and Joshua's men had another day of light to erase the menace.

The longest day in history was also a day for believing in the
Lord for victory. Joshua went against the combined armies of five
kings because he believed the Lord's promise, and he saw God
fight for him. In that spirit, he prayed a great prayer.

May we be emboldened to pray great prayers when we see
the Lord following through in our lives.

---

*Lord, thank You for the amazing miracle You did
for Joshua that day. Increase my faith so that I can
believe for great miracles in my life also. Amen.*

*Each of you should use whatever gift you have
received to serve others, as faithful stewards
of God's grace in its various forms.*
1 PETER 4:10 NIV

There are no useless lives. But there are lives taken out of service. God doesn't do that, and His enemy isn't responsible either. Those lives are put "on the bench" by the people living them.

You might think people incapacitated by illness are taken out of the game by God—but they have a role in bringing out the best in others. People who are swamped by the evil around them might feel unable to do any real good—but their courage is a great example.

This message is for the ones who through fear of failure or worry about their inadequacy deliberately sideline themselves. There are no useless lives. There is a point to your being on this earth. If the least you can offer is a smile, if you can only sit and listen, then smile and listen. The most seemingly insignificant act on your part might be what makes the difference to another struggling soul.

Think you have nothing to offer? You're wrong. Get back on the field and make your play, however feeble it might seem to you. God will take it and do great things with it. He just needs you to be in the game.

*God, help me not to give up and sideline myself from
serving You. May I be willing to do what little I can. Amen.*

So the king gave the order, and they brought Daniel and
threw him into the lions' den. The king said to Daniel,
"May your God, whom you serve continually, rescue you!"
DANIEL 6:16 NIV

Daniel was not a young man when he faced the lions' den. He had
served Nebuchadnezzar and Nebuchadnezzar's son Belshazzar,
and now he served in the court of Darius. His faithful service in
the court of Israel's enemies lasted almost seventy years, and in
all that time, Daniel's service to God always came first. So when
Darius's other advisers plotted the lions' den episode—convincing
Darius that the punishment for praying to anyone beside him
should be death by lions—to get rid of Daniel, the prophet did as
he always had. He trusted God.

The thing Daniel understood, from the moment he was taken
from his people as a young man to the moment he was thrown
in the pit, was this: *Life* is a lions' den. There are no safe places.
If plotting enemies don't get you, illness and grief and stupidity
will. Lions are everywhere, and they're always hungry. The safest
plan is to continue serving God, whom even the lions obey.

Whether or not God closes the mouths of the lions, your
faithful service will ensure the safety of your soul and your witness
to the world will be worth listening to.

Father, may I always trust You more than I fear the lions.

Have I not written thirty sayings for you, sayings of counsel and knowledge, teaching you to be honest and to speak the truth, so that you bring back truthful reports to those you serve?
PROVERBS 22:20–21 NIV

Some aspects of scripture are hard to understand. The frightful visions of the book of Revelation come quickly to mind.

But most instructions for living are quite plain. The things God wants us to do, the things that make us holy (set apart to Him), are not mysterious at all. For example, these "thirty sayings" in Proverbs 22–24. "Haven't I told you clearly," Solomon essentially said to his son, "how to be honest and good?"

The sayings address many issues found elsewhere in Proverbs, just in greater detail—rather than a thought-provoking two-liner, these sayings may be two or three or four times as long. All of them, like the moral teaching of the entire Bible, are designed to improve our own lives, bless others around us, and honor our Creator.

God has made His expectations plain. Having seen His rules and requirements in black and white, we now have a choice to make: to obey and be blessed, or to go our own way and reap the consequences. Human as we are, we might struggle to humbly follow God's instructions. But we can never honestly argue that His desires are mysterious.

Lord, help me to follow scripture's plain instructions while entrusting the truly mysterious to You.

*In the same way, you who are younger, submit yourselves
to your elders. All of you, clothe yourselves with
humility toward one another, because, "God opposes
the proud but shows favor to the humble."*
1 PETER 5:5 NIV

Do you suppose teenagers enjoy hearing this verse? If it was only
for teens, they might have a right to feel put upon. But it isn't. We
can all find someone older and wiser, if we have the eyes to look.

So the question is this: Do we have the humility to learn
from those older people? If we do, our submission becomes a
positive thing. Through it we move onward and upward. If we
don't, we set ourselves up as the authority, as people who know it
all. That's exactly the kind of person the next generation likes to
rebel against and try to topple. So the generations are separated
because of pride.

It's tougher to rebel against humility. If our children see the
benefits of positive submission, the peace and wisdom it brings,
they might follow the example and learn from us. In turn, they
become the teachers. It's a process that never ends. We will always
be younger than someone, so we'll always have more to learn.
And even when we're "old as the hills," we won't be as old as God.

*God, remove pride from my heart, I pray. Keep me humble and
willing to learn from others. In Jesus' name, I pray. Amen.*

*A person can do nothing better than to eat and drink and find
satisfaction in their own toil. This too, I see, is from the hand of God.*
ECCLESIASTES 2:24 NIV

Ecclesiastes has earned a reputation for pessimism in the Old
Testament canon. After all, the teacher (presumed to be Solomon)
repeats the word *meaningless* thirty-five times in twelve chapters.

In the second chapter, he examines the worth of pursuing
pleasure and of work. He concludes, "This too is meaningless"
(Ecclesiastes 2:23 NIV).

In spite of his seeming pessimism, the teacher finds nug-
gets of meaning. Sometimes he compares two items, such as by
saying "wisdom is *better than* folly" (Ecclesiastes 2:13 NIV, italics
added). Four times he uses the formula found in the above verse:
nothing "better than." To borrow a movie title, this is "as good
as it gets" in this life.

What are those rock-bottom sources of satisfaction?

- your work (2:24; 3:22)
- eating, drinking, and all of life (2:24; 8:15)
- being happy (3:12)
- doing good while you can (3:12)

Live each day to the fullest and find joy in the simple things.
If we follow the teacher's advice, we will find the meaning that
escaped him.

*Lord, help me to live each day to the fullest and find joy
in simple things. May I find true meaning in life. Amen.*

Scripture says: "God opposes the proud but shows favor
to the humble." Submit yourselves, then, to God. Resist the
devil, and he will flee from you. Come near to God and he will
come near to you. Wash your hands, you sinners, and purify
your hearts, you double-minded. Grieve, mourn and wail.
Change your laughter to mourning and your joy to gloom.
Humble yourselves before the Lord, and he will lift you up.
JAMES 4:6–10 NIV

Many have described James as one of the Bible's most practical
books, offering "how-tos" for living as a Christian.

Today's scripture includes a list of mind-sets and actions on the
theme of humility. After alluding to Proverbs 3:34, James urged
his readers—in the first century and today—to consciously place
themselves under God's authority. Knowing we are under God's
authority, we can confidently oppose Satan's work in our lives.
Having pushed away sin, we can draw even closer to God, enjoying
an ever-increasing experience of His presence. We'll adopt a heart
attitude that contradicts this world's pattern, choosing the pure,
the serious, and the humble. And, in His time and His way, God
will show us favor and lift us up.

Every one of these how-tos requires action on our part. *Submit,*
resist, come, wash, purify, grieve, change, and *humble* are all
commands. If we choose to obey them, we have the promise of
God's reward.

Father, Your commands are simple if not easy. Help me to obey.

But Ruth replied, "Don't ask me to leave you and turn back.
Wherever you go, I will go; wherever you live, I will live. Your
people will be my people, and your God will be my God."
RUTH 1:16 NLT

During a famine in Israel, a man named Elimelech moved with
his wife, Naomi, and their two sons into the land of Moab. Life
became easier and each son married.

Sadness descended on the family when Elimelech died. Then
each son passed away, leaving behind their widows, Ruth and
Orpah, and their mother, Naomi.

By now the famine in Israel had ended, and Naomi decided to
return home to Israel, with Orpah and Ruth accompanying her.
Along the way, Naomi urged her daughters-in-law to "go back to
your mothers' homes" instead of coming with her (Ruth 1:8 NLT).

Orpah returned, but not Ruth. She refused, determined to
stay with her mother-in-law and take Naomi's God as her own.

What attracted Ruth to this heartbroken woman? During
the years in Moab, Naomi must have radiated an authentic faith
in God. No doubt this faith peeked out even as Naomi worked
through the pain and anger of the grieving process.

Life was hard then; it's hard now. But God is greater. Does your
faith show during difficult times? Trust God to get you through,
and others will notice.

Dear God, life was hard then, but it's hard now too. No matter what,
You're greater—so with Your help, may my faith shine forth.

For the love of money is a root of all kinds of evil.
Some people, eager for money, have wandered from
the faith and pierced themselves with many griefs.
1 TIMOTHY 6:10 NIV

Even if you haven't been an avid Bible reader, you probably have heard this verse.

Two of the most popular topics covered in the Bible are love and money. In fact, out of Jesus' approximately forty parables, nearly half refer to money. Ironically in this verse, the words *love* and *money* are written side by side, forming a simple equation of sorts: love of money equals evil. That's a tough one. Doesn't everybody love money?

In Paul's words to Timothy, it's not money that's evil, rather the extent to which our hearts are involved. What applied to people almost two thousand years ago applies 100 percent to us today.

Our hearts need constant examining when it comes to money. How much commitment and priority do we give to obtaining money? And once we've got it, how passionate are we in getting, spending, or saving more? Paul cautions that some of us who are eager for money have wandered from the faith.

Wandering from faith separates us from God, and separation from God equals grief. No amount of money anywhere is worth that.

Dear Father, help me to be content, whether I
earn little or much. In Jesus' name, I pray. Amen.

Watch out that no poisonous root of bitterness
grows up to trouble you, corrupting many.
HEBREWS 12:15 NLT

Though salvation is entirely a gift of God, our sanctification—growth in grace—takes effort on our part. The warning above is tucked into a whole paragraph of commands: "Work at living in peace," "work at living a holy life," "look after each other," "make sure that no one is immoral or godless" (Hebrews 12:14–16 NLT).

Most of us, at some time, have wrestled with that "poisonous root of bitterness." Maybe we were cheated in a business deal. Maybe we felt disrespected by our wife or kids or someone at church. Maybe we just expected life to turn out better. . .and that noxious root begins to stir deep inside, trying to break through the surface of our lives.

The writer of Hebrews would say, "Stop!" Though our life is a soil and circumstances the seed, we don't have to cultivate bitterness. Don't water the seed by consciously replaying offenses. Don't fertilize it with thoughts of getting even. If that bitterness does take root, use the sharp edge of God's Word (Hebrews 4:12) to hack it to pieces.

The responsibility is ours. God will gladly assist, but the duty of obedience falls squarely on each of us. By choosing to do right, we help ourselves and avoid "corrupting many." This is serious!

Father, I want to grow the fruit of Your Spirit,
not the noxious weeds of bitterness.

Dear friend, you are faithful in what you are doing for the
brothers and sisters, even though they are strangers to you.
3 JOHN 5 NIV

Don't you sometimes wish you were a missionary, devoting yourself completely to God and the Word? All you would do is leave
behind everything you've known to risk the ridicule of strangers, the ill-treatment of antagonistic powers, and perhaps, an
ignominious death.

No? You don't fancy that? Really?

Those whom God calls (the "brothers and sisters" in this
verse) get a sense of mission—a willingness to sacrifice and the
strength to do the Lord's work. Most of us are never asked to do
anything so terribly dramatic.

Before you heave a sigh of relief, though, don't think you have
nothing to do. There are "brothers" and "sisters" risking all for
God right now. Some of them will cross our paths; others we'll
never meet. Most will be strangers, like the men John thanked
Gaius for helping. They are our frontline troops in the battle for
souls—and if we aren't fighting alongside them, we can at least
support them.

Do what you can to help those called to give their all. Never
think of them as strangers. Instead, remember this: Someone
who loves us loves them too.

Lord, please show me how I can help those who serve
You full-time. Help me to give cheerfully, I pray. Amen.

> "As long as the earth endures, seedtime and harvest, cold and
> heat, summer and winter, day and night will never cease."
> GENESIS 8:22 NIV

Amid ongoing environmental debates, there are some God-given absolutes that will never change.

Today's scripture appears at the end of the Noah narrative—when the great flood has done its damage and the water has receded. God invites Noah's family to come out, and He tells them to build an altar and make a sacrifice.

Noah's faithfulness and the sweet-smelling sacrifice he kindles give God new hope in what's left of His creation. He determines never again to destroy His creatures in such a violent manner. And as a pledge of His great faithfulness, the Creator promises to keep His young world spinning on its axis, ensuring the natural cycles and beauty of nature.

In Eden, God instructed Adam to care for that corner of creation—its flora and fauna, all gifts to man from the creative hand of God (Genesis 1).

As Christians, we are called to care for God's earth without worshipping it. Let's be stewards of the environment while honoring its Creator.

God, show me how I can be a better steward of Earth's resources.
May I make my corner of this planet beautiful, I pray.

Jephthah made a vow to the LORD. He said, "If you give me victory over the Ammonites, I will give to the LORD whatever comes out of my house to meet me when I return in triumph. I will sacrifice it as a burnt offering."
JUDGES 11:30-31 NLT

Jephthah's vow has been described as "rash" or "tragic." And why not? This judge of Israel asked God for victory in battle, promising that afterward he would sacrifice whatever stepped out of his house. Was he expecting a goat or chicken? It was, in fact, his only child.

The story warns against foolish promises. But there was a deeper issue for Jephthah, one that we as Christian men today do well to consider: when God has called and empowered a person for service, that's enough. No embellishment is necessary or desirable.

Jephthah had dealt wisely with the king of Ammon, denying his demand for Israelite land. "You keep whatever your god Chemosh gives you," he said, "and we will keep whatever the Lord our God gives us" (Judges 11:24 NLT). When the Ammonite king ignored the message, "the Spirit of the Lord came upon Jephthah" (verse 29 NLT). Heading to battle in this power, though, Jephthah seemed to hesitate, making the foolish vow in today's scripture.

Let's not make a similar mistake. With God's promises and presence, we need nothing more. Our trust honors Him more than any promised sacrifice ever could.

Lord, I trust You. That's enough.

Hear, O Israel: The LORD our God is one LORD.
DEUTERONOMY 6:4 KJV

Deuteronomy 6:4, known as the "Shema," is perhaps the best-known statement of Jewish faith and doctrine, recited at synagogues across the world. Jesus affirmed its importance in Mark 12:29–30.

"Hear," from the Hebrew word *sh'ma*, implies more than can be clearly understood from the English translation. The word *sh'ma* appears more than one thousand times in the Hebrew Old Testament and is translated by more than thirteen different words in the King James Version. Of those translations, the third most common is "obey." The implication is clear: if one hears God, one will also obey God.

When Joshua challenged Israel to stay true to the Lord after his death, the people responded, "His voice we will [*sh'ma*]" (Joshua 24:24 ESV). Centuries later, when Samuel confronted King Saul, he said, "Why then did you not [*sh'ma*] the voice of the LORD?" (1 Samuel 15:19 ESV).

James spoke to the duality of hearing without obeying in his epistle. He exhorted believers: "Be doers of the word, and not hearers only" (James 1:22 ESV).

Let's not deceive ourselves. If we hear the Word of God but fail to obey, we haven't truly heard it at all.

Lord, may I truly hear Your Word—hear it and agree with it, hear it with intent to obey. Help me be wholehearted for You, I pray. Amen.

*"Everyone brings out the choice wine first and then
the cheaper wine after the guests have had too much
to drink; but you have saved the best till now."*
JOHN 2:10 NIV

Today's scripture was spoken by a very relieved master of ceremonies. Overseeing a wedding banquet, he had somehow run
out of wine. Happily for him, Jesus was there, and at His mother's
request performed His first miracle: six twenty- to thirty-gallon
waterpots were suddenly brimful of excellent wine. The bemused
banquet master raved to the groom, "Everyone brings out the
choice wine first and then the cheaper wine after the guests have
had too much to drink; but you have saved the best till now."

As followers of Jesus, shouldn't we also do everything to
the highest level possible? Whether we're performing a task at
work, serving at church, or—dare we say it—posting on social
media, we Christians should be known for our top-quality, bene-
ficial, respectful performances. As the apostle Paul so succinctly
put it, "Whether you eat or drink or whatever you do, do it all
for the glory of God" (1 Corinthians 10:31 NIV).

Earlier, Paul had written, "No one should seek their own good,
but the good of others" (1 Corinthians 10:24 NIV). When we work
hard and carefully, we serve the good of others—and honor our
Lord who does "all things well" (Mark 7:37 KJV).

Father, help me devote my best efforts to Your glory.

"I do believe; help me overcome my unbelief!"
MARK 9:24 NIV

Healing was a significant part of Jesus' ministry. Throughout the four Gospels we read about Jesus healing lepers, the blind, and those possessed with evil spirits.

The verses prior to Mark 9:24 tell of a father who brings his son to the disciples, asking them to cast out an evil spirit. After a failed attempt, an argument occurs. Jesus arrives to witness the chaos. The father explains his plight and informs Jesus that His disciples' healing skills aren't up to par. He then tells Jesus, "If you can do anything. . .help us." Jesus corrects him by saying, " '*If* you can'? . . . Everything is possible for one who believes" (verses 22–23 NIV, italics added).

Interestingly, Jesus didn't always choose to heal upon request (Matthew 13:58). So why did He heal this man's son, despite his doubt? Mark 9:24 may give us the answer. In one breath, the man confidently states his belief, and in the next he honestly confesses his doubt, asking Jesus for help.

The father's contradictory response speaks for us all. Like him, we confidently profess our faith, until tested, then find ourselves slipping into doubt. In times like these, we must be honest about our faith, praying for God to strengthen it. Only then can God truly begin the healing process.

Father, I, too, believe. . .up to a certain point. Please strengthen my faith where it begins to get weak. In Jesus' name, I ask. Amen.

"In that day," declares the LORD, "you will call me 'my husband'; you will no longer call me 'my master.'"
HOSEA 2:16 NIV

This Old Testament book tells the story of the faithful and forgiving Hosea, married to the prostitute Gomer. Hosea represents God's deep love and commitment to His people. Gomer, in her sinful and wandering ways, symbolizes Israel.

God based this illustration on the marriage relationship. God is the loving husband, fully devoted to his wife, even considering her infidelity. He never gives up and continually searches for her, protecting her, restoring her to His side. God's forgiveness and love redeem that relationship.

God also wants *our* hearts. He desires a relationship with us based on love and forgiveness. He enters into a covenant with us, like the marriage between Hosea and Gomer.

God is the loving, faithful husband, constantly pursuing us no matter what we do or where we roam. Though it is difficult to grasp how much He loves us, we find hope in His promise. God will keep His commitment to us. His love song to us is forgiveness, and His wedding vow is unconditional love.

God, I thank You for Your persistent, unconditional love for me. Thank You that, despite my wanderings, You never, ever give up on me. I can barely grasp such love. May I walk worthy of You.

"Nor will people say, 'Here it is,' or 'There it is,'
because the kingdom of God is in your midst."
LUKE 17:21 NIV

For centuries, the Jewish people had waited for their "glory day." Through ancient prophecies came mental pictures of the kingdom of God—a physical kingdom with a real king who would deliver them from Roman rule.

In Luke 17, the Pharisees demanded that Jesus tell them when the kingdom of God would arrive. Jesus' answer, that the kingdom of God already existed, surely confused them. Probably more puzzling to them was *where* it existed!

As Christians, we, too, find ourselves waiting. We wait for good to win over evil and for Christ's second coming. We long to experience the glory of God's kingdom. Jesus' answer applies to us too: God's kingdom is already here.

But where? Some Christians confuse "church" as the kingdom. But church and kingdom are not the same. If we've discovered the kingdom, it means God (our King) has delivered us from the darkness of sin through His prince, Jesus. God sits on a throne, in our very own hearts, governing our souls and consciences. Church is simply a place for those who submit to the rule of the King to come together, proclaim, and invite others to find it.

In that sense, every day is a "glory day."

Thank You, Jesus, that Your kingdom has already come in my heart.
I long for Your kingdom to come on all the earth, however. Amen.

*This made Saul very angry. "What's this?" he said.
"They credit David with ten thousands and me with
only thousands. Next they'll be making him their king!"
So from that time on Saul kept a jealous eye on David.*
1 SAMUEL 18:8–9 NLT

King Saul proved himself to be a valiant and successful warrior. We're told that "he fought against his enemies in every direction. . . . And wherever he turned, he was victorious" (1 Samuel 14:47 NLT).

Then Saul grew prideful and no longer followed God's commands. As a result, God rejected him as king of Israel (1 Samuel 15:26). Saul realized his son would never inherit the throne.

When young David returned victorious from the battlefield and received higher praise than Saul, the king's jealousy flared and quickly turned to anger. Instead of celebrating, Saul became a raving madman, fearful of losing his throne to the valiant young warrior.

Although David proved himself loyal to the king, Saul's suspicion and jealousy blinded him to the talents and accomplishments of his faithful subject. David's success on the battlefield made everyday life in Israel more secure, but Saul couldn't see or appreciate these gains.

Jealousy and suspicion make terrible taskmasters. So let's consciously and intentionally cheer when others succeed. That pleases God and smooths our own way.

*Lord, I thank You that others sometimes excel me, and I
pray for their blessing. And bless me too, I pray. Amen.*

Do not quench the Spirit.
1 THESSALONIANS 5:19 NIV

Fire is a destructive force, showing no mercy on what it consumes. However, fire also gives off warmth and light, enabling us to do many good things.

Paul was instructing his readers not to put out the fire of the Spirit. Continual prayer, a thankful attitude in the midst of their circumstances, whether good or bad, and believing in God's will for their lives were the qualities they were to be displaying.

In addition, they were to speak out against the idle, come alongside the timid, and examine the things they were being taught. They needed to hang on to what was good and stay away from evil. By living in this manner they wouldn't be quenching the Holy Spirit.

Jesus spoke of the importance of the Spirit, especially in the book of John. He preached that the Spirit not only teaches us about God but also brings back to mind the lessons we have already learned (John 14:25–26).

We know that when a fire is neglected it soon begins to go out. With proper attention though, a fire will continue burning, giving off warmth and light to those around it. Are you doing what you should to keep that fire glowing?

Holy Spirit, please glow brightly in me, I pray. Help me to shine with Your radiance. In Jesus' name, I pray. Amen.

But if I say, "I will not mention his word or speak anymore in his name," his word is in my heart like a fire, a fire shut up in my bones.
JEREMIAH 20:9 NIV

The prophet Jeremiah faced a challenge. He'd been called to minister the Word of God to Judah during that nation's final years of decline. With passion and fervor, the prophet preached that unless God's people repented, judgment and calamity would soon follow.

The people resented and ridiculed Jeremiah, treating him with contempt for those unwanted proclamations. Frustrated, the man called "the weeping prophet" lamented, "The word of the LORD has brought me insult and reproach all day long" (Jeremiah 20:8 NIV). So he sought to silence his spiritual stirrings.

No matter how hard Jeremiah tried though, he couldn't suppress the divine message God placed on his heart. Despite the personal cost, Jeremiah continued to proclaim the Word.

In a world that rejects the gospel, God is seeking Christians who are eager and willing to share the truth of His Word—no matter the consequences. The apostle Paul declared, "I am not ashamed of the gospel of Christ: for it is the power of God unto salvation" (Romans 1:16 KJV).

When our love of God exceeds our fear of rejection and reproach, we can't help but proclaim the good news with unabashed boldness.

God, encourage me when others reject Your Word. Help me to continue sharing it. Amen.

> *Turn us again to yourself, O God. Make your face*
> *shine down upon us. Only then will we be saved.*
> PSALM 80:3 NLT

When your car's in a ditch, you don't dial a plumber. If your cell phone gets cracked, you don't rush to the hospital. Should your tax return be selected for audit, you don't call a devotional writer. (Definitely not a devotional writer!) Particular crises require particular helpers, those with the specific skills and abilities to get you out of trouble.

Often, our problems aren't physical but spiritual. We have sinned. We know we're lost. We need forgiveness, guidance, and hope. If we seek help from anyone or anything but God, we'll be disappointed—eternally so.

The psalm writer Asaph recognized this truth, begging God to "show [Israel] your mighty power. Come to rescue us!" (Psalm 80:2 NLT). God's people were being harassed by other nations (verse 6), but the larger issue was spiritual: the people had strayed from their Shepherd, who was angry even with their prayers (verse 4). Asaph implored God to turn the Israelites' hearts back to Him. "Only then will we be saved," he wrote—three times (verses 3, 7, and 19 NLT).

When you find yourself in spiritual need, go straight to God. He may use a friend or pastor or Christian book to help you through—but He is the ultimate source of salvation.

> *Lord, You are my Hope and Salvation.*
> *May I never look to anyone else.*

*Better to have little, with fear for the LORD, than to have great
treasure and inner turmoil. A bowl of vegetables with someone
you love is better than steak with someone you hate.*
PROVERBS 15:16–17 NLT

Everything in this world, it seems, is designed to make you discontent. Phone companies want you to upgrade your device or service, automakers think you need some hotter wheels, pharmaceutical companies imply (even say out loud) that you're too tired, too fat, too bald. What's a guy to do?

Well, a Christian guy should follow the example of the apostle Paul, who "learned how to be content with whatever I have" (Philippians 4:11 NLT). For a man who had enjoyed times of plenty and survived periods of scarcity, Jesus was the key. "I can do everything through Christ, who gives me strength" (Philippians 4:13 NLT).

Paul's words parallel today's scripture. Our "fear for the LORD" makes up any lack we may experience—or any supposed lack the world tries to convince us we're suffering. On the other hand, no earthly treasure could ever make up for the "inner turmoil" of life without God. His love and the love of the friends and family He gives us make whatever we have "better than." But we need to make a decision: Will we be content with what God's given us?

*Father God, You have given me all I need and
much that I want. Help me to be content.*

And I saw that all toil and all achievement spring
from one person's envy of another. This too is
meaningless, a chasing after the wind.
ECCLESIASTES 4:4 NIV

Labor isn't meaningless. Achievement isn't meaningless either. Man's envy of his neighbor is the spoiler. What we do to be like others, what we want because other people have it, those are the meaningless things.

"Keeping up with the Joneses" is all very well in this life, but the Joneses (whoever they might be for you) are mortal, and their example is finite. When they go the way of all mortal things, their works, achievements, and everything we emulated—or wished we were or wished we had because they had it—all of that goes with them, like dust blowing in a good stiff breeze.

For a life's work to be meaningful, its effects should be independent of the life that made it. Great men and women get that for a while—until history forgets them. Humble, faith-filled souls find real meaning not in trying to get what their neighbors have, but by reaching out to those neighbors, and others, in God's name, making their labor the Lord's work.

If you must chase after the wind, make it the Holy Spirit, otherwise known as the Wind of Heaven. Then your achievements will mean something forever.

God, may my heart pursue Your Spirit and the spiritual riches
He bestows, rather than seeking material things. Amen.

*"This is My body, which is broken for you.
Do this in remembrance of Me."*
1 CORINTHIANS 11:24 SKJV

For the most part, when people remember heroes, they celebrate their accomplishments. But with the Lord's Supper, Jesus commands us to remember His death.

Why not let a cup of wine remind us of the time He turned the water into wine? Or have the bread remind us of when He multiplied the loaves to feed five thousand? Instead, He calls us to the circumstances of His death.

At the Passover, a lamb was sacrificed. But Jesus was the Lamb of God who came to take away the sins of the world. That is why we remember His death. Only by His dying on the cross then rising again could we be saved from our punishment of hell and the slavery of sin.

Some things lose their fascination with familiarity. It's normal for a familiar passage of scripture to lose its force over time. Chances are, if we have taken Christ's death for granted, we have accommodated sin too. Let us stir up our hearts over the death, burial, and resurrection of Christ, for it is the bedrock of our faith and will lead us to triumph over all sin.

*Jesus, may I always honor You by remembering that
You died for my sins and that Your resurrection holds
promise of new life for me as well. Amen.*

"What is this that God has done to us?"
GENESIS 42:28 NIV

It was Jacob's bewildered boys who asked this question. The answer blew their minds and brought them face-to-face with forgiveness.

You remember Joseph with the beautiful coat, whose brothers sold him into slavery? They thought they had seen the last of their fair sibling, until a famine drove them to Egypt for a "care package." But lo and behold, who was providing the life-saving supplies? Their brother Joseph.

The irony of this historical incident cannot be misunderstood. Before recognizing Joseph, the brothers were overwhelmed by finding their silver payments returned in the sacks of grain. Rightfully, they gave God credit for such generosity. Of course, it was God working in the heart of Joseph that began the process leading to recognition, renewal, and the reward of reconciliation. No coincidence there.

Perhaps no other biography is as convincing that God is always at work for our good. In many ways, Joseph foreshadows what was to come from another Father. Read Joseph's full story (Genesis 37–50). Open your heart to God's lifesaving provision.

Of the four-hundred-some verses comprising Joseph's story, none are more thrilling than Genesis 50:20 (NIV), where Joseph says to his brothers, "You intended to harm me, but God intended it for good." That's just like Him.

God, thank You that You get good out of bad circumstances.

"But if you remain in me and my words remain in you,
you may ask for anything you want, and it will be granted!"
JOHN 15:7 NLT

Wow. . .is that really true? Is God like a genie who will grant us unlimited wishes?

There are some who pray that way. They assume that they have license to treat God as a concierge of some kind, who is standing by to rush to fulfill our every request.

When we think about our children, we remember that our love for them is so great that we would give them anything they want. In the midst of thinking this, however, wisdom kicks in, and we realize what might happen if we did, in fact, give our kids everything they want. The result would probably be some pretty rotten kids.

As we present our requests to God, we need to realize that He knows what is best for us and that we should never demand "our way." We must not forget the first part of John 15:7 that says, "If you remain in me and my words remain in you." This clearly indicates that our first desires need to be that God's will is done.

Since God only wants to give us the very best, and He knows how to make that happen, why would we pray for anything else?

Lord, may I seek first Your kingdom and Your righteousness,
knowing that then You will give me all that I need. Amen.

But the LORD replied, "Is it right for you to be angry?"
JONAH 4:4 NIV

Jonah is one of the most familiar characters in the Bible.

His adventure began when God told Jonah to go and spread the word in the wicked town of Nineveh that God would soon be passing judgment on them. Jonah refused to go and ran away. He ended up on a boat that he eventually got tossed off of in the midst of a raging storm. Jonah didn't drown though; instead God was merciful and spared Jonah by sending a big fish to swallow him.

Once Jonah repented, God delivered him out of the fish. Jonah then traveled to Nineveh and preached. The people listened and repented. Jonah should have been happy with the results, but that wasn't his reaction.

After seeing God's compassion for people he despised, Jonah got mad. He was so angry that he wanted God to take his life. Instead God taught Jonah about compassion. It was a lesson Jonah refused to submit to.

The wayward prophet had forgotten his role as the clay and God's position as the potter. When we reverse our role with God's, we're going to find ourselves angry and frustrated. We are blessed with many rights, but questioning God isn't one of them.

Father in heaven, help me to obey You. You know what's best in any situation. And give me love and compassion for others. In Jesus' name, I pray. Amen.

Pride goeth before destruction, and an haughty spirit before a fall.
PROVERBS 16:18 KJV

If you ever hear someone say, "Pride goes before a fall," and think, *That's not what the Bible says,* give yourself a pat on the back. This is one of those often misquoted verses like "money is the root of all evil" (it's actually "*the love of* money," 1 Timothy 6:10) or "cleanliness is next to godliness" (which is not in the Bible at all).

Proverbs 16:18 clearly states that pride goes before destruction; it's a haughty spirit that precedes a fall. While we should always be careful to quote scripture accurately, in this case a little mixing and matching seems harmless enough. The Proverbs often make their point by restating an idea in parallel terms—"pride" and "a haughty spirit" are essentially the same thing. So are "destruction" and "a fall." Let's be sure we avoid them all!

Pride is the sin that turned Lucifer into the devil. It's the desire that caused Eve to eat the forbidden fruit. It's the ambition that tripped up countless Bible characters and billions of human beings throughout history. And God hates it (Proverbs 8:13).

So how do we avoid pride? With a regular, conscious effort to chip away the crust that's baked onto our hearts. Here's a helpful verse to remember: "God resisteth the proud, but giveth grace unto the humble" (James 4:6 KJV).

---

*Lord God, turn my self-praise into
praise of You. Only You are worthy.*

These all died in faith, not having received the promises,
but having seen them from afar and were persuaded
of them, and embraced them, and confessed that
they were foreigners and pilgrims on the earth.
HEBREWS 11:13 SKJV

When we are in trouble, we often look to God and His promises. The expectation, of course, is that He will deliver us sooner rather than later. What's so amazing about this verse is that the Bible lifts up Abraham as a man demonstrating great faith—by believing God would fulfill His promise after Abraham's death!

Abraham had rejoiced in God's promise for a son years before he received the baby. Then he rejoiced in receiving a land of his own, even when he came to realize that it wouldn't be in his lifetime. The fulfillment of the first promise—given miraculously—probably helped Abraham to believe God for the other promise.

God calls us to experience the same faith as Abraham, to believe in a better world to come when every righteous promise will be fulfilled. May each promise you believe be a stepping stone to a greater faith.

Lord God, thank You for the many promises You made in
Your Word to me—and to all believers. Help me to cling to
these promises and expect to see them fulfilled. Amen.

*"And I bought the field at Anathoth from
Hanamel my cousin, and weighed out the
money to him, seventeen shekels of silver."*
JEREMIAH 32:9 ESV

It was a very dark hour for Jerusalem and for Jeremiah personally.
He had warned the Jews for decades that if they didn't repent, God
would send the Babylonians to conquer them. Sure enough, a vast
Babylonian army was now camped around Jerusalem, and the siege
ramps were in place. The Jews were trapped inside, couldn't get out
to their fields, and were low on food. Jeremiah was worst-off of all.
The rulers of Jerusalem had thrown him in prison because of his
unpopular message.

In Jeremiah's lowest moment, his cousin showed up. Hanamel
needed money for food and wanted to sell his field. The only
problem was it was in the village of Anathoth, some distance
outside the walls of Jerusalem where it couldn't do Jeremiah any
good. Yet following God's instructions, Jeremiah bought the field.
Why? Because as hopeless as things were at the moment, God
said things would soon get much better (Jeremiah 32:36–44).
Jeremiah believed God, and better things came to pass.

If you're trapped in a corner like Jeremiah was, remember
what God asked him: "I am the LORD, the God of all flesh: is there
any thing too hard for me?" (Jeremiah 32:27 KJV).

*Lord, there is truly nothing too hard for You.
Thank You that in my darkest, most desperate
situation, You are still powerful and able.*

Say to God, "How awesome are your deeds!
Your enemies cringe before your mighty power."
PSALM 66:3 NLT

Today's scripture must be read in ultimate terms. Not all God's enemies are currently cringing before Him. . .in fact, they're more like the angry nations of Psalm 2, with rulers who "plot together against the LORD and against his anointed one. 'Let us break their chains,' they cry, 'and free ourselves from slavery to God' " (verses 2–3 NLT).

But a day is coming when those who oppose God and trouble His children will regret their folly. "The one who rules in heaven laughs. The Lord scoffs at them. Then in anger he rebukes them, terrifying them with his fierce fury" (Psalm 2:4–5 NLT). They'll cringe while the rest of us celebrate.

"Everything on earth will worship you; they will sing your praises, shouting your name in glorious songs" (Psalm 66:4 NLT). Note the future tense of those verbs—we are not at present in this stage of history. But Jesus said He's "coming soon" (Revelation 3:11; 22:7, 12, 20), and the world's current trajectory seems to indicate His return is closer than ever. All the sin and sadness, fear and frustration of this world will be wiped away. God will make everything right in His good time.

Until then, keep your chin up. God is still in control.

Lord, how awesome are Your deeds! Remind me
today of Your greatness and goodness.

*Come and listen, all you who fear God, and I will tell
you what he did for me. For I cried out to him for help,
praising him as I spoke. If I had not confessed the sin in my
heart, the Lord would not have listened. But God did listen!
He paid attention to my prayer. Praise God, who did not
ignore my prayer or withdraw his unfailing love from me.*
PSALM 66:16-20 NLT

These verses describe "3 C's" of effective prayer: first, the confidence
we have in God; second, the conditions we must meet; and third,
the conclusion we'll enjoy.

Through the first fifteen verses of Psalm 66, the writer praises
God for His awesome glory and might. This is a God who could
lead His people out of slavery in Egypt on a dry path through the
Red Sea (verse 6), a God who brought them "through fire and
flood" into "a place of great abundance" (verse 12 NLT).

With confidence in God's power and goodness, the psalmist
ensured his right standing. By meeting the condition of prayer—
confession of sin—he knew God would listen.

The beautiful conclusion? "God did listen! He paid attention
to my prayer." And God never removed His unfailing love.

Thousands of years have passed since this psalm was written.
But God has not changed. He still welcomes the confident, clean-
hearted prayers of His people.

---

*Lord God, You are great and powerful!
Please hear my honest, humble pleas.*

*While Jesus was still speaking, some people came from
the house of Jairus, the synagogue leader. "Your daughter
is dead," they said. "Why bother the teacher anymore?"*
MARK 5:35 NIV

What hopelessness. Jairus, a synagogue ruler, pleaded with
Jesus to heal his sick child. Jesus was en route to the man's home
when they got the news that the child had died. Why trouble the
Galilean teacher any further? It was kind of Him to come, but
there's nothing He can do now, the naysayers thought. Yet Jesus'
response was one of encouragement and hope: "Don't be afraid;
just believe" (verse 36 NIV).

When Jesus entered Jairus' home, He heard the crying. "Why
all this commotion and wailing? The child is not dead but asleep,"
He said (Mark 5:39 NIV). But they laughed. After removing the
doubters, Jesus took the child by her hand and said, "Little girl,
I say to you, get up!" and the child was brought back to life
(verse 41 NIV).

When the odds are stacked against us and circumstances riddle
us with hopelessness, our tendency is to manage our burdens
as well as we can and stop praying. Doubtful, we wonder: Can
God restore an unhappy marriage? Can He heal cancer? Can He
deliver me from financial ruin? *Will* He?

Jesus knows the way out. Only believe—have faith in Him
and never lose hope.

*Jesus, I commit my marriage, my finances, and my health into
Your keeping. May my trust in You never falter, I pray. Amen.*

*For we are His workmanship, created in Christ
Jesus for good works, which God has before
ordained that we should walk in them.*
EPHESIANS 2:10 SKJV

Paul says we are created in Christ Jesus and designed to do God's work. God has a plan for each of us.

Because we are "created in Christ Jesus," Christ is the example of what Christians should be. "Therefore, if any man is in Christ, he is a new creature. Old things have passed away; behold, all things have become new" (2 Corinthians 5:17 SKJV). We are saved through Christ to do the good works that God has planned for us.

How can you know God's plans for your life? First, you should meet with Him in prayer each day and seek His will. Studying the Bible is also important. Often, God speaks to us directly through His Word (Psalm 119:105). Finally, you must have faith that God *will* work out His plan for your life and that His plan is good. Jeremiah 29:11 (NIV) says, " 'For I know the plans I have for you,' declares the LORD, 'plans to prosper you and not to harm you, plans to give you hope and a future.' "

You will accomplish great things as you allow God's plan to unfold in your life. Work with Him, and be amazed.

*God, I choose to walk in the new life You've given
me in Jesus. Help me never to forget that You
have good things planned for me. Amen.*

*But when the kindness and love
of God our Savior appeared. . .*
TITUS 3:4 NIV

Eleven words. Their message is a simple one: when love and kindness from God appear, changes occur.

In Paul's letter to Titus, he addressed the conduct that those who know Christ should have. They should submit to authority, not speak ill of anyone, strive for peace, and have a humble attitude.

Paul also gave a reminder about the approach that they should take with those who don't yet know Christ. Instead of being prideful, they would do well to remember that once upon a time they engaged in jealousy, lying, hatred, disobedience, and foolish living. It was only when Jesus came into their lives that those behaviors changed.

The apostle knew full well what he was writing about. For he once lived in a state of hatred toward others and approved of the mistreatment of those who believed in Jesus. Then known as Saul, he wasn't about peace at all. But then Jesus appeared (Acts 9:1–19). Suddenly the man who would be known as Paul was putting off his bad conduct in exchange for the behavior that showed God was in his heart.

God's love and kindness are powerful things that continuously transform hearts. How has His love changed yours?

*Lord, Your love and kindness changed my life,
and may they continue to change my life each
and every day. I pray this in Jesus' name. Amen.*

"You are the light of the world. A town built on a hill cannot be hidden."
MATTHEW 5:14 NIV

William Holman Hunt portrayed Jesus Christ in a painting called *The Light of the World*. Despite the fact that Jesus is holding a lamp in the painting, there is no doubt that Hunt meant the Lord—not the lamp—was the light referred to.

The title is from a description Jesus used for Himself. He said that whoever followed Him would not walk in darkness. Then Jesus qualified that by saying He would be the light of the world while He was in the world.

Then, in anticipation of His death, Jesus passed the duty of illumination to the disciples and, through them, to us.

In the painting Jesus stands before a door that has no handle on the outside. The implication is that He has to be invited in. But once Jesus is inside you, don't keep Him to yourself—not while others still walk in darkness. As a follower of the Lord, you stand on the "hill" of God's love and shine a guiding light for others.

Bringing people heavenward isn't just a job for pastors and theologians. It's a job for all of us who claim Him—as He said, *you* are the light of the world.

Jesus, help me to faithfully shine forth Your light to the world around me. Help others, when they see me, to see Your presence within me, I pray.

For which cause we faint not; but though our outward man
perish, yet the inward man is renewed day by day. For our
light affliction, which is but for a moment, worketh for us
a far more exceeding and eternal weight of glory.
2 CORINTHIANS 4:16–17 KJV

Paul had a heavenly mindset. In a tone befitting a poet, he encouraged the early church as he compared this earthly life against the ecstasy of the eternal for every Christian.

Our bodies—the temporal temples of the Holy Spirit—are just that. . .temporary. In 1 Corinthians 15:31 (KJV), the apostle wrote, "I die daily." His statement was both figurative and actual. Physically, our bodies deteriorate with age—and spiritually, we seek to "die" to our self-serving, carnal natures. This presents an interesting dichotomy—namely, the death of self leads to life. As the body grows old, the spirit grows young and is invigorated in Christ daily.

With the voice of wisdom, Paul declares that however heavy our sufferings seem to us, they cannot compare to the far more exceeding and eternal weight of glory we will experience with God throughout eternity.

Paul beautifully contrasted things present to things future—a moment to an eternity, lightness to weight, affliction to glory. This is the mindset God wants all believers to attain. This is the mindset He will provide as we pray and obey.

God, thank You that one day You will transform my
weak, weary physical body into a powerful, glorious,
eternal body. I look forward to that day!

But Paul was of the opinion that they should not take along with them this man who had deserted them in Pamphylia and had not gone with them to the work.
ACTS 15:38 NASB

A young man, Mark, accompanied Barnabas and Paul as they set out on the first missionary journey, but he returned to Jerusalem before completing the trip.

When planning the second missionary journey, Barnabas wanted to include Mark again, but Paul adamantly disagreed. The young man had deserted them the first time, dumping his share of the work onto the other team members. Paul had no desire for a repeat performance.

However Barnabas insisted Mark, who was his cousin, come along. Unable to agree on the issue, Paul teamed up with Silas and headed north, while Barnabas took Mark and sailed west to Cyprus.

Barnabas provided Mark with the encouragement and training he needed to reach his full potential. Mark went on to pen the Gospel of Mark, effectively minister in the early church, and even become an appreciated coworker with Paul.

Has anyone failed you? Before completely writing the person off, look for signs of a teachable spirit and growing maturity. Direction and encouragement may be exactly what someone needs to succeed at a task. Perhaps there is a Mark in your life, and Christ is calling you to be a Barnabas.

Lord, it's hard for me to trust people who have failed me. But help me to hold out hope and give them another chance, I pray. Amen.

. . .on the day he comes to be glorified in his holy people and to be marveled at among all those who have believed. This includes you, because you believed our testimony to you.
2 THESSALONIANS 1:10 NIV

In the early part of his letter to the Thessalonians, Paul contrasts the everlasting destruction awaiting those who don't know the gospel with the glory awaiting those who have believed.

Several things will happen on the day "when the Lord Jesus is revealed from heaven in blazing fire with his powerful angels" (2 Thessalonians 1:7 NIV). Among them: God will be glorified in His holy people—in *us* (verse 10). In Paul's letter to the Ephesians, he mentioned that we believed "for the praise of his glory" (Ephesians 1:12 NIV). The more we are transformed into the likeness of the Lord, the more we reflect His glory (2 Corinthians 3:18).

This verse tells us we will also "marvel" at the Lord. A few translations use *admired* instead of *marveled*. Both words have similar implications, but *marvel* suggests a stronger degree of the same feeling. We will do more than look at the Lord with approval and respect. When we come face-to-face with the Lord in all His glory, we will be amazed—surprised and even bewildered.

Let's begin to seek that amazing, surprising, bewildering God in our lives here and now.

Lord, reveal Yourself in me. Show me Your amazing, surprising, bewildering power, starting right now.

These are evil times, so make every minute count.
EPHESIANS 5:16 CEV

Just think: Paul wrote these words to the church at Ephesus almost two thousand years ago. If the times were evil then, what would Paul say about the state of affairs in the twenty-first century? When was the last time you turned on the news without hearing about the evil humanity visits upon itself?

And speaking of the world, it has its own system for time management and making every minute count. The bookstore on the corner has titles galore giving advice on how to best utilize every second of every day in order to become the most productive, best worker/parent/child/human being you can dream of becoming.

But God's plan for time management serves a different goal than self-actualization. And while it may seem tempting to crawl back into bed and hide beneath the covers of denial instead of facing the harsh reality of the world, God has a different idea.

Every minute counts because we, as believers, carry an eternal hope that the world needs to hear. Bad things do happen to good people, but ever present in the trials of this world is a loving God who cares deeply for His children. Who can you share this good news with today?

---

*God, empower me by Your Spirit. Help me to work
diligently for You. Help me to seize all opportunities.
Help me to make every minute count, I pray. Amen.*

"Unless you repent, you too will all perish."
LUKE 13:3 NIV

Many prefer the "gracious" Jesus of the New Testament to the "harsh" God of the Old Testament. They argue that God is angry and vindictive; Jesus is all love and acceptance.

There are sound theological reasons (such as the doctrine of the Trinity) to dismiss that argument. But even a quick skim of scripture reveals many examples of God's patience and tenderness "before Christ," as well as Jesus' own tough approach to sin and holiness. Today's scripture, repeated verbatim in Luke 13:5, is an instance of the latter.

When informed of the Roman governor Pilate's violence against certain Galileans, Jesus didn't criticize the perpetrator or sympathize with the victims. Instead, He told the crowd around Him, "Do you think that these Galileans were worse sinners than all the other Galileans because they suffered this way?" (Luke 13:2 NIV).

Then Jesus mentioned another news headline: "Those eighteen who died when the tower in Siloam fell on them—do you think they were more guilty than all the others living in Jerusalem?" (Luke 13:4 NIV). To both questions He said, "I tell you, no! But unless you repent, you too will all perish" (verse 5 NIV).

Jesus was harsh when warning about sin. But He was actually being gracious, helping us to meet God on His own terms. . .which is the only way we can.

*Holy God, loving Lord, help me honor Your
perfection by my humble submission.*

SCRIPTURE INDEX

BIBLE PERMISSIONS